# EXPLORING THE RELIGION OF ANCIENT ISRAEL

Aaron Chalmers is Head of the School of Ministry, Theology and Culture at Tabor Adelaide, South Australia, where he teaches Old Testament, biblical interpretation and Hebrew. His research interests include the history of Israelite religion and the phenomenon of prophecy in ancient Israel. He has had a number of articles published in various scholarly journals, including *Vetus Testamentum*, *Ugarit Forschungen* and *Tyndale Bulletin*. He is married to Catherine, and they have two young children.

# Exploring the Religion of Ancient Israel

*Prophet, Priest, Sage and People*

AARON CHALMERS

IVP Academic

An imprint of InterVarsity Press
Downers Grove, Illinois

*InterVarsity Press*
*P.O. Box 1400, Downers Grove, IL 60515-1426*
*World Wide Web: www.ivpress.com*
*E-mail: email@ivpress.com*

*InterVarsity Press® is the book-publishing division of InterVarsity Christian Fellowship/USA®, a movement of students and faculty active on campus at hundreds of universities, colleges and schools of nursing in the United States of America, and a member movement of the International Fellowship of Evangelical Students. For information about local and regional activities, write Public Relations Dept., InterVarsity Christian Fellowship/USA, 6400 Schroeder Rd., P.O. Box 7895, Madison, WI 53707-7895, or visit the IVCF website at <www.intervarsity.org>.*

*Scripture quotations, unless otherwise noted, are from the* New Revised Standard Version of the Bible, *copyright 1989 by the Division of Christian Education of the National Council of the Churches of Christ in the USA. Used by permission. All rights reserved.*

*Design: Cindy Kiple*

*Images: Moses and the Brazen Serpent by Sebastien Bourdon at Prado, Madrid, Spain. The Bridgeman Art Library*

*ISBN 978-0-8308-2545-5*

*Printed in the United States of America ∞*

**Library of Congress Cataloging-in-Publication Data**

*Chalmers, Aaron.*
 *Exploring the religion of ancient Israel : priest, prophet, sage, and people / Aaron Chalmers.*
  *pages cm — (Exploring topics in Christianity series)*
 *Includes bibliographical references and index.*
 *ISBN 978-0-8308-2545-5 (casebound : alk. paper)*
*1. Leadership in the Bible. 2. Priests, Jewish. 3. Prophets. 4. Bible. O.T.—Criticism,*
*interpretation, etc. 5. Jews—History—To 70 A.D. I. Title.*
 *BS1199.L4C43 2012*
 *221.9'5—dc23*

*2012038470*

| **P** | 22 | 21 | 20 | 19 | 18 | 17 | 16 | 15 | 14 | 13 | 12 | 11 | 10 | 9 | 8 | 7 | 6 | 5 | 4 | 3 | 2 | 1 |
|---|---|---|---|---|---|---|---|---|---|---|---|---|---|---|---|---|---|---|---|---|---|---|
| **Y** | 29 | 28 | 27 | 26 | 25 | 24 | 23 | 22 | 21 | 20 | 19 | 18 | 17 | 16 | 15 | 14 | 13 | 12 | 11 | 12 | | |

# CONTENTS

| | | |
|---|---|---|
| **List of illustrations** | | vii |
| **Key to panels** | | ix |
| **Preface** | | xiii |
| **List of abbreviations** | | xv |
| **Introduction** | | 1 |
| Notes | | 5 |
| **1** | **Sources for reconstructing the social and religious world of ancient Israel** | 6 |
| | 1.1 Introduction | 6 |
| | 1.2 The biblical text | 6 |
| | 1.3 Ancient Near Eastern texts | 9 |
| | 1.4 Syro-Palestinian archaeology | 10 |
| | 1.5 Summary | 13 |
| | Notes | 14 |
| | For further reading | 14 |
| **2** | **Priests in ancient Israel** | 15 |
| | 2.1 Introduction | 15 |
| | 2.2 How did someone become a priest? | 17 |
| | 2.2.1 Who was eligible to become a priest? | 17 |
| | 2.2.2 What training did priests undergo? | 20 |
| | 2.2.3 Was there an installation ceremony? | 24 |
| | 2.3 What did a priest do? | 24 |
| | 2.3.1 Divination | 26 |
| | 2.3.2 Teaching | 27 |
| | 2.3.3 Sacrifice (and incense offering) | 28 |
| | 2.3.4 Blessing the people | 30 |
| | 2.4 Where were priests to be found? | 32 |
| | 2.5 Summary | 36 |
| | Notes | 36 |
| | For further reading | 38 |
| **3** | **Prophets in ancient Israel** | 39 |
| | 3.1 Introduction | 39 |

| | | |
|---|---|---|
| | 3.2 Where were prophets to be found? | 42 |
| | 3.2.1 Religious centres | 43 |
| | 3.2.2 Political centres | 44 |
| | 3.2.3 Independent prophets | 45 |
| | 3.3 How did someone become a prophet? | 46 |
| | 3.3.1 Who could become a prophet? | 47 |
| | 3.3.2 What took place in a prophetic call experience? | 50 |
| | 3.3.3 What training did prophets undergo? | 53 |
| | 3.4 What did a prophet do? | 55 |
| | 3.4.1 Communicate the word of the Lord | 55 |
| | 3.4.2 Miracle working | 62 |
| | 3.4.3 Interceding | 62 |
| | 3.4.4 Healing | 63 |
| | 3.5 Summary | 64 |
| | Notes | 64 |
| | For further reading (in addition to texts cited in Chapter 2) | 66 |
| **4** | **The wise in ancient Israel** | 67 |
| | 4.1 Introduction | 67 |
| | 4.2 Where were the wise to be found? | 68 |
| | 4.2.1 The royal court | 68 |
| | 4.2.2 Schools | 72 |
| | 4.2.3 The town gates | 74 |
| | 4.3 What did the wise do? | 76 |
| | 4.3.1 Teaching | 76 |
| | 4.3.2 Advising/counselling | 77 |
| | 4.3.3 Arbitrating disputes | 79 |
| | 4.3.4 Composing documents | 80 |
| | 4.4 How did someone become wise? | 82 |
| | 4.4.1 Education | 82 |
| | 4.4.2 Experience and observations of life | 84 |
| | 4.4.3 Divine revelation | 86 |

4.5   Summary                                          87
Notes                                                  87
For further reading (in addition to texts
        cited in Chapter 2)                            88

**Excursus: the role of kings in the religious
life of ancient Israel**                               89
Notes                                                  96
For further reading                                    97

5   **The common people in ancient Israel**            98
5.1   Introduction                                     98
5.2   Whom did the common people
        worship?                                      102
        5.2.1   *The god of the family*               102
        5.2.2   *El and Baal*                         104
        5.2.3   *Asherah and the Queen of Heaven*     107
        5.2.4   *The host of heaven*                  111
5.3   Where did the common people worship?   114
        5.3.1   *Within the household*                115

5.3.2   *Within towns or villages*                   118
5.3.3   *Outside towns or villages*                  119
5.4   When did the common people
        worship?                                      120
        5.4.1   *Regular religious activities
                (annually, monthly, weekly)*          120
        5.4.2   *Regular religious activities related
                to the human life cycle*              122
        5.4.3   *Occasional religious activities
                related to a specific crisis or
                concern*                              131
5.5   Summary                                         132
Notes                                                 133
For further reading                                   136

**Conclusion**                                        138
**Copyright acknowledgements**                        141
**Select bibliography**                               144
**Index of biblical references**                      153
**Index of names and subjects**                       157

# ILLUSTRATIONS

## PLATES

2.1 Terracotta figurine of a woman holding a drum from the Iron II period   21

2.2 Faience die which may have been used in divination, found in the sacred precinct at Tel Dan   26

2.3 Man bringing an offering, from Zinjirli   29

2.4 Assemblage of four-horned incense altars, from Ekron   30

2.5 The inner sanctum of the temple at Arad complete with two *maṣṣēbôt* (rear) and altars (front)   33

2.6 Stone stele depicting a warrior god from Moab (possibly Chemosh)   34

4.1 Relief of Horemheb's tomb depicting Egyptian scribes writing documents (eighteenth dynasty of Egypt, 1328–1298 BC)   70

4.2 King Bar Rakab seated on his throne, with his scribe who is holding writing implements, from Zinjirli   78

4.3 Diorite statue of a seated Egyptian scribe with a papyrus scroll

(nineteenth–twentieth dynasty, 1295–1069 BC)   82

Ex.1 Limestone plaque depicting Ur-Nanshe of Lagash bearing a basket on his head, possibly containing the first brick for the foundation of a temple (*c*.2500 BC)   92

Ex.2 Egyptian stele showing six individuals carrying various standards   93

5.1 Limestone stele from Ugarit depicting Baal with thunderbolt (1900–1500 BC)   105

5.2 An ivory panel depicting an Ugaritic goddess, possibly Asherah, nursing two children (1400–1350 BC)   108

5.3 Judean female terracotta figurine from the eighth century, possibly Asherah   109

5.4 Two silver statuettes, possibly teraphim, found in a jar, from Ugarit (*c*.2000–1800 BC)   112

5.5 Relief showing an Egyptian funeral procession from the tomb of Mermery (*c*. fourteenth century BC)   128

5.6 A funerary stele depicting an elaborately dressed woman

*vii*

(perhaps a queen) with offerings
for the deceased, from Zinjirli    129

## FIGURES

1.1   Female lyre player from
      Kuntillet Ajrud                  12
2.1   The large four-horned altar from
      Beersheba, as reassembled        29
2.2   Artist's reconstruction of a gate
      shrine from Dan, complete with
      set of five *maṣṣēbôt* (top corner)
      and basin structure              35
3.1   Two seals depicting winged serpents  51
3.2   Detail from the Lachish reliefs
      showing the Assyrian army
      attacking the gate area of
      Lachish                          58
3.3   Egyptian hieroglyph showing
      an individual in an ecstatic state,
      from the story of Wen-Amon       61
3.4   Procession of worshippers with
      arms upraised in a gesture
      of prayer, from Kuntillet Ajrud  63
4.1   Plans of city gates of Megiddo (a),
      Hazor (b), Gezer (c), Ashdod (d)
      and Lachish (e)                  75
Ex.1  The Assyrian king Ashurbanipal
      pouring a libation over four
      dead lions before an offering
      table and incense stand          95
5.1   Artist's reconstruction showing
      a large residence in a provincial
      town with people performing
      various everyday activities      100
5.2   Artist's reconstruction showing
      several multi-house compounds
      within a typical Israelite village  102
5.3   Drawing of a bronze and gold
      statuette from Ugarit of a seated
      god, probably El                 105

5.4   Stele from Ugarit depicting an
      individual (perhaps a king or chief
      priest) presenting an offering to
      an enthroned god, probably El
      (1400–1300 BC)                   105
5.5   A Cypriot terracotta cake mould,
      probably representing the
      Queen of Heaven (*c.* Iron II)   110
5.6   Seal from Shechem depicting
      an Assyrian king bringing a
      burnt offering to Ishtar         110
5.7   Terracotta figurine of horse
      and rider from Lachish (Iron II)  111
5.8   Close-up of head of horse
      figurine from Jerusalem with
      (solar?) disk between ears       111
5.9   Isometric drawing of a typical
      'four-room house' at Tell
      el-Far'ah (north)                115
5.10  Partial reconstruction of cult
      room 65 from Ai, including its
      distinctive fenestrated offering
      stand (on podium)                117
5.11  Plan of hilltop cult place from
      the territory of Manasseh with
      bull statue (twelfth century BC)  119
5.12  Female figurines from Lachish
      and Jerusalem (eighth–seventh
      centuries BC)                    124
5.13  Amulets from Lachish depicting
      the Egyptian dwarf god, Bes
      (Iron II)                        126
5.14  Plan of a typical Israelite burial
      cave from the pre-exilic period,
      from north of Jerusalem         128

## MAPS

In.1  The northern and southern kingdoms
      of Israel and Judah *c.*830 BC    4
1.1   Location of Ugarit                9

# KEY TO PANELS

## 'GOING DEEPER' PANELS

Laws and the social world of ancient Israel — 7

Ugaritic and Canaanite religion — 9

Textual remains from ancient Israel — 10

The value of archaeology — 11

The preference for Levitical priests — 19

The roles of priests and Levites in Ezekiel's new temple — 20

Priestly pronouncements — 27

What else was incense used for? — 29

Were *bāmôt* unique to Israel? — 32

Who were Chemosh and Milcom? — 34

The 'sons of the prophets' and Israel's sanctuaries — 43

Female prophets — 49

The meaning of *nābî'* — 50

The roles of Israel's cult prophets — 55

Job 4:12–21 and prophetic revelation — 59

Symbolic actions in the OT — 61

Elijah, Elisha and miracles — 62

The elders in the book of Ruth — 79

Female composition of an OT wisdom text — 81

How were Israelite scribes educated? — 84

What was Nehushtan? — 93

Ahaz's altar and sacrifice — 95

The four tiers of Israelite society — 99

Who were the 'resident aliens'? — 100

The inheritance of the *bêt 'āb* — 101

The relationship between El and Yahweh — 106

Monotheism in ancient Israel — 114

The pre-history of Passover — 120

Who was 'the destroyer'? — 121

The significance of vows — 123

Who did these female figurines represent and how did they function? — 125

Offerings for the dead — 129

Personal piety and the individual psalms of lament — 132

Religious specialists in African societies — 138

## 'HAVE YOU CONSIDERED?' PANELS

The minimalist–maximalist debate — 8

Could Levites be recruited? — 19

Why were there no female priests in ancient Israel? — 22

Priests may have also functioned
as the tax-men of ancient Israel 31

Were some of the canonical prophets
cult prophets? 43

Prophets as members of the divine
council 46

How common was Samuel's
experience? 53

Could you be born a prophet? 54

How did the prophets earn a living? 56

Were the prophets ecstatics? 60

The relationship between scribes
and 'the wise' 71

Who were the 'wise women' and what
did they do? 80

Mothers as instructors in wisdom 83

What constituted old age in ancient
Israel? 86

Why did Manasseh do what he did? 94

Who or what were the teraphim
(těrapîm)? 113

Was necromancy practised in ancient
Israel? 130

Prophets, priests and sages outside
the capitals 139

## 'SCHOLAR FOCUS' PANELS

William Dever (1933– ) 11

Julius Wellhausen (1844–1918) 16

Robert Wilson (1942– ) 45

Max Weber (1864–1920) 48

Gerhard von Rad (1901–71) 69

Albrecht Alt (1883–1956) 103

## 'ANE PARALLELS' PANELS

The priesthood as a hereditary office 17

ANE prophets and the royal court 44

Amos the nōqēd 49

What are the seraphim? 51

The cleansing of Isaiah's lips 52

The roles of court prophets 57

Ahiqar as a court sage 68

Egyptian Instructions and the book
of Proverbs 72

Schools in Ugarit? 73

Old age and wisdom 74

The institution of elders 75

Royal counsellors 77

Wisdom as the product of human
effort and divine gift 86

Phoenician priest-kings 89

Kings and the construction of
temples 91

Kings and cult organization 91

The maintenance of temples
in the Hittite empire 92

The god of the family 104

The Ugaritic Baal cycle 107

Cakes (kawwānîm) for the Queen
of Heaven 110

Rooftops as a location for cultic
practice 116

A Babylonian Sabbath? 122

Who was Bes? 126

## 'ARCHAEOLOGICAL INSIGHT' PANELS

What did the Urim and Thummim
look like? 25

What did an altar look like? 28

A priestly blessing from outside the OT 31

The maṣṣēbôt from Arad 33

The sanctuary at Tel Dan 35

Israelite prophecy outside the OT 40

The Balaam Text from Deir 'Alla   41

a/Asherah inscriptions from ancient
  Israel   108

Horse and rider figurines   111

Tell Halif and the use of domestic
  space   115

Cult room 65 from Ai   116

Ancient Israelite tombs   127

# PREFACE

The ultimate origins of this book can be traced back to my undergraduate studies at Tabor Adelaide. As a student in the Bachelor of Theology programme, I took classes in three major fields: biblical studies, Church history and systematic theology. Both biblical studies and Church history fascinated me, but I never particularly enjoyed systematics. At the time I didn't consciously reflect on why this was the case. Looking back on it now, however, I think a major reason for my lack of interest in systematics was that I found the discipline too abstract and 'ethereal'. Conversely, the reason I enjoyed biblical studies and history was because both disciplines are grounded in an 'earthy', lived reality. When studying the Bible or Church history we are, at least for the most part, concerned with real people who lived at a certain time, in a certain place within a certain socio-cultural context. It is this passion for the groundedness and earthiness of the Scriptures, and my desire to share this with others, that has led to the writing of this book.

The world of ancient Israel is an intriguing and fascinating place. It is also a world which is unlike our own in many respects. Significant differences were present in virtually every aspect of life: socially (whereas the modern West emphasizes the value of the individual, the world of the Bible was dyadic, oriented towards groups and communities), ideologically (whereas the modern West promotes change and is always looking forward to the new and novel, the ancient Israelites endorsed stability and viewed change as a danger or threat) and religiously, including the presence of a variety of religious specialists in ancient Israel for which there are no exact modern equivalents (Matthews and Benjamin, 1993: xiii–xxiii). It is my hope that this book will transport the readers back to the world of the Bible, allowing them to develop a fuller and more accurate picture of the social location, training and roles of Israel's prophets, priests and sages, as well as the religious beliefs and practices of the common people. It will quickly become clear that, in contrast to much contemporary, fashionable biblical scholarship, I believe that the biblical text does, at least in part, reflect the reality of life in ancient Israel, and that through studying the text and other available sources (e.g. archaeology and comparative ANE documents) we can come to some understanding of what life was, in fact, like. At the same time, the more we are able to grasp what life was like, the better the position we are in to understand the biblical text itself.

I would like to thank a number of people who have helped me in the process of writing this book. First of all, I wish to express my gratitude to Philip Law and the team at SPCK for taking a risk with a young author. It is unlikely that this book would have seen the light of day without their commitment to the project. The Revd Dr Stephen Spence, Deputy Principal (Academic) at Tabor Adelaide, ensured that I had time to work on the project and even managed to cast a critical eye over some of the chapters himself. A number of my OT colleagues generously gave of their time to read through draft chapters and offer valuable feedback. I would particularly like to thank Prof. Patrick Miller, Prof. James Crenshaw, Prof. Norm Habel, Prof. Richard Nelson, Prof. William Dever and Prof. Beth Alpert Nakhai. Professor Joseph Blenkinsopp was kind enough to read through my proposal and offer valuable encouragement. The impact of his work, along with that of Lester Grabbe, should be obvious to the attentive reader.

On a more personal note, I would like to acknowledge Janelle Palmer (who manages to occupy my wife while I am busy at work), my family and, in particular, my mother and father who have remained a constant source of encouragement throughout my studies and now work. Finally, this book is dedicated to my wife, Catherine, without whom none of this would be possible.

# ABBREVIATIONS

ABRL    Anchor Bible Reference Library

ALASP    Abhandlungen zur Literatur Alt-Syrien-Palästinas and Mesopotamiens

ANE    Ancient Near East/Ancient Near Eastern

*ANEP*    James B. Pritchard (ed.), *Ancient Near East in Pictures relating to the Old Testament*, Princeton: Princeton University Press, 1954

*ANET*    James B. Pritchard (ed.), *Ancient Near Eastern Texts relating to the Old Testament*, 3rd edn with sup. Princeton: Princeton University Press, 1969

*BASOR*    *Bulletin of the American School for Oriental Research*

BRS    Biblical Resource Series

BS    The Biblical Seminar

FRLANT    Forschungen zur Religion und Literatur des Alten und Neuen Testaments

HBIS    History of Biblical Interpretation Series

*HdO*    *Handbuch der Orientalistik /* Handbook of Oriental Studies

IBT    Interpreting Biblical Texts

JSOTSS    Journal for the Study of the Old Testament Supplement Series

KTU    M. Dietrich, O. Loretz and J. Sanmartín, *The Cuneiform Alphabetic Texts from Ugarit, Ras Ibn Hani and Other Places*, 2nd enlarged edn, ALASP 8. Münster: Ugarit Verlag, 1995

LAI    Library of Ancient Israel

*NEA*    *Near Eastern Archaeology*

OBS    The Oxford Bible Series

OBT    Overtures to Biblical Theology

OT    Old Testament

OTL    Old Testament Library

SBTS    Sources for Biblical and Theological Study

SBLABS    Society of Biblical Literature Archaeology and Biblical Studies

SBLMS    Society of Biblical Literature Monograph Series

SBLSS    Society of Biblical Literature Supplement Series

SHANE    Studies in the History of the Ancient Near East

SWBAS    The Social World of Biblical Antiquity Series

*ZAW*    *Zeitschrift für die alttestamentliche Wissenschaft*

# INTRODUCTION

The past is a foreign country: they do things differently there. (L.P. Hartley, *The Go-Between*)

For many people, even those raised in religious families, the OT is a foreign country. Apart from a few famous stories, such as Adam and Eve, Noah and the flood, David and Goliath, there seems to be a general lack of familiarity with many of the key people, places and events of the OT. When I initially mention figures like Manasseh, Josiah or Cyrus to my first year OT students more often than not I am confronted by blank stares, in spite of how important these individuals are to the OT narrative. This situation is probably not helped by the 'classic' status of the Bible (which essentially means that we all think it is important, we all think we should read it, but relatively few of us, in fact, do!).

In addition to lack of knowledge, there is also the problem of widespread misconceptions. People may have a general acquaintance with the key people, places and events of the OT, but their knowledge is sometimes distorted or skewed, whether by the influence of the media, broader culture or even Church tradition. Perhaps

the best example of this is Israel's prophets. The all too common view of these individuals as prognosticators of the (distant) future owes more to the figure of Nostradamus, I would suggest, than it does to the biblical text. In spite of the 'evidence' of many Christian bookstores with shelves labelled 'prophecy' there is little (if anything!) in the biblical prophets that foreshadows contemporary events in the Middle East. And while prophets may have at times announced God's future activity, this was usually the imminent future or, to put it another way, the *future* for the prophets is the *past* for us. In some ways, such misconceptions are potentially more harmful than lack of knowledge because they distort our reading of the biblical text (we go looking for things that the author never intended us to look for) and blind us to our ignorance (we think we know more than we actually do).

In order to understand the message of a text, especially a narrative text, it helps to have some ideas of the characters involved. Take *The Lord of the Rings*, for example. The story would be virtually incomprehensible without some knowledge of who Frodo, Gandalf and Sauron are and what their

*1*

respective roles involve. Or consider *Pride and Prejudice*. To appreciate fully this work we need to familiarize ourselves with Mr Darcy, Elizabeth Bennet, Mr Wickham and the complex and changing relationships between them. The same principle applies to the OT: to understand this text we need to have some idea of the key characters involved, including the prophets, priests, sages and common people. In order to do this, I hope to transport you, the reader, back to the world of ancient Israel. Imagine, if you will, that time travel is possible and we could return to pre-exilic Israel. If you had wanted to track down a prophet, where would you have found one? If you had stumbled across a priest, what may he have been doing? If you had encountered someone who wanted to be recognized as a sage, what form of education and training might he (or she) have been undergoing? My hope in doing this is that the world, and thus the text, of the OT will come alive for its readers.

While this may sound like a relatively modest goal, the challenges are numerous. Our main source of evidence for reconstructing the social and religious world of ancient Israel, the OT, is not without its problems. Much of the OT, at least in its final form, clearly postdates the events it is recording, leaving its accuracy as a historical source open to debate. Furthermore, the OT itself is not primarily concerned with 'social world' questions, but instead focuses on religious and theological issues. Thus, it often does not address the questions we are asking in this study in a clear or explicit fashion. Our other main source of evidence, the archaeological record, while potentially helpful for shedding light on the faith and practices of the common people, will be less productive when it comes time to discuss

the religious leadership of the nation (esp. the prophets) as there are relatively few preserved remains that relate directly to these groups. Because of these challenges, I shall address the issue of our sources and their potential strengths and weaknesses in Chapter 1. To anticipate what I have to say there, I believe the available sources do allow us to shed some light on social world questions, even though these 'answers' are not as comprehensive or definitive as we might perhaps like them to be.

The rest of this book is divided into two main parts. In the first, we look at some of the key positions of leadership within the religious and social world of ancient Israel: prophet, priest and sage (along with a brief discussion of Israel's kings). I have chosen these groups because they are frequently encountered in the OT, their roles lay at the heart of the practice of Israel's faith (at least at a corporate level), and they are associated with, and perhaps responsible for, large portions of the OT text. For each of these figures we ask three key questions. How did you become recognized as a prophet, priest or sage? Where would you have found a prophet, priest or sage in ancient Israel? And what did a prophet, priest or sage actually do? By the end of each chapter, the reader should have a good idea how such people fitted within and contributed to the social and religious world of ancient Israel. Although each of these groups (esp. the prophets) has come under scrutiny in previous works, what I hope to achieve here has not yet been done: to consider not only the roles of such people but also their social location/s and training, and to condense and summarize relevant, contemporary OT scholarship in a way that is accessible to the non-specialist.

In the second part of the book we shift our focus from those who held positions of leadership to the 'common people'. Even though such people made up the *vast* majority of ancient Israel's population (by my estimates more than 98 per cent), they have traditionally received little attention in studies of Israel's religion. One of the main reasons for this is that biblical scholarship has usually reflected the primary concerns of the OT text, with its dominant focus on important men and key events in the life of the nation. A study which attempts to do justice to the religion of ancient Israel as a whole, however, cannot afford to overlook this significant group. In this chapter we ask three questions. Who did the people worship (apart from Yahweh)? When did they worship? And where did they worship? Archaeology is in a unique position to help us answer these questions as the material remains preserve a record of the lives of all classes of the Israelite people, and thus allow us to hear the voices of a wider cross-section of the population than the biblical text alone.

Before we get underway, however, I need to acknowledge a couple of the key limitations of this study:

1 This book is intended for beginning students and educated, interested non-specialists – thus I have kept footnotes and technical comments to a minimum and assumed little or no prior knowledge of the field on the part of my audience. Key terms are usually defined and I have tried to introduce the reader to the work of important scholars at relevant points. Given the intended audience, I have attempted to make the work as accessible and engaging as possible, yet all the while grounding it in contemporary biblical, ANE and archaeological scholarship. I trust the result is easy to understand but not simplistic. If the reader is after more detailed treatments of the key religious specialists, I would recommend the works of Grabbe and Blenkinsopp.

2 This book is not a full-scale study of the religion of ancient Israel[1] – thus there will be little explicit treatment of 'standard' topics such as the sacrificial system, life and death, and the relationship between God and humanity. My goal in this book is far more modest: to approach Israelite religion through the lens of its leaders (prophets, priests, and the wise) and to consider the religious beliefs and practices of the common people.

Finally, a few comments on the choice of the title 'ancient Israel' are required. The decision to use the descriptor 'Israel' is potentially problematic as it is employed in a variety of different ways within the biblical text. For example, it can refer to the nation as a whole, the northern kingdom during the period of the divided kingdom, or the southern kingdom following the loss of the north in 722 BC.[2] For the sake of convenience, I will use it in its most general sense to include the nation and people as a whole. If greater precision is required, I will employ the terms 'kingdom of Israel' or the 'Northern Kingdom' and 'kingdom of Judah' or 'the Southern Kingdom'. From a chronological perspective, the boundaries of this study are, in biblical terms, from the establishment of the monarchy through to the Babylonian exile or, in archaeological parlance, the Iron II period (*c.*1000–586 BC). I have chosen to focus particularly on this period as it provides the implied historical context for much of the biblical narrative and books and, thus, is likely to be of most interest to students of the OT.

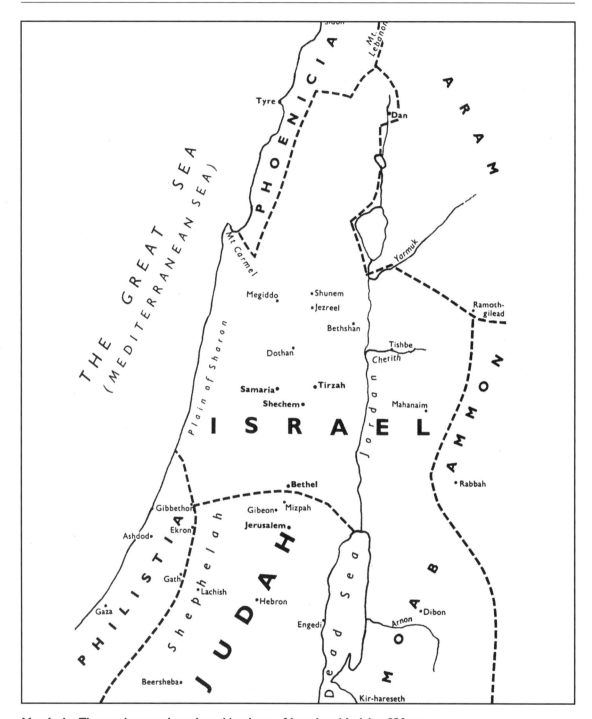

**Map In.1  The northern and southern kingdoms of Israel and Judah c.830 BC**

## NOTES

1 The pluriform nature of Israelite religious belief and practice during the pre-exilic period is a good argument for speaking of the religions (plural) of ancient Israel, rather than religion (singular) (cf. the title of Zevit's work (2001)). My use of the terminology 'religion' does not seek to downplay this diversity, but rather recognizes that religions themselves actually happen to be heterogeneous entities.

2 For a fuller discussion of the various ways in which the title 'Israel' is used in the biblical text, see Davies, 1992: 49–59.

Chapter 1

# SOURCES FOR RECONSTRUCTING THE SOCIAL AND RELIGIOUS WORLD OF ANCIENT ISRAEL

## 1.1 INTRODUCTION

Before we begin discussing the religious and social world of ancient Israel, we first need to consider the various sources we have at our disposal. Each of these has its own strengths and weaknesses and can contribute to our discussion in different ways. Broadly speaking, the two main sources of evidence are the biblical text and archaeological remains.[1] The latter can be divided into textual and non-textual finds.

## 1.2 THE BIBLICAL TEXT

Our main source of evidence for reconstructing the religious world of ancient Israel is the biblical text, especially the Pentateuch (Genesis–Deuteronomy), which tells the story of the origins of the nation from creation through to the exodus from Egypt, covenant at Sinai and journey to the borders of the promised land,[2] the Deuteronomistic History (Joshua, Judges, 1 and 2 Samuel, 1 and 2 Kings) which focuses on the period of the entrance of the tribes into the land through to the nation's exile to Babylon (c.586 BC) and the pre-exilic prophets (esp. Hosea, Amos, parts of Isaiah, Jeremiah), who were operative from

shortly before the fall of the northern kingdom of Israel (c.750 BC) until shortly after the loss of the southern kingdom of Judah. It needs to be recognized, however, that the use of the biblical text as a source for historical reconstruction, particularly of the pre-exilic period, is a debated topic in contemporary biblical scholarship.

A number of influential scholars, including Davies, Lemche and Thompson, have argued that the majority of the OT is little more than 'pious fiction', reflecting an image of Israel that was current in the Persian and Hellenistic periods (i.e. the fourth–second centuries BC) rather than the earlier, pre-exilic period. Although there may be some truth to the claims of these so-called 'minimalists' (e.g. the final form of the OT text was probably not reached until this period), correlations of biblical lore, contemporary extra-biblical inscriptions and archaeology lead me to believe that we should not simply write off the biblical text as a source for historical reconstruction – much of what we find in the OT does, in fact, faithfully represent life from the Iron Age period (c.1200–586 BC). Dever (2001: 97–243), in particular, has done much to draw attention to so-called 'convergences' between the biblical text and archaeology, highlighting the fact that the Bible does contain valuable historical information, at least from the time of the monarchy onwards. Thus, although these OT texts may not have reached their *final form* until the exilic or post-exilic periods, they undoubtedly contain significant *earlier traditions* that shed light on the religious leadership, beliefs and practices of the pre-exilic period, and therefore can and should be used in a study of this sort.

Furthermore, the claim of traditional, critical scholarship that the OT narratives contain fictional elements need not overly concern a study of this sort. It is well recognized that even writers of fiction tend to describe what they know to be true and thus often give a broadly accurate representation of society even while inventing characters and events along the way (Grabbe, 1995: 19).[3] For example, the modern novelist Ken Follett describes his one rule for writing historical fiction as follows: 'Either the scene did happen, or it might have; either these words were used, or they might have been. And if I find some reason why the scene could not have taken place in real life, or the words would not really have been said — if, for example, the character was in another country at the time — I leave it out' (2010: 851). As King and Stager (2001: 7) have pointed out, the OT narratives must have passed a certain test of verisimilitude (i.e. of having the appearance of being real or true) on the part of the ancient Israelites for them to be transmitted and accepted. At the very least, they must have *seemed* to be real for their original (and subsequent) audience. Thus, even though some modern scholars may choose to label such narratives as 'fiction', they still have the potential to shed much light on the social and religious institutions of ancient Israel.

> **Going deeper:**
> **LAWS AND THE SOCIAL WORLD OF ANCIENT ISRAEL**
>
> Law can be a particularly valuable genre for reconstructing the social world of ancient Israel. As Kessler (2008: 29) has pointed out, the intention of the laws is to shape the world as they find it and therefore they must take into account both the institutions that are present within the society at the time and the problems society faces. 'Since laws only regulate things that are socially relevant', we may assume that the issues and situations they addressed 'happened often' (Kessler, 2008: 29).

Nevertheless, the OT is not without its own limitations when it comes to analysing the social world of ancient Israel. The text's primary theological and kerygmatic focus means that almost everything that interests us in our attempt at socio-historical reconstruction appears only peripherally or incidentally. Rarely, if ever, are such concerns its major focus. To put it a different way, the text is more interested in significant events and their theological message than the circumstances in which these take place. For example, the prophetic books are dominated by the divine messages the prophet speaks but contain relatively few references to the concrete, historical world in which those messages were first spoken (note, e.g., the lack of narrative in prophetic texts in comparison with the overwhelming focus on the word of the Lord). This means, therefore, that we will need to use the OT carefully when it comes to socio-historical reconstruction. We will need to read between the lines, to bring to the fore that which is in the background, and to consider what is handed on unintentionally. Information about the social world of

## Have you considered?
## THE MINIMALIST–MAXIMALIST DEBATE

There is much debate in contemporary OT scholarship regarding the place of the Bible in writing histories of ancient Israel. Two main approaches or options dominate the scene: maximalist and minimalist (sometimes also referred to as 'revisionist').* Essentially, these options are differentiated by the way they approach the various sources of evidence and, in particular, the biblical text, in order to reconstruct Israel's history.

*Maximalists* (who largely represent the traditional approach) generally trust the biblical text as a historical source. They suggest that the majority of the historical portions of the biblical text were written during the monarchic period and thus the stories have a direct link to the events they describe.** The biblical text is essentially reliable because it comes from the same time period as (or shortly after) the events themselves. Other potential sources of evidence (e.g. archaeology and inscriptions) are usually viewed as being of secondary importance to the biblical text and maximalists generally argue that the archaeological and inscriptional remains tend to confirm the descriptions we find in the biblical text. The maximalist view can be summarized as follows: 'everything in the biblical text that cannot be disproven by external sources has to be accepted as historical'.

*Minimalists*, however, are generally sceptical about the historical claims of the biblical text. They suggest a late date for the biblical text as a whole and thus view the OT as an unreliable historical source for

the pre-exilic period as it is far removed from the events the narrative describes. Rather than recording contemporary history, the biblical authors were imagining and creating a past whose shape was determined by their present context (which may range from the Persian to Hellenistic periods, depending on the particular scholar's preference). The starting point for such minimalist reconstructions is external data (i.e. archaeology and ancient inscriptions), which they argue directly contradict large and important parts of the OT, especially the sections that describe Israel's origins (e.g. not only the Pentateuch, Joshua and Judges but also extending into the books of Samuel). The minimalist view can be summarized as follows: 'nothing in the biblical text can be accepted as historical unless it can be verified by external sources'.

Rather than approaching these as two mutually exclusive options, we need to recognize that they are, in fact, two ends of a continuum. Most historians of ancient Israel would sit somewhere between these two camps, seeking to draw responsibly upon both sources of evidence in their reconstructions and not necessarily privileging one over the other.

* Geographically, maximalists tend to be located in Israel and the United States whereas the minimalist option is more popular in Europe, especially in Germany, Italy and Denmark.
** Maximalists may accept post-monarchical editing for the biblical books.

ancient Israel *is* contained within the text, but we will need to search to find it.

Apart from the biblical text, our main source of evidence for reconstructing the social and religious world of ancient Israel

is the work of archaeologists. Significant textual and non-textual remains have been discovered in excavations from both Israel and the broader ANE which have the potential to shed much light on ancient Israel's religious institutions and practices.

## 1.3 ANCIENT NEAR EASTERN TEXTS

Archaeologists have unearthed a significant body of comparative texts from the surrounding regions of Syria, Mesopotamia and Egypt that can help shed light on the social and religious world of ancient Israel. These include mythological, ritual, psalmic and prophetic texts, many of which share strong literary and conceptual parallels to the OT. The potential value of these for reconstructing the religious and social world of ancient Israel is immense. For example, such texts may help provide a better understanding of a specific Hebrew word, fill gaps in the fragmentary biblical record or allow us to check hypotheses based on the biblical text by comparison with similarly functioning societies.

Perhaps the most significant body of ANE texts for this study comes from Ugarit, a coastal city located in northern Syria. Ugarit was an important Phoenician trading centre that was destroyed some time around 1200 BC and never rebuilt. Modern excavations were begun by the French in 1929 and archaeologists quickly discovered an entire library of texts from the royal

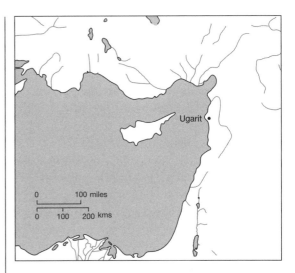

**Map 1.1   Location of Ugarit**

palace and various houses. While many of these documents deal with standard economic and political issues, archaeologists also unearthed a number of tablets containing important liturgical material and religious myths, the most famous of which is the Baal Cycle. These provide a first-hand account of the kind of religion Israel encountered in the land of Canaan; for the first time we can hear the 'Canaanites' speaking with their own voices (and not just the Hebrew authors of the OT speaking for them!). These documents have been particularly valued in OT scholarship owing to the fact that Ugarit was located in relative close proximity (both temporally and geographically) to ancient Israel.

When approaching this potential source of evidence, however, we need to walk a path between *parallelomania* (widespread, uncritical comparison of texts from one society with another), on the one hand, and *parallelophobia* (general refusal to compare texts from one society with another), on the other. Both approaches can be problematic. *Parallelomania* often fails to realize that texts

---

**Going deeper:**
**UGARITIC AND CANAANITE RELIGION**

Hess (2007: 95) has correctly pointed out that we should not simply equate Ugaritic and Canaanite religion. Although Ugarit was geographically proximate to Canaan, it did not identify itself or its inhabitants as Canaanite. Nevertheless, Ugarit belonged to the broader, West Semitic cultural world of both Canaan and Israel, and its texts contain mythological and cultic information that seems to be closely related to and broadly representative of that found in Canaan.

must be understood within the original context in which they were produced as surface similarities may, in fact, mask deeper differences. *Parallelophobia*, in contrast, fails to recognize that the various people groups of the ANE shared a broadly similar intellectual and conceptual world-view, and thus texts may shed light on realities which extended beyond the borders of the society that produced them. Potential problems can be minimized by ensuring that texts are interpreted contextually and that any comparisons that are made are with societies that are as chronologically and geographically close to ancient Israel as possible. When approached responsibly, the use of comparative texts is a very valuable exercise. 'Regardless of the problems it poses, comparative inquiry provides new ways of thinking about issues for which traditional approaches are ill equipped. It offers new models and theoretical insights for thinking about Israelite practices and beliefs' (McNutt, 1999: 29). In particular, ANE texts have the potential to provide significant insight into the religious beliefs and practices of the common people. As Albertz has argued, 'Because of the fundamental functional orientation towards the needs of families, which were similar among the people of the ancient Near Eastern cultures, the family religions of that region are less different than the religions of the nations to which family members belonged' (Albertz, 2008: 93). Thus, comparative texts dealing with family religion in Mesopotamia or Syria may well shed light on practices which were present in ancient Israel.

## 1.4 SYRO-PALESTINIAN ARCHAEOLOGY

Syro-Palestinian archaeology has a long and rich history, and offers a valuable

> **Going deeper:**
> **TEXTUAL REMAINS FROM ANCIENT ISRAEL**
>
> Unfortunately, apart from the OT itself, textual remains from pre-exilic Israel are not abundant. There are a number of reasons for this dearth of written material. Ancient Israelite society was much smaller in size and had less developed structures than the great empires of the ANE and thus produced fewer writings in the first place (Kessler, 2008: 22). Furthermore, the writing materials that were commonly used in Syro-Palestine (e.g. papyrus and ink on ostraca, i.e. broken pottery sherds) do not last as well as the incised clay tablets from Mesopotamia, while the wetter climate of the region leads to greater degradation than we find, for example, in the warm and dry environment of Egypt.

source of evidence for reconstructing the social and religious world of ancient Israel. In particular, excavations have yielded important *textual* remains (e.g. inscriptions), *iconographic* (i.e. pictorial) remains (e.g. drawings and artwork) and *other material* remains (e.g. building remains, pottery etc.). Such remains are particularly significant for this study as they constitute a primary, contemporary and direct witness to the beliefs and practices of the time.

The potential value of archaeological evidence for reconstructing the social and religious history of ancient Israel has been particularly emphasized by William Dever. In fact, Dever has suggested that archaeological research constitutes a source of evidence not only equal but also superior to the biblical texts (2001: 89–90, 2005: 74–6). Dever argues that, in contrast to the biblical text, the archaeological evidence is:

**Scholar focus:**
## WILLIAM DEVER (1933– )

Dever is one of the leading north American Syro-Palestinian archaeologists and a key player in the current debate regarding the history of ancient Israel (see 'Have you considered? The minimalist–maximalist debate', above). Although originally intending to complete a doctorate in OT theology under leading biblical scholar and archaeologist G.E. Wright, Dever transferred to archaeology, beginning a more than forty-year career which combined archaeological fieldwork, research and teaching. It is Dever's knowledge of both biblical scholarship and archaeological theory and practice which distinguishes him from many of his contemporaries. Some of Dever's key contributions include:

1. his role in helping to establish Syro-Palestinian archaeology as a distinct discipline, independent from biblical studies;
2. his study of Israelite 'folk religion' and recognition of the importance of the goddess Asherah to popular Israelite belief;
3. his analysis of the emergence and nature of early Israel which he describes as a 'frontier agrarian reform movement'. This is one of the main points of his following work (Dever, 2003: esp. 167–90).

- more *extensive*: while the canonical biblical text is static, a 'closed book', archaeology is dynamic, open-ended, constantly generating new discoveries and insights into ancient Israel;
- more *varied*: while the biblical text is the result of an ongoing process of intentional selection and editing, the archaeological remains are incredibly diverse, covering the whole gamut of Israelite society and thus providing a more comprehensive picture of what life was really like in ancient Israel;

- more *contemporary*: while the biblical text was produced after the events it describes, archaeological artefacts offer a contemporary, 'eye witness' source of evidence and can usually be dated with a relatively high degree of precision;
- more *representative*: while the biblical text was produced by a relatively small circle within ancient Israel (i.e. by educated, male, elites), the archaeological data is broadly representative of every class of society, of every group, and, in particular, of women;
- more *objective*: while the 'facts' in biblical scholarship often seem to be in dispute, there tends to be less debate regarding the interpretation of tangible material remains (but see below).

**Going deeper:**
## THE VALUE OF ARCHAEOLOGY

Dever (2005: 63) has suggested a division of labour between biblical study and archaeology claiming that the former reveals religious *beliefs* whereas the latter primarily sheds light on religious *practices*. Such a broad generalization contains an element of truth. Further nuancing, however, is perhaps warranted. As Dever has himself pointed out, we cannot definitively separate religious belief from practice – belief shapes practice and practice shapes belief. Furthermore, the biblical text has a lot to say about religious practice (think, e.g., of the book of Leviticus with its focus on cultic, especially sacrificial, rites, or the prophets with their references to popular religious activity) while material remains can contribute to our understanding of religious beliefs (the discovery of hundreds of female figurines from ancient Israel and Judah, e.g., has required scholars to rethink the importance of themes of fertility, pregnancy and childbirth within popular religion).

Thus, according to Dever, archaeology allows us to reconstruct a religious history of Israel that is 'more realistic, more comprehensive, better balanced, and ultimately more satisfying' than that provided by the biblical text (2005: 76).

Dever's work offers a valuable corrective to traditional, purely text-focused reconstructions of Israelite history, society and religion. In response, however, I would emphasize that one source of evidence, whether the Bible or archaeology, is not unambiguously better than the other. It all depends on precisely *what* we are trying to reconstruct. For example, if our focus is on the religious beliefs and practices of the common people then archaeology will be very useful. The archaeological remains preserve a record of virtually every segment of Israelite society, thus potentially shedding tremendous light on the faith of the regular, everyday people, the kind of people who are largely ignored in the biblical text with its focus on the state cult and religion of the nation as a whole. It is largely thanks to the findings of archaeology, for example, that scholars have been forced to re-assess the place and role of the goddess Asherah in the popular religion of ancient Israel. In this case, archaeology can and does function as a source of evidence not only equal but also superior to the biblical texts.

It is virtually impossible to develop any sort of picture of the nature, role and place of the leaders of Israel's religion, especially the prophets, however, on the basis of the preserved archaeological remains alone. There is simply not enough evidence to do so – there are very few remains that can be plausibly connected with such individuals and the material that we do have sheds relatively little light on who they were and

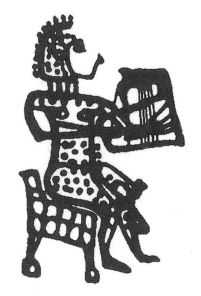

**Figure 1.1    Female lyre player from Kuntillet Ajrud**

what they did. Thus, we are going to be almost entirely reliant on the biblical text for reconstruction of the social locations and roles of these people. It needs to be emphasized, therefore, that the findings of archaeology (like the biblical text) are themselves partial and limited and thus require augmentation from other sources.[4] Thus, 'archaeology alone' is clearly not the answer.

Furthermore, it needs to be kept in mind that archaeology itself is not a hard, objective science, even though scientific processes are frequently employed. The remains do not speak for themselves – interpretation is required. Thus, there can be debate about the meaning and significance of a discovery. Take, for example, the thirteenth–twelfth-century structure excavated at Mount Ebal, located just north of Shechem. The archaeologists involved in the dig interpreted this as the remains of a sanctuary, complete with altar and a wall surrounding the sacred space (cf. Josh. 8). Other scholars, however, have suggested that we are dealing with a farmstead with work buildings and an enclosure fence to hold in the animals (Kessler, 2008: 21). Or take the image of a female lyre player from Kuntillet Ajrud. While there is widespread agreement regarding the figure's gender, her exact identity remains debated: is she the goddess Asherah, a human worshipper, or a royal figure seated on a throne? In both cases, we have only one set of archaeological remains, but multiple interpretations of these are possible.

It should be emphasized, however, that this need to interpret archaeological evidence (and thus the possibility of conflicting interpretations that ensues) is *not* an inherent weakness of the discipline. After all, virtually all human activities, including reading the Bible, require some level of interpretation. It is, however, to recognize that archaeology will not offer the definitive, 'objective' answers for which we might sometimes hope. Archaeology yields probabilities rather than proofs (Dever, 2001: 71).

## 1.5 SUMMARY

The strengths and weaknesses of the various sources of evidence are summarized in Table 1.1.

The starting point for our reconstruction of the social and religious world of ancient Israel is the biblical text. While this approach may not appeal to the so-called 'minimalists', it is a decision born both of conviction (that the biblical text *does* shed light on pre-exilic Israel) and necessity. The biblical text alone provides sufficient data to generate any sort of meaningful picture of the place, nature and function of Israel's prophets, priests and sages, as well as providing some insight into the religious beliefs and practices of the common people. As Grabbe declares, 'For the question of religious specialists, we either use the text or we abandon the subject' (1995: 214). Our two other main sources of evidence – ANE documents and archaeological remains – will play an important twofold role: corrective and supplementary. Because archaeological remains and comparative texts provide an external, independent

**TABLE 1.1**

| Source | Strength | Weakness |
|---|---|---|
| **Biblical text** | Most detailed source. | Social world of ancient Israel is not its primary focus. |
| **ANE documents** | Provide additional evidence which may help shed light on aspects of Israelite society and religion not explicitly discussed in the Bible, and which we may be able to use to test our reconstructions. | Each text reflects its own socio-historical context and thus comparison with a different society is a potentially problematic endeavour. |
| **Archaeological remains** | Constitute a primary, direct and contemporary witness. Such evidence is potentially more extensive, varied, representative and objective than the biblical text. Has the potential to shed much light on the religious beliefs and practices of the common people, in particular. | Have yielded relatively little evidence regarding the key religious leaders of ancient Israel (esp. the prophets). |

voice, they will help to correct and control historical reconstructions based on the biblical text. Furthermore, these sources will help to supplement the picture provided by the biblical text, shedding light on aspects of religious beliefs and practices that were overlooked or even distorted by the authors of the biblical text itself.

## NOTES

1 In addition to the biblical text and textual and non-textual archaeological remains, we may wish to add social scientific research as another possible source of information. Essentially, all our attempts to reconstruct ancient societies are based on the principle of analogy. We make inferences on the basis of a known reality: in other words, we reconstruct ancient societies (the unknown) on the basis of better-known, usually modern, equivalents. For example, parallels are often drawn between life in modern Arab villages or Bedouin society and the biblical world. While the potential value of this research for shedding light on some aspects of Israelite society is clear (e.g. the religious practices of Israelite women), overall, I have not made considerable, direct use of such research because of the significant chronological gap between the modern societies under investigation and ancient Israel. Thus, social scientific research will play an implicit rather than an explicit role in this study.

2 Although the origins of some of the Pentateuch may predate the specific period under discussion in this book, it is clear that this is a composite work that has undergone modification and revision over time (e.g. Gen. 37:25 describes camels as beasts of burden used in caravan trade yet the archaeological evidence suggests that these animals were not domesticated earlier than the late second millennium and were not widely used in trade until well after 1000 BC). Thus, the text still has the potential to shed light on the later time period.

3 Elsewhere, Grabbe comments, 'Yet fiction may be a true representation of its own age, and stereotypes too may have their uses; however much they misrepresent the character of a historical individual, they still often show types of persons or institutions. Even when distorted and unbalanced, they may convey certain truths about society in general' (1995: 9).

4 Kessler, for example, speaks of 'the accident of archaeological finds and the restricted realm of social reality that reveals itself only in material remains' (2008: 23).

## FOR FURTHER READING

P. Davies (2008), *Memories of Ancient Israel: An Introduction to Biblical History – Ancient and Modern*, Louisville: WJKP.

W. Dever (2001), *What Did the Biblical Writers Know and When Did They Know It? What Archaeology Can Tell Us about the Reality of Ancient Israel*, Grand Rapids: Eerdmans.

R. Kessler (2008), *The Social History of Ancient Israel: An Introduction*, trans. L. Maloney, Minneapolis: Fortress Press.

P. McNutt (1999), *Reconstructing the Society of Ancient Israel*, LAI, Louisville: WJKP.

M. Moore and B. Kelle (2011), *Biblical History and Israel's Past: The Changing Study of the Bible and History*, Grand Rapids: Eerdmans.

I. Provan, V.P. Long and T. Longman III (2003), *A Biblical History of Israel*, Louisville: WJKP.

# Chapter 2

# PRIESTS IN ANCIENT ISRAEL

## 2.1 INTRODUCTION

The priests of ancient Israel do not have a good reputation within some Christian circles. We don't need to dig too deep to discover some of the reasons for this antipathy:

- We struggle to make sense of much of the priestly regulations found in Leviticus 1—14 (including the various laws of sacrifice found in chapters 1—7 or the need to distinguish between clean and unclean in chapters 11—14) and therefore fail to appreciate fully the roles and significance of the priests to Israel's faith.
- We allow our (largely negative) view of the law to spill over to the priests who are closely connected with this.
- We allow the prophetic critique of the priestly and sacrificial system to shape our view of what was normative for these institutions, rather than realizing that the prophets are not necessarily condemning the systems per se but rather the abuse and distortion of these.
- We view the priests as proponents of a religion that is static, legalistic and restrictive and which stands in complete opposition to spontaneity and a religion of the heart.
- Within some Protestant circles, the Israelite priesthood has come to embody much of what was believed to be wrong with contemporary Roman Catholicism (e.g., a concern with ritual at the expense of relationship, and an insistence that an individual's access to God can be mediated by another).

It's fair to say, however, that the poor reputation of Israel's priests has not been restricted simply to popular circles. Much biblical scholarship, especially following the work of the influential German OT scholar, Julius Wellhausen (see 'Scholar focus: Julius Wellhausen (1844–1918)'), has fostered a negative appraisal of the priests, their work and writings. Wellhausen's influence, whether overt or implicit, can be seen in subsequent Protestant OT scholarship, particularly that produced in twentieth-century Germany. For example, while acknowledging some of the positive roles of priests in the development of religious faith and practice, Eichrodt could conclude,

> [I]t is also the priesthood that can provide the most serious obstacles to the development of healthy religious life. A rapid florescence of the priestly class is precisely what

**Scholar focus:**
## JULIUS WELLHAUSEN (1844–1918)

Wellhausen was a noted German biblical scholar and orientalist, particularly well known for his theory regarding the origin of the Pentateuch. In his *magnum opus Prolegomena to the History of Israel*, he advanced a definitive formulation of the Documentary Hypothesis, arguing that the Pentateuch should not be attributed to Moses, its traditional author, but that it instead had its origins in a redaction of four, originally independent texts dating from several centuries after the time of Moses (http://en.wikipedia.org/wiki/Julius_Wellhausen). According to this reconstruction, the Pentateuch's priestly and cultic laws came relatively late in Israel's history (following the return from exile) reflecting a move to legalism which was a departure from the heart of Israel's earlier, prophetic religion. Wellhausen's views of the work of the priestly author and, by inference, the priests behind it, can be glimpsed in the following quote: 'By its taste for barren names and technical descriptions, the Priestly Code comes to stand on the same line with the Chronicles and the other literature of Judaism which labours at an artificial revival of the old tradition . . . Of a piece with this tendency is an indescribable pedantry, belonging to the very being of the author of the Priestly Code . . . He selects a long-drawn expression wherever he can; he does not weary of repeating for the hundredth time what is a matter of course (Num. viii.) . . . What is interesting is passed over, what is of no importance is described with minuteness, his exhaustive clearness is such as with its numerous details to confuse our apprehension of what is in itself perfectly clear' (1885: 350–1).

encourages it to separate itself from the community at large, and become a caste, thrusting itself between the secular and religious life of society, and proving instead of a mediator more of a hindrance to direct intercourse with God . . . Furthermore, the high value set on tradition turns into a rigid adherence to forms long suspended, stifling any new religious growth; and for this reason the influence of religion on the shaping of public life is either directed along false paths, or completely neutralized. (1961: 405)

In more recent OT scholarship, however, there has been a renewed appreciation for the critical role the priesthood played within ancient Israel and its religious life.[1] Despite their occasional failings, the priests were holders of a divinely instituted office and stood at the heart of the practice of ancient Israel's faith. As Miller concludes:

> Throughout Israel's history, the priests and the priestly community exercised a fundamental role in maintaining the order of life in the community and stood at the centre of religious practice, whether carried out in a family setting or at local or state levels . . . The priestly instruction and setting forth the norms for community life, individually and corporately, insured that the community would not fall apart by failure to keep the stipulations of the covenantal agreement between Yahweh and Israel and thus damage relations between people and deity and among members of the community. (2000: 162, 163)

Similarly, Nelson has highlighted the key role the priests played in maintaining the faith of the Israelite people throughout their long and difficult history. 'The priests were a fundamental factor in Israel's existence before Yahweh. More durable than either the kings or the prophets, the priesthood as an institution originated in the pre-monarchic period and flourished until the devastation of the temple by the Romans, bridging all the momentous transitions in Israel's national life' (1993: 88). Thus while their conservatism and traditionalism has often been viewed in a negative light, it was precisely this reluctance to change that saw the priests preserve and safeguard the faith of Israel, transmitting it from one generation to the next.

But who actually were the priests? How did you become one? What did they do? Where were they to be found? This chapter will answer these questions.

## 2.2 HOW DID SOMEONE BECOME A PRIEST?

Unlike the prophets, Israel's priests received no special, individual divine calling to fulfil their role. Their path, while no less important, was a bit more mundane. In fact, on a number of occasions the biblical text specifically speaks not of God but of other human beings, often the king, appointing individuals to be priests (for more details about the role of the king in the religious life of ancient Israel see the Excursus). In order to address the issue of how someone became a priest in ancient Israel we need to consider three related questions:

- Who could become a priest (in other words, who were the eligible candidates for the position)?

- Did one have to undergo training to become a priest (in other words, what was the required education for the position)?
- Was there a formal rite by which one became 'ordained' as a priest?

### 2.2.1 WHO WAS ELIGIBLE TO BECOME A PRIEST?

At first glance, this appears to be a relatively simple question to answer. Most

**ANE parallels:**
**THE PRIESTHOOD AS A HEREDITARY OFFICE**

The priesthood was a hereditary office not only in Israel but also throughout the ancient Near East. For example, in Egypt the priesthood appears to have been hereditary from the nineteenth dynasty (i.e. early thirteenth century BC) onwards, in Assyria there were certain types of priestly office for which succession passed from father to son, and from Phoenicia there is evidence that points to the presence of priestly houses. De Vaux has argued that such a hereditary system was particularly suited for the priesthood, for 'it ensured that sanctuaries were well looked after and kept in good repair, and that religious rites were left unchanged: the father would initiate his son into the skills required of him' (1965: 359). The fact that individuals inherited the office, however, could also have a negative effect. According to Sabourin, 'it could also lead to excessive institutionalism, crass conservatism, and a lack of zeal in performing the sacred duties' (1973: 137). In particular, the hereditary nature of the office meant that it could sometimes be taken for granted, giving rise to a lack of care in the performance of priestly duties. This is seen, for example, in the case of Eli's sons, Hophni and Phinehas, who treated their sacrificial responsibilities with contempt (1 Sam. 2:12–17).

readers of the OT will be aware that the biblical text, and in particular the book of Numbers, suggests that only the sons of Aaron, Moses' brother, could function as priests in ancient Israel. The priesthood was essentially a hereditary office (as were most professions in the ancient Near East) with eligibility determined by lineage.

When we look at the biblical text as a whole, however, it is clear that this answer is inadequate in and of itself. During Israel's early history, a number of people of non-Aaronic descent performed priestly roles and appear to have been viewed as legitimate priests. Thus, three answers to the question of eligibility are, in fact, possible: (1) any male Israelite could function as a priest; (2) only a Levite (i.e. member of the tribe of Levi) could perform priestly roles; and (3) priestly responsibilities were restricted to only one branch of the Levites, the sons of Aaron.

### Any Israelite

The biblical text is quite clear that in the early period of Israel's history, from the time of the Judges through to the beginning of the monarchy, any male could potentially function as a priest. Although Levitical descent may have been preferred, this was not a rigid requirement. The clearest evidence for this is found in Judges 17 where Micah, a member of the tribe of Ephraim (17:1), appoints one of his own sons as priest in the shrine that he has just established (17:5). Other priests of non-Levitical descent include Samuel (who was also an Ephraimite, cf. 1 Sam. 1:1),[2] some of the sons of David (who, like their father, must have belonged to the tribe of Judah, cf. 2 Sam. 8:18) and Ira the Jairite, David's priest (2 Sam. 20:26).[3]

It is quite possible that non-Levites continued to function as priests (at least in the northern kingdom) even into the period of the divided kingdom (c.922 BC onwards). Although such claims need to be viewed with a certain degree of suspicion, the Deuteronomist asserts that Jeroboam I appointed priests who were not of Levi's line to the various sanctuaries that he had established throughout the northern kingdom.[4] 'Even after this event Jeroboam did not turn from his evil way, but made priests for the high places again from among all the people; any who wanted to be priests he consecrated for the high places' (1 Kings 13:33; cf. 12:31). (For a discussion of 'high places' see 2.4.) It should be recognized, however, that the negative appraisal of such actions clearly suggests that by the time that Kings was composed it was commonly accepted (at least in the south) that only Levites could function as priests.

### Levites

A more restrictive view of eligibility for the priesthood is provided within the pentateuchal legislation, especially in the books of Numbers and Deuteronomy. Both of these texts emphasize that only members of the tribe of Levi, the tribe specially dedicated to God for holy service in place of the first-born of Israel (Num. 3:12; 8:16), could perform priestly functions. Beyond this point of agreement, however, the two books are not completely unanimous in their perspectives. Deuteronomy implies that any Levite could perform priestly functions, whereas Numbers restricts this privilege to the sons of Aaron. Let's look at Deuteronomy first.

Deuteronomy suggests that any Levite was able to fulfil priestly responsibilities. While

## Going deeper:
## THE PREFERENCE FOR LEVITICAL PRIESTS

While Levitical descent may have not been a fixed requirement for all priests in ancient Israel, it is quite clear that there was a preference for Levites from a very early time. For example, in the above-mentioned story from the book of Judges, Micah does not take long to replace his son as priest with a wandering Levite (17:7–13). This predilection for Levitical descent is clearly indicated in verse 13 where Micah declares, 'Now I know that the LORD will prosper me, because the Levite has become my priest.' As Miller states, 'Levitical descent is not required but seems to be a clear plus in that Micah believes himself to be in better stead with Yahweh for having now a Levite as priest and not just a member of the family' (2000: 172).

the issue is hotly disputed, this book appears to equate priests and Levites (cf. the reference to 'the levitical priests' in Deut. 17:9, 18; 24:8; 27:9, the reference to 'the levitical priests, the whole tribe of Levi' in 18:1 and 'the priests, the sons of Levi' in 21:5 and 31:9), attributes to the Levites priestly roles (e.g. to minister in the name of the Lord, Deut. 18:5–7, cf. Deut. 33:8–10), and grants them priestly privileges (e.g. they are allowed to eat the priest's portion of the sacrifices, Deut. 18:3; cf. Num. 18:8–20). In other words, Deuteronomy appears not to draw a rigid distinction between the Levites as a whole and the priestly office – any Levite could function as a priest.

Evidence for Levites functioning as priests is also found outside the book of Deuteronomy. For example, Joshua 13:14 speaks of the

## Have you considered?
## COULD LEVITES BE RECRUITED?

While we may be accustomed to think of Levitical identity as being determined by genealogy (i.e. you had to be born into the tribe of Levi), there is some suggestion that this may not have always been the case, especially during Israel's early history. Stager has suggested that the priesthood in early Israel performed an important socio-economic function, helping to '"absorb" a surplus of young males, especially for those who were not firstborns and, as the frontier was closing, stood little chance of inheriting much of the patrimony or of pioneering new land' (1985: 27).

Without access to land, some non first-born males, in particular, would have found life exceedingly difficult. Parents may thus have made the decision to dedicate their sons to the Levitical order knowing that when they grew up they could be employed as a priest by

a wealthy, landed patron who would be able to provide for their needs (cf. the story of the young Levite attached to the house of Micah in Judges 17).

Stager sees further evidence for this practice in the example of Samuel, who is from the tribe of Ephraim, but who goes to train under the priest Eli at Shiloh, and in the blessing of the tribe of Levi in Deuteronomy 33:9 (which he translates 'Who said of his father (and his mother) "I have not seen him"; He was not acquainted with (nkr) his brothers nor knew his own children.') Stager thus concludes that, while some individuals were indeed born into the priesthood, it is also possible that others were 'recruited' across clan and tribal boundaries, joining the Levitical order as a result of economic factors (1985: 28).

tribe of Levi being given the inheritance of 'offerings by fire' and in 18:7 they are specifically given the 'priesthood of the LORD' as their heritage. In Judges, the Levite Jonathan (a descendant of Moses) and his sons served as priests in the temple at Dan (Judg. 18:30). From a later time, Jeremiah speaks of Levitical priests offering burnt and grain offerings and making sacrifices as a virtual divine ordinance (Jer. 33:18).

### Son of Aaron

Numbers also suggests that membership of the tribe of Levi was a key requirement for

---

**Going deeper:**
### THE ROLES OF PRIESTS AND LEVITES IN EZEKIEL'S NEW TEMPLE

The distinction between the priests and the Levites is also found in Ezekiel's description of the new Jerusalem temple (Ezek. 44). Although the Levites are given a recognized standing within the temple bureaucracy, their roles are restricted because some of their number participated in and led Israel's idolatry (v. 10). Hence, they are forbidden from serving as priests and coming near any of the sacred offerings but are instead appointed 'to keep charge of the temple, to do all its chores, all that is to be done in it' (v. 14). This is in contrast to the group Ezekiel labels the 'levitical priests, the descendants of Zadok'* who are the only ones allowed to perform priestly functions, that is, they may approach Yahweh, offer up fat and blood on the altar, and go into the sanctuary (vv. 15–16).

* Zadok was one of David's priests who supported Solomon in his claim for the throne. Following Solomon's succession, he was appointed as Solomon's sole priest and his family held a monopoly on the Jerusalemite priesthood throughout the pre-exilic period.

---

priestly office. Its perspective, however, appears to be more restrictive than that found in Deuteronomy. Here only members of one family from the tribe of Levi – Aaron and his sons – are given the title 'priest' and are allowed to perform the key priestly functions, including service at the altar (Num. 18:1–7; cf. Exod. 29:9). The rest of the Levites, then, are placed at the service of Aaron and his sons (Num. 3:6–9) and are restricted to the less important functions of the cult, including transportation and maintenance of the Tabernacle (1:47–53).

The secondary position of the Levites to the sons of Aaron is graphically illustrated in the story of the rebellion of Korah found in Numbers 16. Here the Levite Korah, along with 250 other Israelites, complains about the exaltation of Aaron (and his sons) over the rest of the Israelites. The Levites appear to be unhappy over their secondary role in the cult and want to take on priestly duties as well (vv. 8–11). The Lord, however, acts in judgement against Korah and his company as 'a reminder to the Israelites that no outsider, who is not of the descendants of Aaron, shall approach to offer incense before the LORD' (v. 40). (For a discussion of incense offering see 2.2.)

### 2.2.2 WHAT TRAINING DID PRIESTS UNDERGO?

When one considers the specialized knowledge and technical skills required to be a priest, it seems likely that potential candidates must have undergone some form of training. The range of ritual and cultic matters that had to be mastered (e.g. the use of the Urim and Thummim (for more details see below), decisions regarding clean and unclean, oversight of sacrifices etc.) could hardly have been covered and learned without some process

**Plate 2.1   Terracotta figurine of a woman holding a drum from the Iron II period**

of formal instruction. Unfortunately, however, we have practically no information on how priests were educated in ancient Israel.

Given the hereditary nature of the priesthood, it is likely that the majority of instruction was provided by the young man's father. It was a common ANE expectation that fathers would train their sons in the trade or occupation they would pursue. Alternatively, some young men may have been apprenticed to a well-known priest for instruction. For example, 1 Samuel 3:1 speaks of Samuel ministering to the Lord 'under' Eli, a situation perhaps to be expected given that Samuel's father was probably not a priest himself.

It is also possible that more formal instruction may have taken place within an institutional context. While direct evidence for such priestly 'schools' in ancient Israel

is minimal, it is undeniable that they existed within other ANE nations. For example, in Egypt there was a 'house of life' (*pr-'nk*) attached to most of the major temples. This functioned as a college for the training of priests and included a curriculum that covered the entire range of ritual and cultic law. Instruction was provided by a faculty composed of scribes who had the status of priests. Such scribes / priests could also be called on to provide guidance for the conduct of festivals or the authentication of sacred animals. They were also responsible for writing annals, laws and rituals (Blenkinsopp, 1995a: 100). From Mesopotamia, we also have examples of schools attached to temples. These functioned as libraries and educational centres for the priests, especially those responsible for healing.

While little direct evidence for such a process of formal, priestly instruction in ancient Israel has yet been found, we could well imagine that a similar practice may have been adopted, especially following the construction of the temple in Jerusalem and the growth of institutional structures under the monarchy. André Lemaire, in particular, has argued for the existence of such a priestly school within Jerusalem.

In Jerusalem, the building of the temple carried with it the need for trained personnel for the temple who had to receive a formative education for their service (reading, writing, singing, music, rites, feasts, calendar, national religious traditions, etc.) This instruction was probably given at or near the temple perhaps under the supervision of the high priest . . . After a possible general training in reading, writing, the scribal arts, and national traditions, future priests were

21

## Have you considered?
## WHY WERE THERE NO FEMALE PRIESTS IN ANCIENT ISRAEL?

Both legal and narrative sections of the OT suggest that only males could function as priests of Yahweh in ancient Israel. Contrary to popular opinion, however, this refusal to allow women to hold priestly office was not unique to Israel but, in fact, conforms to common ANE practice (Bird, 1997: 94).

So why were females not allowed to become priests? The obvious answer is that the law that was given by God only sanctioned a male priesthood. Sociologists and historians of Israelite religion, however, have put forward a number of additional suggestions that are worth considering. These include:

1 The sexual division of labour located women within the household rather than in public spaces and institutions, such as the cult. Ethnographic studies of ancient and modern societies have highlighted the almost universal phenomenon of sexual division of labour, which is particularly pronounced in preindustrial agricultural societies such as ancient Israel (Bird, 1997: 86). Essentially, these studies suggest that the work someone does is largely determined by their gender. Thus, in ancient Israel the primary work of females was reproduction (and associated household tasks) whereas for males this involved protection and agricultural production.

This fundamental sexual division of labour has far-reaching consequences for the location, status and roles of women in society (Bird, 1997: 86). Because of their primary responsibility for reproduction, women were located (both physically and ideologically) within the domestic sphere. Males, in contrast, inhabited the public domain, and thus could be involved in the military, legal and cultic institutions of their society. Because the official cult belonged to the public, male sphere it is unsurprising to find that women only held limited or marginal roles within this, and could not occupy a formal position of leadership (i.e. function as a priest).

2 The periodic impurity of women during their reproductive years made them unfit for continual cultic service and leadership. Israelite religion, following widespread ancient practice, excluded all persons (whether male or female) who were deemed to be unclean from participation in cultic activities. Various circumstances could give rise to this state, including childbirth and the woman's monthly period (cf. Lev. 12; and 15). These regular occurrences would have disqualified a woman from access to those spaces and items dedicated as holy, especially the altar and sanctuary, and thus made it virtually impossible for her to perform priestly duties on a continual basis.

3 Women were related to the Israelite cult through a male and, therefore, they were less likely to have a direct leadership role. Israelite society as a whole was essentially patriarchal and patrilineal (tracing descent through the male line) and so too was its religion. For example, according to texts such as Genesis 17:9–14 and Exodus 12:44, 48 the covenant community is essentially the community of the circumcised, and in Exodus 23:17 it is only males who are required to participate in the three great pilgrimage festivals (cf. Deut. 16:16). Females related to the cultic community through the male (whether a husband or father) and thus their involvement was mediated rather than direct.* The fact that women had no 'independent existence' in terms of the cult itself meant that it was unlikely that they would hold a leadership role within it.

4 The patrilineal nature of the priestly office meant that female priests would have created serious difficulties in identifying who was and was not a priest. Nelson (1993: 97) has suggested that the decision not to employ women as priests in ancient Israel probably had more to do with kinship structures than with theology. From the period of the monarchy onwards, genealogy, and in particular patrilineal descent, was crucial to hold priestly office. In other words, to be a priest you had to be the son of a priest. The precise

genealogy of a priest's mother, however, was irrelevant. According to Nelson, 'The inclusion of priests' daughters into priestly office would have strained this patrilineal descent system beyond capacity' (Nelson, 1993: 97). All sorts of problems could have arisen. For example, would the son or daughter of a non-priest father and a priest mother be recognized as a priest? Since a married woman's position in the cult depended on her husband (see above), would the marriage of a female priest to a layman erase her priestly status? Such potential difficulties to a patrilineal system meant that it was unlikely that women would hold priestly office in ancient Israel.

Although they could not function as priests, there is some evidence to suggest that women played various other roles in the Israelite cult. It seems, however, that their service was confined largely to maintenance and support duties (Bird, 1997: 94). These may have included:

1  weaving and sewing of cloth, hangings and other textiles – according to Exodus 35:25–26 the material of the Tabernacle hangings was spun by women;**
2  preparation of cultic foods and meals – this was the standard work of women in the domestic sphere and there is no reason to believe that they would not have performed this task in the cultic sphere as well. Jeremiah 7:18 explicitly describes the women as kneading dough and making cakes for the Queen of Heaven, indicating an association between women and food preparation in a religious context;
3  involvement in corporate worship as singers (Exod. 15:20), dancers (1 Sam. 18:6–7) or musicians (Ps. 68:24–26);
4  attendance in the sanctuary – Exodus 38:8 and 1 Samuel 2:22 point to the involvement of women who 'ministered (*šĕbā'ôt*) at the Tent of Meeting'. The Hebrew term *ṣābā'* is used elsewhere in the OT to describe the service of the Levites (cf. Num. 4:3, 23, 35, 39, 43), suggesting that these women

fulfilled a specific role within the Israelite cult. Unfortunately, however, there is little evidence to suggest what this role may have actually entailed, and how long this position lasted.

There are also a number of references to *qĕdēšôt* in the biblical text (e.g. Gen. 38:21–22; Deut. 23:17–18 and Hos. 4:14) although such women are usually viewed as operating outside the Yahwistic cult. Traditionally, this term has been rendered as '(cult) prostitute' suggesting that they were involved in some form of ritual sexual activity. Such an interpretation, however, has been questioned in more recent scholarship with opponents arguing that there is no clear evidence for sacred prostitution within West Semitic religion in general (including at Ugarit where the same term is also used) and that the classical sources (e.g. Herodotus) which do suggest that such a practice was found in the ANE are late and unreliable (Nelson, 1993: 98). This would seem to be one of those areas, therefore, where caution is warranted. *qĕdēšâ* (the singular, feminine form of the noun) simply means 'consecrated one' and points to the existence of female cultic functionaries within West Semitic religion. As with the 'women who ministered at the tent of meeting', however, the exact nature of their role remains unclear.

For more details about the roles of women in the Israelite cult, see Bird (1997). For a nuanced discussion of the possible role of prostitution in ANE cults, see Hess, 2007: 332–6.

* This principle can also be seen in the example of a woman from a priestly family who had rights to eat certain sacrifices because of her association with a priestly father of husband (Lev. 22:12–13; Num. 18:11, 13).
** Although 2 Kings 23:7 refers to non-Yahwistic religious practices, this passage also associates women with weaving in a religious context.

probably taught more specific subjects concerning rites, sacrifices, calendar, the temple (buildings, furnishings etc.), distinctions between clean and unclean, the singing of psalms, and the playing of sacred music. Priestly instruction could well be reflected in biblical books such as Leviticus (especially chaps. 1—7; 11; 13—14; 25) or the end of Exodus (chaps. 25—31; 35—40). In fact, these biblical texts may have been used as a reference work, a kind of text book, in the priestly school of Jerusalem, a learning center probably situated in the temple complex having some kind of library (cf. 2 Kings 22:8) as known from Egypt. (1992: 309–10)

While such a suggestion must remain conjectural, the comparative evidence, especially from Egypt, renders such a hypothesis possible, if not likely.

### 2.2.3 WAS THERE AN INSTALLATION CEREMONY?

Although it is impossible to know how widespread the practice was, Exodus 29 and Leviticus 8—9 suggest that at least some of Israel's priests underwent a rite of installation or ordination that set them apart to fulfil their unique role. The common Hebrew expression for this process was 'filling (*millu'îm*) the hand'. While the exact meaning of this phrase is debated,[5] it may refer to a priest's rights to the portions of the sacrifices upon which he and his family survived.[6]

The rite described in the books of Exodus and Leviticus takes place over a period of seven days and involves a number of different stages. Initially, the priests were washed with water, probably as a means of purifying and cleansing them. They were then clothed in special garments including tunics, sashes and headdresses.[7] These garments were viewed as being holy in their own right and thus could only be put on after the priest had taken a purificatory bath. A number of sacrifices were offered and some of the blood was daubed on the priest's right ear lobe, thumb and big toe. While the significance of this act remains debated, Milgrom has argued that 'in the ANE, incantations recited during the ritual smearing of persons, statues of gods, and buildings suggest that its purpose is purificatory and apotropaic – to wipe off and ward off the incursions of menacing forces' (1993: 164). Perhaps locating the blood on the ear, hand and foot also points to the necessity of the priest hearing the divine word and putting this into action. Blood and anointing oil were then sprinkled on the priests and their clothes, sanctifying and dedicating them to God's service.[8] Finally, the priest consumed some of the sacrifice.

While the exact significance of some of the elements of the rite may elude us, it is clear that as a whole the process was a profoundly transformative experience. By such a rite the priests were made holy – they were set apart from the common run of humanity and thus 'could venture into sacred space, handle holy objects, and eat the holy sacrifices without jeopardy to themselves or Israel' (Nelson, 1993: 50). The priests no longer simply lived in the ordinary, everyday world; they could now operate in the realm of the sacred.

## 2.3 WHAT DID A PRIEST DO?

Many people operate with a rather simplistic view of the roles of Israel's priests. The dominant perception is that their primary responsibility was to perform the

**TABLE 2.1**

| Task/Text | Deut. 33:8–11 | Lev. 10:10–11 | I Sam. 2:28 |
|---|---|---|---|
| Divination via the use of Urim and Thummim or ephod | √ | | √ |
| Teaching the law | √ | √ | |
| Involvement with sacrifices and offerings (incl. incense) | √ | | √ |
| Distinguishing between holy and common, clean and unclean | | √ | |

various sacrifices, a role which included killing the sacrificial animal itself.

While this perspective contains an element of truth, it needs to be qualified in two important ways.[9] First, priestly involvement in the sacrificial system was not the sum and total of their responsibilities. In fact, if we take Deuteronomy 33:8–11 as broadly representative of the priestly role during the pre-exilic period, sacrifice may have been the *least* important of their responsibilities (as suggested by its location last on the list of priestly duties). As we will see, priests performed a multi-faceted role within ancient Israel's religious and economic systems which included, but was certainly not limited to, involvement in sacrificial rites. Second, it is quite clear that in the majority of cases the priests themselves were not actually involved in the killing of the sacrificial animal. The legislation in Leviticus 1—7 suggests that the priests usually became involved in the sacrificial rite only after the animal had been killed.[10] The actual task of killing (sometimes referred to as 'immolation') was the responsibility of the person who had brought the offering; after all, it was *this* person's sacrifice.

So what did a priest actually do? Several texts from the OT (Deut. 33:8–11; Lev. 10:10–11; 1 Sam. 2:28) provide us with the basic outline for a priestly 'job description'.

Comparing these texts produces the results shown in Table 2.1. Other passages suggest that a key priestly responsibility included blessing the people (Num. 6:23; cf. Deut. 10:8; and 1 Chron. 23:13). While this list may not provide an exhaustive picture of the duties a priest would perform, it certainly highlights the key tasks which priests were generally expected to complete.

**Archaeological insight:**
**WHAT DID THE URIM AND THUMMIM LOOK LIKE?**

King and Stager (2001: 330) have suggested that the Urim and Thummim may have resembled modern day dice. Excavations of a sanctuary at Dan have uncovered a number of cultic objects, including a large die made of blue frit or faience (earthenware or pottery covered with a glaze). Because of the location of the die within the sanctuary and the fact that the dots on opposing sides add up to the sacred number seven, King and Stager argue that 'dice were an important part of the priestly paraphernalia at the Danite sanctuary' (King and Stager, 2001: 330). Given the tradition preserved in the book of Judges which connects this site with a Levitical priest who was skilled in divination (cf. Judg. 17—18), it is possible that the Urim and Thummim may have been dice that were used for discerning the will of the Lord.

## 2.3.1 DIVINATION

This activity essentially involved seeking the will of the Lord in a given situation. Through the use of various means, the priest sought a divine response to a request for specific information made by a third party. Such requests ranged from the identification of wrongdoers or divinely chosen people through to tactical decisions during times of conflict.

How did discerning the will of the Lord take place? Some passages imply that a priest had a number of technical instruments at his disposal, including the Urim and Thummim and ephod.[11]

During the pre-monarchic and early monarchic periods, the Urim and Thummim appear to have been consulted regularly by Israel's priests (cf. Num. 27:21; 1 Sam. 14:41, 28:6).[12] The exact nature of the Urim and Thummim, however, remains a point of debate (see box on previous page). Whatever their form, whether dice or two stones engraved with distinctive symbols, the biblical text indicates that they were used when someone wanted an answer to a simple, binary question (i.e. a question in which only two answers are possible).

**Plate 2.2  Faience die which may have been used in divination, found in the sacred precinct at Tel Dan**

A good example of the use of the Urim and Thummim to answer simple, two part questions is found in 1 Samuel 14:36–46. In this passage the device is employed to determine why the Lord has not responded to Saul's query whether he should fight the Philistines or not. Two basic answers are suggested: the Lord has not responded due to the sin of Saul and Jonathan (to be indicated by Urim) or because of the sin of the people (to be indicated by Thummim). Following the identification of Saul and Jonathan, the Urim and Thummim are consulted a second time. Again, only two answers are possible (i.e. whether it is the sin of Saul or Jonathan that is responsible), and this time Jonathan is singled out. On some occasions, however, it appears that the Urim and Thummim could fail to provide an answer (cf. 1 Sam. 14:37; and 28:6). No-one is sure how this was indicated, however, one suggestion is that it may have involved both the Urim and Thummim appearing at the same time.

Another element of priestly paraphernalia which appears to have played a role in divination was the ephod. As with the Urim and Thummim, however, the exact nature of this item or how it was used is unknown. Complicating matters is the fact the Hebrew term *'ēpōd* can carry three different meanings in the OT (for more details see de Vaux, 1965: 349–52). It could be used to refer to:

1  a linen garment, worn round the waist, part of the priest's vestments;
2  a special part of the high priest's outer clothing, worn over the tunic and cloak;
3  a portable, cultic object usually made of gold.

In those narrative passages in which the ephod is specifically connected with divination (i.e. Judg. 17:5—18:6; 1 Sam.

23:6–12; 30:7–8), the third option seems to fit the context best. For example, in 1 Samuel 23:6–12 the priest Abiathar brings the ephod in his hand to answer David's questions. Here the ephod does not appear to be an item of clothing. Like the Urim and Thummim, the ephod is consulted to determine the answer to a simple binary question: will Saul come down to Keilah to destroy the city or not?

Although divination appears to have been an important priestly role, particularly during Israel's early history, over time we witness a decreasing emphasis on this practice. The most likely reason for this is the emergence of the prophets as the authoritative spokespeople of God's will. In fact, de Vaux (1965: 353) argues that later kings (such as Ahab and Joram of Israel) consulted Yahweh through prophets in circumstances where earlier kings, such as Saul and David, used to consult him by ephod.

### 2.3.2 TEACHING

During the pre-exilic period the teaching of the *tôrâ*, the ordinances and the law of the Lord, was the special domain of the priests.[13] In fact, Jeremiah 18:18 suggests that this may have been *the* key priestly role – prophets brought the word of the Lord, the wise brought counsel, the priests gave instruction. The centrality of *tôrâ* to the priestly office is reinforced by the fact that the prophetic critique of the priests characteristically centres on their failure to fulfil their responsibilities in guarding and teaching this material to Israel (Hutton, 1994: 154).[14]

In their role as teachers of *tôrâ*, priests seem to have performed three specific functions. First, the priests were expected to *read the law* and make it known to the people.

> **Going deeper:**
> **PRIESTLY PRONOUNCEMENTS**
>
> Although the book of Haggai clearly dates to the early postexilic period, it may provide an example of what priestly instruction in the law looked like during the pre-exilic period. In Haggai 2:10–13 the prophet is instructed by the Lord to 'ask the priests for a ruling' regarding issues of holiness and uncleanness. He does so and in both cases the priests provide a definitive answer. Leviticus 10:10–11 also suggests that a key role of the priests was to distinguish between the holy and the common, the clean and the unclean, and that they were to 'teach the people of Israel all the statutes that the LORD has spoken to them through Moses' (cf. Deut. 24:8).

Deuteronomy 31:9 suggests that the law had been entrusted to the priests and that they were responsible for its public dissemination. Furthermore, the priests were expected to *make authoritative pronouncements regarding the law's application* to specific situations. In particular, priests were 'authorized' to provide their fellow Israelites with instruction and guidance about ritual or cultic concerns including, for example, issues of purity and holiness. Hence, Nelson concludes, 'The local priest was the average Israelite's closest source of Yahweh's will for daily living' (1993: 87). Finally, the priests *served as judges*. As a result of their knowledge of the law and ability to interpret its regulations, priests may have been consulted to resolve difficult judicial issues. While the OT as a whole does not suggest that this was a major function of the priests (most legal decisions would have been made by the elders at the city gate), Deuteronomy indicates that priests could fulfil this role if required.[15] For example, Deuteronomy 21:5 suggests that in 'all cases of dispute and assault' the priest's decision shall be authoritative. A similar picture is given in 17:8–13 where the Israelites are instructed to 'go up to the place that the LORD your God will choose' and 'consult with the levitical priests' regarding difficult and disputed judicial decisions. Note the binding nature of the priests' judgement:

> Carry out exactly the decision that they announce to you from the place that the LORD will choose, diligently observing everything they instruct you. You must carry out fully the law that they interpret for you or the ruling that they announce to you; do not turn aside from the decision that they announce to you, either to the right or to the left. As for anyone who presumes to disobey the priest appointed to minister there to the LORD your God, or the judge, that person shall die. (Deut. 17:10–12)

It appears, however, that akin to their role as diviners, the place of the priests as teachers of *tôrâ* also became less important over time. During the exilic and post-exilic periods we have the emergence of a new social group within Judaism, the scribes, who would gradually assume increasing responsibility for this role.

### 2.3.3  SACRIFICE (AND INCENSE OFFERING)

The priest's involvement in ancient Israel's sacrificial system is well known but what they actually did is often misunderstood.

As suggested previously, the priest did not normally kill the sacrificial animal himself. The laws of sacrifice which we find in the book of Leviticus stipulate that, in the majority of cases, the animal was to be killed by the person who was making the offering. The main exceptions to this were (1) if the person

---

**Archaeological insight:**
**WHAT DID AN ALTAR LOOK LIKE?**

Archaeologists have discovered dozens of altars of varying sizes, shapes and styles from ancient Israel. Perhaps the most famous comes from Tel Beer Sheba. This altar was very large in size (1.57 m high) and was constructed of ashlar masonry, contrary to the biblical prescriptions that altars be fashioned from earth or unhewn stones (cf. Exod. 20:24–25; Deut. 27:6; and Josh. 8:31). A horn appears to have been located on the top of each corner, perhaps symbolizing the strength of the altar. Unfortunately, archaeologists could find no evidence of burning on the stones of the altar which means that its exact function is unclear. Two options have been put forward: its size suggests that it was used for animal sacrifice: but its shape suggests that it may have been used to offer incense. Interestingly, the altar was not found in situ. Rather it had been broken down and some of the stones reused in the construction of a storehouse wall. It has been suggested that this process of decommissioning may have been connected with Hezekiah's cultic reforms which took place during the eighth century. (For more details about such reforms see the Excursus.)

---

was ritually unclean or (2) if the animal to be sacrificed was a bird. In both these instances the priest himself was directly involved in the killing of the animal. In the case of the latter, this was because the birds had to be killed on the altar itself and this was the specific domain of the priests.

Once the animal had been killed, the offerer brought the body to the priest. The priest would then perform the various

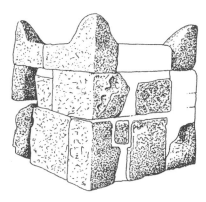

**Figure 2.1    The large four-horned altar from Beersheba, as reassembled**

**Plate 2.3    Man bringing an offering, from Zinjirli**

rites connected with the altar, the place of most direct contact with the divine. According to the laws of sacrifice provided in Leviticus 1—7 these rites included:

1  The priest presented the sacrifice on the altar – specifically, the priest was responsible for placing the part of the sacrifice that belonged to God upon the altar.
2  The priest burned the sacrifice – by turning the offering into smoke, the priest transferred the animal from the human realm to that of the divine.
3  The priest dealt with the blood (and body) of the sacrifice – the blood, which was believed to contain the life-force of the animal (cf. Lev. 17:11), could be splashed on or poured around the altar.

In addition to the sacrifice of animals, priests oversaw offerings of various cereals, liquids and incense. Incense usually consisted of frankincense (a costly, fragrant, whitish gum resin), and several other minor ingredients including sweet spices and myrrh (a reddish gum resin that is bitter to taste) (King and Stager, 2001: 347). The burning of incense was a privilege of the priests because the incense had to be burnt on the altar (cf. Deut. 33:10; and Num. 16:40).

In addition to its overtly religious dimension, the sacrificial system was also

29

**Plate 2.4    Assemblage of four-horned incense altars, from Ekron**

a major source of income and economic support for the priesthood in ancient Israel. While texts such as Judges 17:10 suggest that priests could be paid a wage for their services, there were also specific portions of the various offerings set aside as the 'priest's due' (cf. Lev. 2:1–10; 6:14–18; Deut. 18:3; 1 Sam. 2). Consumption of this portion (even unintentionally) by non-priestly individuals carried with it a significant financial penalty (cf. Lev. 22:10–16).

In contrast to their other two roles (divination and teaching), the priests' involvement in sacrifice actually became more important over time. While people came to look to the prophets for a revelation of the divine will and scribes took on the role of instruction, sacrifice became *the* domain of the priests. Such a development, however, could only ever be a mixed blessing for the loss of the temple and its sacrificial cult would inevitably also lead to a diminishment in the importance of the priests themselves.

### 2.3.4    BLESSING THE PEOPLE

Given their location between both the divine and human realms, the priests were responsible for pronouncing blessing from God upon the Israelite people (Deut. 10:8; 1 Chron. 23:13). These blessings could be spoken over the people as a whole on significant public occasions (Lev. 9:22) or over individuals in response to specific petitions or requests, usually during a time of distress. Such declarations were highly regarded as they were considered to be authoritative pronouncements of God's will and not merely the human opinion of the priest (Nelson, 1993: 46).

## Archaeological insight:
## A PRIESTLY BLESSING FROM OUTSIDE THE OT

During the late 1970s, Israeli archaeologists excavated a series of late seventh- to early sixth-century-BC burial chambers from the Hinnom Valley, just outside Jerusalem. Among the various items left with the deceased, they discovered two small silver scrolls that had been rolled up to be worn on a leather strap around the neck. When the scrolls were unrolled (a process which took almost three years!) they measured 3 × 10 cm and 1 × 4 cm. Both scrolls appear to contain a version of the so-called Aaronic or Priestly blessing that Aaron and his sons were commanded to say over the Israelites (Num. 6:24–26). The end of the larger scroll reads: 'May blessings be on you from Yahweh, and may he keep you, may Yahweh cause to shine his countenance . . .', while the end of the smaller finishes 'above you and grant you peace' (Keel and Uehlinger, 1998: 364).

## Have you considered?
## PRIESTS MAY HAVE ALSO FUNCTIONED AS THE TAX-MEN OF ANCIENT ISRAEL

Matthews and Benjamin (1993: 187) have emphasized the important *economic* role that priests played within Israel's society because of their involvement in collecting agricultural produce as sacrifices or taxes during harvest times. In particular, Matthews and Benjamin suggest that the priests had three key responsibilities.

Initially, the priests *determined how much produce could be used by the households* which produced it and how much was to be collected by the state. Then they *supervised the collection and processing of the sacrifices* so that they could be stored in sanctuaries until the beginning of the next agricultural season or until the king redistributed them to state workers and soldiers. (Matthews and Benjamin argue that most of the farm produce that was given as an offering would not have been destroyed by fire but stored. 'The wholesale destruction of produce contradicts the strong sense of limited foods that predominated in Mediterranean culture . . . even with their surplus economies it is unlikely that states could afford, much less value, the regular loss of a percentage of their gross national product' (1993: 192).) Finally, the priests *supervised any borrowing from their sanctuary's treasury* by Israelite households to pay for animals and seed and to prepare for the next season.

Perhaps the best-known example of a priestly blessing is found in Numbers 6:24–26. Here Moses instructs Aaron and his sons to bless the Israelites with the following words: 'the Lord bless you and keep you; the Lord make his face to shine upon you, and be gracious to you; the Lord lift up his countenance upon you, and give you peace'. Further examples can be found embedded within certain psalms (e.g. Pss. 115:14–15; 121:7–8; 128:5; and 134:3; cf. 1 Sam. 1:9–20). A good specimen is Psalm 118:26, which was probably spoken by a priest over an individual who had approached the temple in Jerusalem to worship: 'Blessed in the name of Yahweh is the one who comes. We bless you from the house of Yahweh.'

If we had to summarize the role of Israel's priests in one word it would be 'mediation'. Priests stood in the dangerous boundary zone or 'no man's land' between the holy God and sinful people (Duke, 2003: 651–2). As a diviner of God's will and teacher of God's *tôrâ*, the priest represented God before humanity. As one who oversaw the sacrificial system, served at the altar and offered incense, he represented humanity before God. The priests thus stood at the heart of the practice of ancient Israel's faith, ensuring that the people's relationship with Yahweh was kept healthy and strong.

## 2.4 WHERE WERE PRIESTS TO BE FOUND?

It is commonly assumed that the majority of Israel's priests were located in the Jerusalem temple. This assumption is partially correct; many priests did, in fact, work and serve in the temple at Jerusalem, the hub of cultic activity (at least in Judah) from the reign of Solomon onwards. Overall, however, this preconception is far too simplistic as it fails to recognize that the Jerusalem temple complex was only one employer of priests in ancient Israel. In fact, priests would have been spread throughout Israel and Judah ministering in the various sanctuaries that dotted the nation.[16] The short answer to the question 'Where were priests located?' therefore is wherever the sanctuaries (which required their knowledge and skills) were located.

During the pre-exilic period there were dozens of local sanctuaries scattered throughout both the northern and southern kingdoms, each with their own priest/s. Some of these are specifically named in the biblical text, including Shechem, Bethel, Beersheba, Gilgal, Shiloh, Mizpah, Gibeon, Ophrah and Dan. In addition to these named sites, priests could probably also be found ministering at the various *bāmôt* (sing. *bāmâ*), commonly translated as 'high places', within Israel. For example, during the time of David the *bāmâ* at Gibeah clearly had its own priests (1 Chron. 16:39–40), 1 Kings 13:33 describes how Jeroboam I appointed priests for the

> **Going deeper:**
> **WERE *BĀMÔT* UNIQUE TO ISRAEL?**
>
> The answer is an unequivocal 'no'. Textual evidence, both biblical and extra-biblical, clearly indicates that *bāmôt* were also located in the kingdoms surrounding Israel, including Moab. For example, the Mesha Stele (a ninth-century-BC text written to commemorate the achievements of the Moabite king Mesha); Isaiah 16:12 and Jeremiah 48:35 all suggest that high places were a key part of Moabite religious practice.

high places he established throughout his kingdom, and 2 Kings 23:5 speaks of the kings of Judah appointing priests to make sacrifices at the various *bāmôt* throughout the cities of Judah and around Jerusalem.

Even though *bāmôt* are mentioned more than a hundred times in the Bible, their exact nature, appearance and architecture remains disputed. Essentially, a *bāmâ* seems to be an artificially constructed raised platform or mound where religious rituals were performed.[17] These may have served the religious needs of a family, clan, town or larger regional community. Such sites could be adorned with a variety of cult objects, including altars for the offering of sacrifices and incense, *maṣṣēbôt* (sing. *maṣṣēbâ*, commonly translated as 'standing stones' or 'stone pillars') and *'ašērîm* (the meaning of which is greatly disputed). Let's look at the last two.

A *maṣṣēbâ* is an upright standing stone erected by human hands. The stone itself could be worked or remain unhewn. The *maṣṣēbâ* may have been set up as a sign of divine presence (cf. Jacob's construction of a *maṣṣēbâ* at Bethel in Genesis 28:18

## Archaeological insight:
### THE *MAṢṢĒBÔT* FROM ARAD

Perhaps the most famous examples of *maṣṣēbôt* discovered by archaeologists were found in the temple at Arad, an Israelite fortress located about twenty kilometres west of Beersheba and forty kilometres south of Hebron. A total of three stones were uncovered in the temple's smallest of three rooms, often referred to as the Holy of Holies. The first of these, a well-finished and rounded piece of limestone (0.9 m high), with the remains of red paint still attached, was resting on a raised podium. The other two, both flint and cruder in finish, had been leant against the walls and covered with plaster. While the significance of these items remains disputed, their location in such an important position suggests that they played a key role in the cult at Arad.

**Plate 2.5    The inner sanctum of the temple at Arad complete with two *maṣṣēbôt* (rear) and altars (front)**

following his vision of God) or even as a symbol of the deity. The OT possesses a somewhat ambivalent attitude towards these stones: in earlier texts they are accepted as a legitimate element in the worship of the Israelite God (in addition to the example of Jacob, see Josh. 24:26–27, where Joshua sets one up in the sanctuary at Shechem), whereas in other texts they are condemned, probably the result of their close association with Canaanite religious beliefs and practices (cf. Deut. 16:22; Lev. 26:1).

There is significant debate among scholars regarding the meaning and significance of the objects referred to as *'ašērîm*. The one point of agreement is that this item was connected in some way with the Canaanite goddess, Asherah, consort to the supreme god, El. The most common suggestion is that the term refers to a wooden cult object (perhaps a pole) or a symbol (perhaps of the goddess herself) that was connected with her worship. Alternatively, *'ašērîm* may have denoted a sacred tree or grove that grew in the courtyards and surroundings of temples and high places (King and Stager, 2001: 352). The vocabulary which is used to describe the construction of such *'ašērîm* (i.e. 'to make', 'to build', 'to erect'), however, tends to favour the former interpretation. Unlike the *maṣṣēbôt* which are sometimes viewed in a positive light, *'ašērîm* are never accepted in the OT as a legitimate element in Israel's worship of Yahweh.

Along with their accompanying cultic assemblage, *bāmôt* could be found in both rural and urban contexts. Hilltop locations were particularly popular and there are

**Plate 2.6  Stone stele depicting a warrior god from Moab (possibly Chemosh)**

numerous references in the OT to *bāmôt* being found on the hills or mountains of Israel. For example, in 1 Kings 11:7 Solomon is said to have built a *bāmâ* for the gods Chemosh (the national god of the Moabites) and Milcom (the national god of the Ammonites) on the mountain east of Jerusalem (cf. 2 Kings 16:4; and 17:9–10, note how the worship conducted on the *bāmôt* is set alongside worship on the hills). This preference for mountain top sites is probably because such locations were believed to be specially favoured by the gods. In Canaanite thought, for example, Mount Zaphon was the site of Baal's royal palace and a place where the gods were believed to meet together. In the biblical text, God appears on Mount Sinai and establishes his earthly residence – the Jerusalem temple – on Mount Zion. *bāmôt* were not restricted to the countryside, however, nor hilltop locations. They could also be found inside cities (1 Kings 13:32; and 2 Kings 23:5) and even at the gate of Jerusalem (2 Kings 23:8). Such installations 'probably were utilized by travellers desiring a blessing or by those wishing to consult or swear to the deity with respect to legal matters' (Petter, 2005: 416).

The majority of *bāmôt*, particularly those found in the countryside, were probably open-air structures. The OT repeatedly speaks of them being located 'under every green tree' (Deut. 12:2; 1 Kings 14:23; 2 Kings 16:4; and 17:10). In some locations, however, buildings were associated with them.[18] According to 1 Samuel 9:22 the *bāmâ* near where Samuel lived at Ramah had a 'room' (*liškâ*) which could hold thirty guests. Several texts also speak of a *bêth bāmâ* (lit. a house of a *bāmâ*) which King

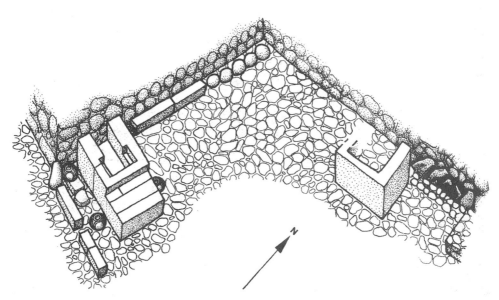

**Figure 2.2    Artist's reconstruction of a gate shrine from Dan, complete with set of five *maṣṣēbôt* (top corner) and basin structure**

### Archaeological insight:
## THE SANCTUARY AT TEL DAN

Following the division of the kingdom in the late tenth century, Jeroboam I established Dan and Bethel as key places of worship in the northern kingdom of Israel (1 Kings 12). Archaeological excavations at Dan have revealed a cultic structure and surroundings that can almost certainly be identified with Jeroboam's sanctuary. The most prominent feature of the site is a beautifully built podium of ashlar blocks which, at its greatest, was about 18.5 m square and 3 m high. On the basis of the presence of stone socles (square blocks that formed the base for a column), King and Stager (2001: 327) have argued that a two-storey temple stood atop the podium. This may have contained the golden calf that Jeroboam is said to have placed in Dan (1 Kings 12:29). In front of the temple was an enclosure, 12.5 m × 14 m in size, which contained two horned altars. The first was a small limestone incense altar, the second was a massive ashlar construction about 6 m square × 3 m high. This appears to have been used for animal sacrifices and came complete with its own staircase that the priests must have climbed in order to ascend to the top. Other buildings located in close proximity also contained various cultic items including more altars, three iron shovels, perhaps used for incense and/or the removal of ashes and coals from the altars, a ritual bowl and a large die. (For a discussion of the latter, see 'What did the Urim and Thummim look like?' above.)

and Stager define as 'a kind of sanctuary building where a priest was required to serve' (2001: 321). For example, in 1 Kings 12:31 we read that Jeroboam

I built numerous *bêth bāmôt* within the northern kingdom of Israel as part of his establishment of a cult that was distinct from the influence of Jerusalem. Likewise,

2 Kings 17:29–32 speaks of a *bêth bāmâ* in which the newly arrived citizens of Samaria installed their idols and conducted their services. Such a *bêth bāmâ* would have been a natural 'home' for Israel's priests who were not serving in the Jerusalem temple.

Such *bāmôt* were probably viewed by the majority of the population as legitimate and acceptable places of worship. For example, both David and Solomon visited the 'great' (or principal) *bāmâ* at Gibeah (1 Kings 3:3–4), while Samuel appears to have had no qualms attending the *bāmâ* in his home town (1 Kings 9 – here the NRSV renders *bāmâ* as 'shrine'). As de Vaux argues, 'Neither Dan nor Bethel, the official sanctuaries of the kingdom of Israel, nor Jerusalem, the official sanctuary of the king of Judah, ever replaced the other centres of worship. Everyone continued to attend the "high place" of his own town, and the ancient sanctuaries of the pre-monarchic period continued to attract pilgrims' (1965: 335).

Following the construction of the temple in Jerusalem, however, it is clear that some elements within Israelite society began to view the *bāmôt* in a negative light. This hostility eventually culminated in attempts to destroy the high places, first during the reign of Hezekiah (*c.* end of the eighth century) and again during the reign of Josiah (*c.*622/621 BC). Josiah's programme of religious reforms was particularly wide reaching. He demolished the *bāmôt* throughout the land, had their priests deposed, brought to Jerusalem, or, in the case of those who had been involved with the idolatrous northern *bêth bāmôt*, killed, and centralized religious worship in the temple at Jerusalem (2 Kings 23:8). From this time onwards, the Jerusalem temple was the only place where sacrifices were to be offered and the only legitimate place of worship within Judah where priests were to be found.

## 2.5 SUMMARY

Priests lay at the heart of the practice of Israel's religion, at least at a corporate level. They could be found throughout the sanctuaries of the nation, performing a variety of roles, including divination, teaching, blessing and sacrifice. Their knowledge and skills were required for the effective functioning of the Israelite cult, which, in turn, ensured that the relationship between God and the Israelites remained healthy. Although much maligned in traditional (especially Protestant) OT scholarship, the priests played an invaluable role in preserving and maintaining Israel's religion throughout the nation's long and difficult history, and thus decisively shaped the heirs of ancient Israel's faith, both Judaism and Christianity.

## NOTES

1  In fact, Nelson concludes that 'from the ecumenical and global perspective of the last years of the twentieth century, these earlier criticisms seem to reveal more about the prejudices of the critics than about the values inherent in Israel's priesthood. As adherents of a progressive ideology convinced that tradition stifles individual freedom and religious development, our scholarly predecessors naturally favoured prophets over priests' (1993: 103).
2  It is not until the post-exilic period that Samuel is assigned Levitic ancestry (1 Chron. 6:18–23).
3  It is also possible that Zabud, the 'son of Nathan' (1 Kings 4:5) was a non-Levitical priest: however, since

the identity of the Nathan who is mentioned in this passage cannot be firmly established this is impossible to prove one way or the other.

4  It needs to be acknowledged that some scholars are unwilling to accept this claim at face value. For example, de Vaux (1965: 362) suggests that this particular indictment may have been a result of the fact that the text was edited by men whose home lay in Judah and who were anxious to condemn a hated rival to the Jerusalem temple. For more details see Toews, 1993: 86–99.

5  For further discussion regarding the meaning of this expression, see Hutton, 1994: 146.

6  Priests serving at the larger, central sanctuaries would have had additional sources of income including regular tithes of produce and livestock usually given at the major agricultural pilgrimage festivals, census taxes, private gifts, vows, dedications and redemptions, and judicially imposed fines and forfeitures (Hutton, 1994: 148).

7  In addition to these pieces of clothing the priest was also required to wear 'linen breeches', which covered his nakedness in the presence of God. The preference for linen (as opposed to wool) was probably owing to the fact that it was viewed as a ritually clean fabric (cf. the prohibition of wool in Ezekiel's temple legislation, 44:17).

8  It should be acknowledged, however, that some scholars, e.g. de Vaux (1965: 347), have suggested that priests were not anointed during the pre-exilic period, with this rite instead being restricted to the king.

9  Of course, this perspective also overlooks the fact that non-animal sacrifices were practised in ancient Israel.

10  It should be acknowledged that not all OT scholars, especially those who adopt a more critical approach to the text, would accept that Leviticus 1—7 provides insight into pre-exilic practice. They argue that the text reached its final form in the post-exilic period and thus the rites that it describes reflect practices in the Second, and not necessarily the Solomonic, temple. My own perspective is that such rites were not created out of thin air, and that their origins are, in fact, to be found in pre-exilic practice.

11  Of course, the fact that these devices are not always mentioned suggests that priests could sometimes receive divine revelation without using any technical instrument at all.

12  The lack of references to the Urim and Thummim after 1 Samuel suggests that their usage was not as common during the period of the monarchy, except possibly in relation to the selection of the goats for the Day of Atonement (Lev. 16:8–10).

13  Exilic or post-exilic texts which emphasize the teaching function of priests include Ezek. 7:26 and Mal. 2:4–9.

14  Taken at face value, 2 Kings 17:27–28 suggests that the teaching function of Israel's priests was widely known. Here the king of Assyria sends an exiled Israelite priest back to Samaria in order to instruct the newly settled population in the law of the God of the land (i.e. Yahweh).

15  See also Ezek. 44:24. Although Ezekiel is specifically talking about priests who will serve in the new, rebuilt temple it is highly likely that he has constructed their job description based on the role of priests in the period of the Solomonic temple.

16  For a recent discussion of sanctuaries outside Jerusalem see Edelman, 2010.

17 The suggestion that they were a natural feature is hard to maintain given the numerous references to them being 'built', 'torn down' and 'destroyed' in 1–2 Kings.

18 Miller suggests that the high places may have originally started out as open-air shrines before gaining a 'structural character' during the period of the monarchy (2000: 251, n. 184).

## FOR FURTHER READING

J. Blenkinsopp (1995a), *Sage, Priest, Prophet: Religious and Intellectual Leadership in Ancient Israel*, LAI, Louisville: WJKP.

L. Grabbe (1995), *Priests, Prophets, Diviners, Sages: A Socio-Historical Study of Religious Specialists in Ancient Israel*, Valley Forge: Trinity Press.

R. Hutton (1994), *Charisma and Authority in Israelite Society*, Minneapolis: Fortress Press.

V. Matthews and D. Benjamin (1993), *Social World of Ancient Israel, 1250–587 BC*, Peabody: Hendrickson.

R. Nelson (1993), *Raising Up a Faithful Priest: Community and Priesthood in Biblical Theology*, Louisville: WJKP.

L. Sabourin (1973), *Priesthood: A Comparative Study*, Leiden: E.J. Brill.

Chapter 3

# PROPHETS IN ANCIENT ISRAEL

## 3.1 INTRODUCTION

The prophets stir up all kinds of excitement within some Christian circles. Go down to your local Christian book shop and you will probably find a shelf labelled 'prophecy' filled with various titles which seek to correlate so-called 'predictions' of the prophets with contemporary events in the Middle East. Such books imply that a prophet was an individual who foretold the (distant) future. Other Christians are also excited by the OT prophets but for entirely different reasons. Some, especially within liberal traditions, have viewed Israel's prophets as early political and social activists whose primary goal was to bring about change within Israel's society. Others, especially the early Church Fathers, emphasized their role as heralds of the coming Messiah, divinely inspired messengers sent to announce the appearance of Jesus of Nazareth.

But if someone in ancient Israel had referred to an individual as a 'prophet' is this what they would have had in mind? In other words, do these three perspectives (prognosticator, social reformer, herald of the Messiah) encapsulate what it meant to

be a prophet in the world of the OT? The short answer to these questions is 'no'. While the above three perspectives may each contain a degree of legitimacy, they emphasize only a (small) part of the prophetic role. We must be willing, therefore, to widen our understanding if we hope to grasp what a prophet actually did in ancient Israel, as well as considering the key questions of how one became a prophet and where prophets were to be found.

Before we attempt to answer these important questions, however, we need to deal with a few introductory issues. The first has to do with the size of the phenomenon of prophecy in ancient Israel. When I ask my students to name the OT prophets, common responses include Isaiah, Jeremiah, Ezekiel and perhaps Amos. In other words, we tend to focus on those prophets who have books attributed to them. But we need to be aware that these individuals account for only a very small (and often anomalous) minority of the total number of prophets who were at work in ancient Israel (Blenkinsopp, 1995a: 47). In addition to the 55 or so named prophets in the OT, the text itself recognizes the presence of literally *hundreds* of other prophets who remain unnamed (e.g. 1 Kings 22:6). Furthermore, even the earliest of our canonical prophets (Amos and Hosea) see themselves as standing within the context of a much wider and older phenomenon (cf. Amos 2:11–12; Hos. 6:5). In short, the canonical prophets provide only a very small window into the nature of prophecy as it was found within ancient Israel.

Furthermore, there has been a tendency among some OT scholars to focus on the work of Israel's 'classical' prophets (those who operated in the period *c*.750–450 BC) at the expense of their early or 'primitive' forebears (those who were at work in the period *c*.1000[1]–750 BC).[2] This is often coupled with the desire to draw a sharp distinction in terms of the nature of prophecy as it was practised during these two periods.[3] Contemporary scholarship, however, has tended to emphasize the continuity between the various prophets who were at work throughout this six-century span. 'While one may be tempted to draw sharp lines suggesting different types of prophecy or differences between early and later prophecy, the continuity of character and activity is more evident than any major distinctions, whether in terminology, manifestation of possession, function, or relation to official religion' (Miller, 2000: 179).[4] Hence, if we wish to do justice to the phenomenon of prophecy as it was present in Israel, we will need to consider both named and unnamed prophets, those who have books attributed to them and those who appear in the historical narratives of the OT, early and classical prophets. Furthermore, since prophecy was not restricted to Israel but was, in fact, present among many societies of the ANE (a point the OT itself acknowledges,

## Archaeological insight:
## THE BALAAM TEXT FROM DEIR 'ALLA

One of the most significant ANE texts that refers to the phenomenon of prophecy outside Israel comes from the Transjordanian site of Deir 'Alla. This text is particularly important because of its geographical and chronological proximity to the OT prophets (it is dated to the eighth century BC, making it roughly contemporaneous with the work of Israelite prophets such as Amos, Hosea and Micah). Unfortunately, interpretation of the text is difficult owing to the fact that it has been broken into more than a hundred pieces of various sizes (think of a large puzzle but without the finished picture to know whether you have got it right or not!). It does, however, appear to recount the experiences of a seer (ḥzh – one of the titles used for the Israelite prophets, see below) of the gods named Balaam son of Beor. During the night, Balaam is visited by the gods and receives a vision 'like an oracle of El'. This prophetic word appears to be of a negative character (perhaps divine judgement) as it describes the loss of fertility and life on the earth, and the reversal of the normal order of things (a motif also found in the OT prophets). Balaam then communicates these revelations to his community. Most scholars identify the prophetic figure mentioned in this text with Balaam, the Aramean diviner from Pethor, mentioned in Numbers 22—24 who ends up blessing the Israelite people after being hired by the Moabite king to curse them as they journey towards the promised land.

The tremendous breadth of prophecy both within and outside Israel creates its own unique set of problems. The sheer spread and variety that is present within the phenomenon (a much greater spread and variety than we see, for example, with the priests) means that it is sometimes difficult to come up with overarching statements regarding the roles, places and development of Israel's prophets. And when overarching statements are made, it is always going to be possible to point to exceptions to the general rules – what may have been true for one prophet, or group of prophets, may not necessarily have been true for another. In what follows, therefore, I have tried to take into account some of the variety that was obviously present within the movement, without losing sight of the commonalities that unite the various prophetic figures and groups.

Second, it is worth being aware of the variety of terminology that the OT authors could use to refer to the individuals we dub prophets. Four Hebrew labels are particularly important: $nābî'$ (prophet), $rō'eh$ (seer), $ḥōzeh$ (seer) and $'îš$ $'ĕlōhîm$ (man of God). At one stage these titles may have had their own distinctive connotations. For example, Blenkinsopp has suggested that the title 'man of God', which we find applied to key early prophetic figures such as Samuel, Elijah and Elisha, originally denoted 'a person of preternatural and potentially dangerous power; recall, for example, how Samson's mother, cowed by the awe-inspiring appearance of her heavenly visitor, took him to be a man of God (Judg, 13:6, 8)' (1995a: 125–6).[5]

cf. Jer. 27:1–15 which mentions the presence of prophets in the surrounding nations of Edom, Moab, Ammon and Phoenicia), it may also be necessary to draw on comparative insights where relevant.

It would be unwise, however, to conclude too much purely based on the usage of these various labels. Overall, it is relatively hard for the modern interpreter to detect any unique nuances preserved in the OT usage of such descriptors. For example, within David's court, Gad is described as a *ḥōzeh* while his colleague Nathan is a *nābî'* yet there is no discernible difference in the roles the two played. In Amos 7:10–17 the priest Amaziah calls Amos a *ḥōzeh*, to which Amos replies that he is *not a nābî'* 'as though the two terms were, for all practical purposes, indistinguishable' (Hutton, 1994: 116).[6] Thus scholars speak of a process of flattening out, whereby the individual designations lost their distinctive nuances and *nābî'* increasingly became used as a catch-all term to refer to all forms of Israelite prophetic intermediation. This process is suggested by 1 Samuel 9:9, which implies that even from a relatively early date any clear role distinction that may have been originally associated with the various titles had been forgotten: 'the one who is now called a prophet (*nābî'*) was formerly called a seer (*rō'eh*)'.[7]

The final introductory issue concerns the difficulty of what we plan to do in the following chapter. A significant problem is created by the source material that we have at our disposal – the prophetic books themselves and the historical texts that make reference to Israel's prophets. None of these were ever designed to serve a quest for the historical Isaiah, Micah, Amos etc., or to function as source material for reconstructing a picture of ancient Israelite society. Hence they do not often deal (at least in an explicit fashion) with the kind of questions that I am concerned with addressing in this study. Yet at the end of the day this is the evidence we have and we must make the most of it. As Blenkinsopp has previously recognized, when it comes to examining the social world of the prophets

the likelihood of arriving at satisfactory answers is obviously restricted by the nature of the sources at our disposal, none of which was designed to impart the kind of information we are seeking. We have some stories about prophets (prophetic legends) of very uneven value as source material. The prophetic books themselves contain some biographical and autobiographical passages, but they consist, for the most part, of sayings attributed to named prophets. Both kinds of material have undergone extensive editing over a period of several centuries, with the result that we cannot be optimistic about the chances of reconstructing the social world in which a prophet like Amos acted and spoke. But this is what we have, and we have to make the best of it. (1995a: 32)

Thus we must proceed with care. While the relatively meagre evidence that is available to us does shed some light on the questions I have posed, it certainly does not provide the definitive answers that we might like.

## 3.2 WHERE WERE PROPHETS TO BE FOUND?

When asked to picture a prophet, many people have in mind a solitary figure on the periphery of Israel's society 'despised and rejected' by men (Isa. 53:3). While such a picture may contain an element of truth (it is clear, e.g., that a number of Israel's writing and non-writing prophets were not at home in the key religious and political institutions of their day),[8] it needs to be challenged. In fact, on closer reading of the OT text it appears that this image probably represents the exception rather than the rule! Instead of existing as solitary, isolated individuals, there is much evidence to suggest that the majority of Israel's prophets would have been located either in one of Israel's sanctuaries or at the royal court. In other words, they were to be found at the heart of Israel's society rather than on its periphery.

### 3.2.1 RELIGIOUS CENTRES

The most common place to find a prophet in ancient Israel would have been at one of the nation's various sanctuaries, including the Jerusalem temple. Both writing and non-writing prophets are associated in various ways with Israel's cultic establishments. For example, during the early phase of prophecy in Israel we find prophetic bands or guilds, the 'sons of the prophets' (*bᵉnē hannᵉbî'îm*), living together in or near Israel's major cultic centres such as Bethel (2 Kings 2:3) and Gilgal (2 Kings 4:38). In a similar vein, 1 Samuel 10:5 speaks of 'the band of prophets coming

down from the high place with harp, tambourine, flute and lyre before them, prophesying' (for a discussion of 'high places' see 2.4). It is unclear, however, whether this group of prophets had taken up residence at the high place or were simply travelling from one sanctuary to the next. Either way, had an Israelite wanted to find such a group then the likely place to start would have been at the local cultic centre.

At a later stage, Amos travels to the northern sanctuary in Bethel in order

---

**Going deeper:**
**THE 'SONS OF THE PROPHETS' AND ISRAEL'S SANCTUARIES**

Second Kings 4:8–37 may shed some light on the connection between the prophetic bands or guilds and Israel's religious centres. Following the death of her son, the Shunammite woman makes preparations to seek out the prophet Elisha, a leader of a prophetic guild, who appears to be staying at the sanctuary on Mount Carmel. Her husband, however, raises objections declaring that 'it is neither new moon nor sabbath' (v. 23). Lindblom concludes from this that on festival days in particular the members of the prophetic associations 'were to be found at the sanctuaries performing their cultic duties. At other times they were travelling throughout the country' (Lindblom, 1962: 80).

---

**Have you considered?**
**WERE SOME OF THE CANONICAL PROPHETS CULT PROPHETS?**

While it has long been accepted that some of Israel's prophets may have had a close association with the cult, the suggestion that this may have been the case for those with whom biblical books are associated has been a hotly debated topic. Following the work of the Scandinavian scholar Sigmund Mowinckel, however, various scholars have proposed that at least three of the OT writing prophets – Joel, Nahum and Habakkuk – may have been more-or-less permanently attached to the Jerusalem temple. What is the evidence for this suggestion? Three features of these books are generally emphasized: the presence of hymnic or liturgical elements within their oracles, the absence of any criticism of the cult and other state institutions, and oracles of salvation against the enemy (Miller, 2000: 176). While it would not necessarily be surprising to discover that one (or more) of these three were closely connected with the Jerusalem cult, Miller's cautious conclusion that 'the evidence is more suggestive than definitive' seems best (2000: 176).

to announce his message. While such sites may have been attractive because of their specifically religious function, it must also be kept in mind that they were important social hubs, places where people met and gathered together. Thus they provided the prophet with a large, ready-made audience.

Given the size and importance of the Jerusalem temple, it is highly likely that many prophets would have been found in or around its precincts. There is evidence to suggest that some prophets may have lived within the temple itself (cf. Jer. 35:4), and most scholars now recognize the existence of specialized 'cult prophets' whose primary prophetic activity would have been carried out within the Jerusalem temple, and who would have derived their livelihood from the temple itself. In fact, a number of texts clearly indicate that the House of the Lord was a hub not only of priestly but also prophetic activity (cf. Jer. 23:11; and Lam. 2:20). From the writing prophets, it is clear that Jeremiah delivered a number of his oracles at the Jerusalem temple (Jer. 7 and 28), even though he seems to have had no formal ties to the institution. At the same time, it is possible that Joel, Nahum and Habakkuk were themselves cult prophets (for more details see 'Have you considered? Were some of the canonical prophets cult prophets?').

### 3.2.2  POLITICAL CENTRES

In addition to religious sanctuaries, prophets were also located at key political centres and, in particular, the royal courts of both the southern and northern kingdoms. In fact, Hutton has suggested, 'Because of its ideological centrality in the social structure and because of its control of revenue, the court was naturally the chief patron of prophetic intermediation' (1994: 109).

---

**ANE parallels:**
**ANE PROPHETS AND THE ROYAL COURT**

Many of the prophets mentioned in the literature of Israel's ANE neighbours had some connection with the royal court. For example, in the eighteenth-century Mari texts there are a number of prophecies which directly address the king. According to Grabbe (1995: 88), at least two of these came from prophets who received some form of support from the court, perhaps suggesting that they held an official position within the king's retinue. Like the biblical prophets, oracles could arise spontaneously or could be the result of formal inquiry by the king (Grabbe, 1995: 88). Unlike the biblical court prophets, however, it appears that the majority of prophetic messages that were addressed to the monarch were actually delivered in the temple, often accompanied by sacrificial rites (Blenkinsopp, 1996: 43). They were then collated by the high officials of the court (including the queen) before being forwarded to the king.

---

The best-known examples of such 'court prophets' are Nathan and Gad who both played significant roles during David's reign. In fact, the close connection between King David and his prophets is suggested by the fact that Gad is specifically called 'David's seer' (2 Sam. 24:11) rather than Yahweh's prophet. But there is also plenty of evidence to suggest that such court prophets were active not just during David's reign but throughout Israel's history. For example, 1 Kings 22 points to the existence of a significant retinue of prophets (no fewer than 400!) which the king of Israel could consult before engaging in military conflict. Further evidence for significant numbers of (non-Yahwistic) prophets who were at home within the royal court may be found in 1 Kings 18:19.

While it is unlikely that any of the writing prophets were 'court prophets' in a formal sense, it is clear that on occasion their work could bring them into direct contact with the nation's kings. For example, Isaiah seems to have been involved with a number of Judah's kings (esp. Hezekiah) over a period of approximately 30 years; while Jeremiah is consulted by King Zedekiah (Jer. 21) and is commissioned by the Lord to go to the palace to speak a prophetic word (Jer. 22).

### 3.2.3 INDEPENDENT PROPHETS

While there is clear evidence to suggest that many of Israel's prophets, including some of the writing prophets, could have been found within the key religious and political institutions of their day, a minority chose to exist independently of these. These prophets preferred to move about to perform their role or would have people specifically seek them out.

The prophet Elisha is a good example of such an independent prophet. Although he has a house in Samaria, he is frequently depicted as a peripatetic figure, travelling throughout Israel and the surrounding countries performing his prophetic role. Sometimes this involved the prophet taking the initiative in providing guidance to the king of Israel (2 Kings 6:8–23). On other occasions, however, Elisha himself was sought out. For example, upon his arrival in Damascus, King Ben-hadad of Aram sent Hazael to meet Elisha in order to find out whether he would recover from his illness (2 Kings 8:7–10). Another example of this type of prophet is Micaiah (1 Kings 22). Even though he is known and sought out by the king of Israel, Micaiah is clearly

**Scholar focus:**
**ROBERT WILSON (1942– )**

In his important work, *Prophecy and Society in Ancient Israel* (1980), Robert Wilson has argued that Israel's prophets could be *central* to the political and religious establishments of their society – helping to maintain order and stability – or *peripheral* to these key institutions – working often to effect change and to destabilize the existing social and religious structures. An example of the former may be Samuel, while Elijah is often taken to be representative of the latter.

While Wilson's categorizations are helpful, such distinctions should not be applied too rigidly. For example, prophets could move from a more peripheral status to a more central role, as we perhaps see in the case of Elisha who starts out as the head of a peripheral prophetic guild before moving closer to the political establishment (see Wilson, 1980: 202–6). On other occasions, we see peripheral prophets such as Elijah and Amos appearing (often uninvited, unannounced and unwanted) in the central political and religious establishments.

unencumbered by formal ties to the royal court.

Overall, it is probably fair to locate the majority of Israel's writing prophets within this category. Even though they may have occasionally visited one of the nation's sanctuaries or royal courts in order to perform their prophetic activity, the vast majority did not have a permanent connection with such institutions (with the exception of the possible cult prophets, see above). For example, while Amos probably spent much of his time prophesying at the

---

**Have you considered?**
## PROPHETS AS MEMBERS OF THE DIVINE COUNCIL

In answering the question 'Where would you find a prophet?' I have primarily focused on the human, earthly institutions which Israel's prophets were commonly associated with (e.g. the royal court and religious sanctuaries). This, however, is only a partial answer.

As messengers from God to humanity, prophets could also be 'located' within the realm of the divine. Or as Miller has correctly emphasized, 'The social world of the prophet was to be found in heaven as much as on earth.' (2000: 183).* In particular, a number of Israel's prophets claimed to have stood in the presence of God and those supernatural creatures who composed God's deliberating council. This is a unique claim on the part of the prophets – no other individual is ever described as being allowed to attend God's council meeting (Meier, 2009: 21).

So what did this 'divine council' look like? The text which provides the most detailed description is I Kings 22:19–23. Here the Lord is portrayed as sitting on his throne with all the 'host of heaven' in attendance surrounding him. These beings interact with the Lord (vv. 20–21) and carry out his will on the earth (v. 22). A similar picture is presented in Job 1—2 where the council members are referred to as 'sons of God' (or 'heavenly beings' (NRSV), cf. Ps. 29:1; 82:6; 89:7 etc.). It seems as if the heavenly realm is depicted as operating along similar lines to an ANE royal court with the monarch surrounded by counsellors and envoys who advise the king and perform his will.

Various texts from the OT suggest that prophets could play a threefold role within the divine council:

1 Prophets could function as *observers* of the council – this seems to be the case for Micaiah in I Kings 22. Here the prophet simply observes the proceedings of the council and reports their deliberations to the king of Israel but does not get involved in any way.

---

key cultic centre of the northern kingdom, Bethel (cf. Amos 7), there is nothing to suggest that he was officially connected with this establishment. It needs to be emphasized, however, that the example of the writing prophets was not normal – it was the exception rather than the rule. The *vast* majority of Israel's prophets would have been found in the key religious and/or political centres of the nation. In fact, if we are to take the example of the above-mentioned Micaiah (1 Kings 22) as representative, we could hypothesize that the ratio of institutional prophets to non-institutional prophets was at least 400 to one!

## 3.3 HOW DID SOMEONE BECOME A PROPHET?

The common answer to this question is that Israel's prophets received a special divine calling to fulfil a specific divine commission. It is this dramatic 'call experience' that marked out someone as a prophet. In scholarly circles, this focus on the supernatural, charismatic dimension of entrance into the prophetic office received significant impetus from the work of Max Weber (see 'Scholar focus: Max Weber (1864–1920)'). Weber argued that the prophets were essentially charismatic figures who were neither 'designated by a

2  Prophets could function as *'advisers'* to God – some prophets take a more active role in the workings of the divine council, engaging with God regarding the decisions he will make. The best example of this appears to be Amos. In Amos 7:1–9 the prophet argues with God concerning his proposed judgement on the northern kingdom and actually prompts God to consider alternative courses of action.**

3  Prophets could function as *envoys* for the council – the best example of this is Isaiah 6. Here the prophet is given a vision of the divine council with God enthroned and seraphs in attendance (for more discussion of the seraphim see below). Of particular importance is verse 8. In this verse the Lord appears to be addressing the divine council (note the parallels with 1 Kings 22:20–21), seeking someone who will carry out his will. Isaiah responds and accepts the role – he is now an envoy for the Lord.

The importance of access to the divine council by Israel's prophets is emphasized by Jeremiah. In fact, he makes this a key criterion by which one is able to distinguish genuine prophets from their counterfeits (Jer. 23:16–22). A true prophet stands in the divine council – he/she has access to the transcendent world of the deity – and thus speaks God's word. False prophets, however, are unable to gain admission to this council and thus can only speak their own word.

* Elsewhere Miller recognizes 'Israelite prophecy – and perhaps ancient Near Eastern prophecy generally – cannot be understood simply in terms of its social, religious, or political world. It has to be understood from a frame of reference outside the realia of social existence though never separated from them' (2000: 182).

** At the same time, however, it must be kept in mind that whenever we encounter extended descriptions of the divine council, God is typically seated on his throne (cf. Isa. 6:1; and Ezek. 1:26). As Meier has recognized, this is 'an emphatic reminder that the cosmos is not a democracy and that God is in control' (2009: 22).

predecessor, nor ordained, nor installed in office, but *called*' (Blenkinsopp, 1996: 35).

As with many of the questions we are considering in this book, the standard answer to this question, although not necessarily wrong, is inadequate in and of itself. In recent years there has been increasing recognition of the institutional dimension of prophetic activity and the fact that at least some of Israel's prophets may have undergone a period of training to fulfil their role. So how did one become a prophet? To answer this question we will need to consider who exactly could become a prophet, what training the prophets may have undergone, and the nature and role of their special divine call.

### 3.3.1  WHO COULD BECOME A PROPHET?

This question is more difficult to answer than it first appears. The prophetic books as a whole show relatively little interest in the life of the prophets apart from the message they proclaim, and references to their social and economic background are few and far between. From the evidence that is available, however, it appears that there were virtually no restrictions on who could become a prophet.

The majority of Israel's early prophets appear to have been drawn from the lower

## Scholar focus:
## MAX WEBER (1864–1920)

Weber was a leading German intellectual who pioneered a sociological approach to the study of the OT. Weber's (1978: 439) definition of a prophet as 'a purely individual bearer of charisma, who by virtue of his mission proclaims a religious doctrine or divine commandment' has been particularly influential for study of the OT prophets. In particular, Weber is generally associated with two key emphases.

First, Weber argues that the prophets were marked out by the possession of charisma, which he defines as 'a certain quality of an individual personality by virtue of which he is set apart from ordinary men and treated as endowed with supernatural, superhuman, or at least specifically exceptional powers or qualities' (1978: 241). The possession of this elusive, extraordinary personal quality and its acknowledgement by the prophet's audience legitimated the prophet's status, claims and mission.

Second, the prophets were distinguished from the other religious specialists of ancient Israel (and the priests, in particular) by their call to a special mission, rather than by occupying a socially acknowledged, religious office.

While Weber's work has been subject to criticism and revision (esp. his overemphasis on the charismatic dimension of prophecy to the neglect of the institutional), his insights remain pivotal to much modern scholarship. For more details and critical engagement with the work of Weber, see Hutton, 1994: 105–37.

socio-economic strata of Israelite society (with the obvious exceptions of some of the royal court prophets such as Nathan and Gad). The reference to Elisha's involvement in ploughing (1 Kings 19:19) prior to his becoming Elijah's disciple suggests that he came from an agrarian background. Blenkinsopp (1995a: 133–4) has argued that the prophetic associations, 'the sons of the prophets,' were primarily composed of those who were socially and economically marginalized, perhaps as a result of external pressures (such as the Philistine push into the hill country heartland of Israel) or internal pressures (brought about by limited resources, overpopulation, or a series of poor harvests). Such prophets

may have been recruited from the ranks of males (perhaps especially younger sons)

set adrift when the households to which they belonged fell apart as a result of economic or military pressures. Others, like Samuel, appear to have been dedicated to a sanctuary at an early stage in the manner of the monastic oblates of the Middle Ages . . . All the indications are that they were low on the economic and social scale and, in the eyes of some of their contemporaries, eccentric to the point of insanity. (Blenkinsopp, 1996: 32, 33)

In contrast, it appears that Israel's writing prophets generally came from the higher end of the socio-economic spectrum. Isaiah seems at home in Jerusalem court circles, Jeremiah is said to come from a Benjaminite priestly family claiming descent from the Shiloh priesthood (Jer. 1:1), and Ezekiel was also a priest or a member of a priestly family (Ezek. 1:1–3).[9] Amos, although not of priestly descent, appears to have been relatively prosperous. He is referred to as a sheep-breeder (*nōqēd*, Amos 1:1 – see 'ANE parallels: Amos the *nōqēd*') in the title of the book and in 7:14 he is further identified as a 'herdsman' and 'dresser of sycamore trees'. While we might be initially tempted to think of Amos as a poor and uneducated agriculturalist, it is worth keeping in mind that the title *nōqēd* is applied to only one other individual in the OT – King Mesha of Moab (2 Kings 3:4). It appears, therefore, that Amos was no ordinary, run-of-the-mill shepherd, but a relatively well-off breeder of sheep, in charge of large flocks and other shepherds. Thus, most scholars now conclude that Amos would have belonged to the notable men of his community, a substantial and well-respected individual.

Perhaps the exception to this picture of the writing prophets as members of Israel's upper classes is Micah, whose association with Moresheth suggests that he came from a 'provincial', agrarian background.

In addition to the (admittedly) meagre pieces of biographical data that we find within the prophetic books themselves, the oracles that are attributed to these prophets also imply that they came from Israel's educated, upper classes. Blenkinsopp (1995a: 141–2) points to their relatively high level of literary/rhetorical skill, their familiarity with world affairs and history, and knowledge of Israel's involvement in this as evidence to support this claim.

So, in short, virtually any Israelite – male or female – could become a prophet. There were no restrictions based on gender, lineage, social or economic class. Having said this, however, it is quite likely that the majority of Israel's writing prophets (and some of the non-writing prophets as well) came from the educated, upper classes suggesting that the benefits that this background brought may have also been advantageous to someone becoming a prophet.

If an individual's background was not the decisive factor in whether or not they became a prophet, what then was important? Can we identify a decisive impetus that moved them to assume the prophetic mantle? In a number of cases, this driving force appears to have been a special divine call.

### 3.3.2 WHAT TOOK PLACE IN A PROPHETIC CALL EXPERIENCE?

A number of Israel's writing prophets highlight a unique encounter with the Lord,

often referred to in the secondary literature as the prophet's 'call', as the determinative factor in generating their prophetic ministry. This experience of the divine appears to be completely unexpected and marks a decisive transition point within the prophet's life. References to such call experiences include Amos 7:15 (where Amos declares that he was taken from his previous occupations of herdsman and dresser of sycamore trees in order to announce God's word) and Exodus 3 (where Moses – Israel's prophet par excellence – is commissioned by God to go down to Egypt, hence leaving behind his life as a shepherd in the wilderness of Midian). After receiving the call, the prophet understands him/her self to be specially set apart by God in order to fulfil a specific task or role.

In addition to the examples cited above, accounts of a prophetic call experience are found in all of the major prophets (Isa. 6; Jer. 1; and Ezek. 1—3). In fact, Jeremiah views this as an essential qualification of the true prophets of Israel. According to Jeremiah 14:14 the false prophets are marked out by the fact that 'I [Yahweh] did not send them, nor did I command them or speak to them' (cf. Deut. 18:20; and Ezek. 13:6). Thus, while no exact equivalent to the prophetic call accounts are found in the minor prophets (perhaps a result of the much shorter length of these works), it is quite possible that these prophets also experienced a similar divine encounter and commissioning which generated their ministry.

What did this call experience actually involve? Before we can answer the question we need to offer two important words of caution. First, our only access to the *experience* of Israel's prophets is via reference to the *stylized literary reports* they have left us. And working

---

**Going deeper:**
**THE MEANING OF *NĀBÎ'***

It has been suggested that the common Hebrew word for 'prophet', *nābî'*, in fact means 'one who is called' or 'one who is appointed' (with the implication that the individual is called by God). Most scholars associate the Hebrew word with its Akkadian equivalent *nabū(m)*, meaning 'to name, proclaim, call'. It is still debated, however, whether the noun should be understood with an active sense (e.g. 'speaker, proclaimer') or passively ('one who is named, called'). While either definition would fit the picture of the prophets that is found in the OT, overall there is a general preference for the passive understanding within scholarly circles. For more details see Müller, 1998.

## ANE parallels:
## WHAT ARE THE SERAPHIM?

Although not described in detail in the OT, the seraphim (possibly meaning 'burning ones') appear to be supernatural creatures that can fly and are serpentine in form. The five other passages where a form of the Hebrew word *śārāp* is used (Num. 21:6, 8; Deut. 8:15; Isa. 14:29; 30:6) all seem to have a serpent or snake-like creature in mind (cf. Num. 21:6; and Deut. 8:15, in particular, where the word is used in close association with *nāḥāš*, the standard Hebrew word for 'snake'). Archaeologists excavating in Israel have discovered a number of images of winged serpents drawn on scarab seals, some of which come from the approximate time of Isaiah.

Mettinger (1999: 743), following O. Keel, has suggested that the seraphim are similar to the Egyptian Uraeus serpent which was worn on the forehead of gods and kings and which was responsible for protecting them. If this is the case, then 'Isa. 6 displays a noteworthy mutation of the uraeus motif: instead of protecting Yahweh the seraphim need their wings to cover themselves from head to feet from Yahweh's consuming holiness; Yahweh does not need their protection' (Mettinger, 1999: 743). If anything, the reverse is true – the seraphim need to be protected from Yahweh!

back from stylized literary report to actual experience is always going to be a difficult process. For example, von Rad argues that 'these narratives are probably not simply transcripts of what was experienced at the time. They are as well accounts designed to serve certain definite ends and they no doubt to a certain extent stylize the call' (1968: 34). Therefore, the degree to which they capture and reflect the precise experience of the prophet is always going to be a matter of debate.[10] Second, we need to be wary of over-generalizing. Even a cursory survey of the various accounts quickly reveals that the

**Figure 3.1　Two seals depicting winged serpents**

*51*

prophetic call experiences were not uniform. While they all share some points in common, there is also significant variation between them, perhaps reflecting the unique character and situation of each prophet.

With these cautions in mind, we can suggest that a typical prophetic call experience might have taken place along the following lines:

1 God appears to and confronts the individual – this divine appearance, however, can take a number of different forms. For example, God appears to Moses in the midst of the burning bush, Isaiah sees the Lord sitting on his throne with seraphs in attendance, while Ezekiel is confronted by the radiant glory of the Lord astride the divine chariot.
2 God commissions the prophet – the prophet is characteristically told two things: to whom they must speak (i.e. their intended audience) and what they must speak or do (i.e. the basic content of their message). For example, Moses must bring the Israelites out of Egypt, while Jeremiah's message is summarized in six antithetic verbs: 'to pluck up and to pull down, to destroy and to overthrow, to build and to plant' (Jer. 1:10b, cf. 18:7–9; 24:6 etc.).
3 The prophet responds – while Isaiah volunteers to fulfil the divine commission, this appears to be an anomaly. More often than not, the prophet's initial response is negative in tone. In fact, the prophet may object to his calling, usually on the basis of his perceived unworthiness or inadequacy to fulfil the divine commission that he has been given. For example, Moses' initial response to the sweeping divine declaration that he will be sent to Pharaoh to bring the Israelites out of Egypt is not to embrace the divine mandate but to cry 'Who am I?' (Exod. 3:11). Likewise, when told that

he has been appointed as a prophet to the nations, Jeremiah laments that he does not know how to speak for he is 'only a boy' (Jer. 1:6). Such objections, however, are usually quickly countered.
4 The prophet is prepared or equipped for his ministry – again this activity can take a variety of different forms. Isaiah's mouth is cleansed to make it fit to utter the divine word, the Lord touches Jeremiah's mouth putting the divine word inside him, and Ezekiel eats a scroll with writing on both sides of it. All three accounts thus emphasize the external and objective character of the prophetic word – 'what a prophet speaks does not come from himself but from God' (Lindblom, 1962: 189). This preparation may also include an element of divine reassurance with the Lord promising to be with the prophet no matter what situation he may face.

This experience of being called by God was important not only for the prophets

---

**ANE parallels:**
**THE CLEANSING OF ISAIAH'S LIPS**

Lindblom (1962: 186) has suggested that the cleansing of Isaiah's lips as part of his preparation to fulfil a prophetic role has parallels in the ceremonies for the purification of the mouth which we find in Akkadian and Egyptian texts. In particular, he cites the examples of the *bārû* – priests from Mesopotamia whose task included delivering divine oracles. These priests underwent extensive purificatory rites in order to prepare themselves for this role, including 'washing, putting on clean clothes, anointing with oil, and purifying the lips with cedar wood, meal, and other ritually cleansing substances' (Lindblom, 1962: 186).

themselves but also for others. Without a formal, hereditary office to fill there would always be questions about who was and who was not a legitimate prophet. While various criteria may have been considered (e.g. a track history of fulfilled prophecies, possession of charisma, demonstrations of power etc.), the announcement and later recording of such call experiences could also have functioned as a form of 'social legitimation', justifying the individual's status as a prophet and the authority of his message. Habel (1965: 323) has suggested that the origin of such accounts can be connected with the practice of a human ambassador or messenger publicly presenting his credentials before the appropriate audience (cf. Gen. 24:35–48). If this is the case

> then it seems logical that the goal of the prophetic formulation of the call in the *Gattung* is to announce publicly that Yahweh commissioned the prophet in question as His representative. Thus the words of the call narrative give the individual's credentials as a prophet, messenger and ambassador from the heavenly council. (Habel, 1965: 323)

While some scholars (including von Rad) have sought to differentiate between the *experience* of being called and the later *writing down* of this, arguing that it was only the latter that served as a means of justification for the prophet, the example of Amos suggests that such a neat distinction cannot be maintained.[11] Amos' reference to his call in the context of the attempt by the priest Amaziah to stop him prophesying in Bethel (7:10–17) shows that the prophetic call experience itself could be used as a means of legitimation (Miller, 2000: 182). In effect, Amos rejects Amaziah's attempt to tell him what to do and say on the basis that he has been commissioned by God to speak a word of judgement against the northern kingdom of Israel.[12]

### 3.3.3 WHAT TRAINING DID PROPHETS UNDERGO?

The question whether or not prophets received any kind of formal instruction is usually answered in the negative. The line of reasoning goes that because the prophet had been called by God and given the divine word there was no need for any prophetic tuition. This, however, is an issue that requires further thought for it is highly likely that at least some (if not all) of Israel's prophets were educated in some fashion.

Temple or cult prophets, for example, may well have received formal instruction at significant cult centres, including the Jerusalem temple. If the example of the priests is anything to go by (see 2.2), then it is likely that other important members of the temple personnel (such as cult prophets) would also have received some form of official training in order to fulfil their responsibilities. And if we are to postulate the existence of a school associated with the Jerusalem temple

**Have you considered?**
**HOW COMMON WAS SAMUEL'S EXPERIENCE?**

Both Lang (1983: 97) and Blenkinsopp (1995a: 133) have argued that Samuel's experience in the sanctuary at Shiloh (1 Sam. 3) may have been typical for a temple prophet. Here we see formal instruction under the priest Eli (v. 1) combined with a direct commission from God – 'in other words, even a "called" prophet is a "taught" one' (Lang, 1983: 97).

**Have you considered?**
## COULD YOU BE BORN A PROPHET?

One common way of differentiating between the priestly and prophetic offices is to suggest that only the former was hereditary. Given the fact that members of the prophetic guilds could be married (cf. the reference to the wife of one of the 'sons of the prophets' in 2 Kings 4:1),* it is possible that any offspring born into the community would have been raised and trained as a prophet. Furthermore, considerations such as the hereditary nature of many cultic occupations in the ANE, and the general preference for certain family lines to perform religious observances, means that it would be reasonable to postulate that at least some of the temple prophets may have held their position on a hereditary basis. In the biblical text, however, there is only one clear example of two generations of prophets within the same family – both Hanani (father) and Jehu (son) are recognized as such (cf. 1 Kings 16:7; and 2 Chron. 16:7).

* Of course, Isaiah himself was also married (Isa. 8:3) as were Ezekiel and Hosea.

prophetic figure. Samuel (1 Sam. 9:18–24), Elijah (2 Kings 2:1–18) and Elisha (2 Kings 4:1–7, 38–41; 6:1–7 etc.) are all said to provide leadership to such groups and this probably included teaching their followers. Both 2 Kings 4:38 and 6:1–2 speak of the members of the guild as 'sitting at his (i.e. Elisha's) feet' which seems to imply a process of at least semi-formal instruction. In fact, Baumgartner translates the expression 'to sit at someone's feet' as 'to be a pupil of' (cited in Lang, 1983: 95). Unfortunately, the exact content of this teaching is not indicated. Lang (1983: 95), however, is probably not too far off the mark when he speaks of 'the conveying of the prophetic tradition and general practice in meditation and ecstasy', which are characteristic features of these groups.[13]

But what about the writing prophets? Is there any evidence to suggest that they underwent a process of formal instruction? To answer this question fully it would probably be best to approach the individual prophets on a case-by-case basis. As a group, however, it is clear that they demonstrate a good grasp of common prophetic modes of speech, a knowledge of prophetic traditions and Israel's history (cf. Jer. 28:8–9 which suggests an awareness of the work of previous prophets), and a general awareness of the geo-political realities of their day. While such knowledge *could* have been acquired simply by immersion within ancient Israelite society, on balance it would seem more likely that this was gained through some form of education. Certainly there is little in the prophetic books that would *preclude* the prophets receiving instruction along with their divine call. On the basis of the available evidence before us, however, it is impossible to determine whether this was undertaken

for the training of the priests, then it is possible that there was a similar institution for prophets as well. Here the potential prophets could have learned the basic forms of prophetic speech and come into contact with various prophetic traditions.

Members of the prophetic guilds or associations (*bᵉnē hannᵉbîʾîm*) may have undergone a different form of training. These associations seem to have employed more of an apprenticeship or discipleship model of instruction, with the various members of the guild sitting under a senior on a formal or informal basis, and whether this education was specifically prophetic or more general in nature.

## 3.4 WHAT DID A PROPHET DO?

It is well known that Israel's prophets were responsible for speaking the word of the Lord and this is, without doubt, an important aspect of their role. Yet as we have already seen with regards to the priesthood, the popular understanding does not always capture the full picture. In fact, this perspective needs to be expanded in two key ways.

First, a prophet was indeed responsible for communicating the word of the Lord but he/she was not restricted to *spoken* utterances. Israel's prophets perform numerous 'symbolic actions' which are designed to communicate God's revelation in a primarily *visual* fashion.

Second, while sharing God's message to his people was a primary responsibility of the prophets, their role often extended beyond this. In fact, there is a whole dimension of the prophetic role that such an understanding overlooks: the prophets were not only responsible for representing God to humanity but also represented humanity before God. This is demonstrated, for example, in the involvement of various prophets in healing and interceding for the people.

Before we can consider the various roles of Israel's prophets, however, a word of caution is again required. This is one area, in particular, where the variety that was present within Israelite prophecy makes it difficult to come up with legitimate overarching statements. So while what follows may be true for the phenomenon

of prophecy in Israel as a whole, we should not necessarily expect that an individual prophet would have performed all these different roles.

### 3.4.1 COMMUNICATE THE WORD OF THE LORD

The primary function of Israel's prophets was to reveal the deity's word and will to humanity. The actual content of this revelation could be quite diverse. It might include advice regarding the nation's military activities, responses to queries regarding an individual's illness, proclamations centring on cultic faithfulness, and teaching the king and people, the leaders and populace, to serve

**Going deeper:**
### THE ROLES OF ISRAEL'S CULT PROPHETS

As explained in 3.2, it is likely that a significant number of Israel's prophets were to be found in the nation's cult centres, including the Jerusalem temple. A primary responsibility of these prophets would have been the provision of oracles to those who had come to seek the will of Yahweh regarding a significant issue or life problem. On a communal scale, such prophets may have given a word during significant cultic celebrations and gatherings. 'Unlike the priests they are not responsible for the sacrificial cult, but offer advice to the individual supplicant or appear in larger community services of worship, in order to give to the congregation a comforting, promising or admonishing word of god' (Lang, 1983: 96). The Scandinavian scholar Sigmund Mowinckel identified four psalms (Pss. 60; 65; 82; 110) which he believed contained examples of prophetic oracles of assurance that would have been delivered within the context of an Israelite worship service.

the deity in an appropriate fashion (Miller, 2000: 186).[14]

We may often think that the prophets took the initiative in approaching their audience to deliver the divinely inspired word. But there is also a lot of evidence to suggest that the reverse was true – sometimes the word of the Lord could be sought out by an individual who took the initiative in directly approaching the prophet. This individual may have had a question which required a response from God or may have been seeking divine guidance on a specific issue. Examples of this practice include the Israelites coming to the prophetess Deborah 'for judgement' (Judg. 4:4–5); the king's officials consulting Huldah in order to

**Have you considered?**
## HOW DID THE PROPHETS EARN A LIVING?

The book of Amos suggests that prophecy was essentially a full-time vocation. In Amos 7:15 the prophet declares 'the Lord took me from following the flock, and the Lord said to me, "Go, prophesy to my people Israel."' (cf. the example of Elisha who leaves behind both his job and family, 1 Kings 19:19–20). But how did Israel's prophets survive if they were required to give up their occupation? A number of answers to this question are possible.

The example of Elijah suggests that *God could directly provide* for the needs of his prophets. In 1 Kings 17 the Lord sends ravens in the morning and evening with bread and meat to feed the prophet while there is a drought in the land. Later in 1 Kings 19 an angel brings Elijah cake and water while he is on the run from Jezebel.

Alternatively, the *prophet may have been employed by a wealthy patron*, usually the Israelite king or queen. First Kings 18:19 speaks of the 'four hundred and fifty prophets of Baal and four hundred prophets of Asherah, who eat at Jezebel's table'. It is reasonable to assume that the prophet Gad, who is explicitly described as 'David's seer', was in the employ of the king. Second Kings 4, on the other hand, may contain an example of a non-royal patron. Here, Elisha is provided with meals and a room with furniture by a 'wealthy woman' of Shunem.

The third, and probably most common means, was through *payment for the prophet's services.** This remuneration usually took the form of basic foodstuffs. In 1 Kings 14 Jeroboam sends ten loaves, some cakes and a jar of honey to the prophet Ahijah in order to discover whether his son would recover from his sickness or not. In 1 Samuel 9 Saul initially refuses to consult the prophet Samuel about his lost donkeys because 'the bread in our sacks is gone, and there is no present to bring to the man of God' (v. 7), implying that one would normally have to pay a prophet for his/her services. In the place of food, money could be provided. After hearing Saul's objection, his servant offers to pay Samuel a fourth of a shekel of silver for his assistance (1 Sam. 9:8; cf. Mic. 3:11). There are examples, however, of prophets being offered more exorbitant sums. For example, the king of Aram sends Elisha ten talents of silver, six thousand shekels of gold and ten sets of garments to cure the commander of his army, Naaman (2 Kings 5). In this instance, however, Elisha refuses payment, possibly because such a source of financial security may have undermined his daily dependence on God's provision (Meier, 2009: 189–91).

* Sometimes an individual may make a voluntary payment to a prophet even though he/she requires no service in return (cf. 2 Kings 4:42–44).

## ANE parallels:
## THE ROLES OF COURT PROPHETS

As suggested above, a close connection between kings and prophets is found not just in Israel but throughout the ANE.* For example, when facing the armies of the Aramean king Barhaddad, Zakkur, king of Hamuth and Luash, prayed to the god Baalshamyn who answered him through 'seers' (hzyn) and 'messengers'. Similarly, the Neo-Assyrian kings regularly consulted their court prophets at Nineveh, with the deity responding to the king's prayers for deliverance from enemies and promising the continuation of his rule. It is commonly argued that a key point of difference between Israelite and ANE prophecy was that the latter was primarily supportive of the monarch and status quo, whereas the former could be quite critical. Walton, for example, suggests that 'support clauses [which] express intended future actions by deity in support of the king . . . are the dominant feature of ancient Near Eastern prophecy' (2006: 248). This assumption, however, may need to be re-evaluated. As Grabbe (1995: 89, 92) has pointed out there are a number of prophecies from Mari that are quite critical of the king and some of his practices, while an Assyrian document such as the *Treaty of Esarhaddon* clearly recognizes the presence of prophets who speak an 'evil, improper, ugly word which is not seemly nor good' to the monarch, even if their actual words have not been preserved.

* The close association between prophets and foreign kings is also suggested by the biblical text itself. For example, Jeremiah urges rulers from the neighbouring lands of Edom, Moab, Ammon and the Phoenician cities not to heed their prophets and other intermediaries who were backing the planned rebellion against the Babylonian king, Nebuchadrezzar (27:1–15).

determine the appropriate response to the discovery of the book of the law (2 Kings 22:12–20); and the numerous times where a prophet was consulted to determine whether someone who was sick and near death would recover or not (e.g. 1 Kings 14:1–18; 2 Kings 1:2–4; 8:7–10; 20:1).

This custom of directly approaching a prophet or group of prophets to discover the divine will seems to have been a common practice of Israel's kings. In terms of the writing prophets, Isaiah was consulted by Hezekiah during the Assyrian invasion of Judah (Isa. 37:1–7). Similarly, Zedekiah sought out Jeremiah on a number of occasions as the Babylonian army besieged Jerusalem (Jer. 21; 37:3–10). In addition, prophets were often consulted by reigning monarchs before engaging in a military campaign in order to determine their chance of success.[15] A good example of this practice is found in 1 Kings 22. Here the king of Judah asks the king of Israel to 'inquire for the word of the LORD' via his 400 prophets before committing his forces against the neighbouring state of Aram. It is therefore possible to view the court prophets, in particular, as consultants for the king, bringing the divine input they required before significant decisions were made.[16]

While individuals, including Israel's kings, could come to a prophet to seek out God's will, more often than not the writing prophets were directed by God to take the initiative and directly approach their audience. For example, Amos travels from his home town of Tekoa in Judah to Bethel in order to address the problems that plague the northern kingdom (Amos 7:13). Likewise, Moses is sent to the Hebrew people who are enslaved in Egypt (Exod. 3:10). In this regard, Israel's prophets have been likened to ancient diplomats

**Figure 3.2  Detail from the Lachish reliefs showing the Assyrian army attacking the gate area of Lachish**

or envoys who were responsible for transporting an important message or command from one individual (or in the case of the prophets, the deity) to another.

A key text which sheds light on the role of the prophet as a messenger is 2 Kings 18 (Lang, 1983: 70–1). This describes how, in 701 BC, the Assyrian military juggernaut overran the tiny state of Judah, capturing all the significant towns before eventually laying siege to Jerusalem. As the Assyrian army sat encamped around Jerusalem a period of feverish diplomacy between Hezekiah, the king of Judah, and Sennacherib, the king of Assyria, ensued. Instead of personally meeting and engaging in direct negotiations, however, these kings sent a series of messengers, envoys and diplomats who communicated their will to the enemy. The kings never negotiated in person but made use of their delegates.

The similarity between the recorded speeches of the ancient envoys and the prophet Isaiah is noticeable. The use of a common messenger formula in particular highlights the close relationship between the role of envoy and that of prophet. For example, in 2 Kings 18:19 the messengers of the Assyrian king declare, 'These are the words of the King of Assyria', and in 2 Kings 19:3 the messenger of Hezekiah begins his speech to Isaiah with 'These are the words of Hezekiah'. The correspondence with Isaiah's response in 2 Kings 19:6 is immediate and obvious: 'These are the words of Yahweh'. This overlap suggests that the prophet viewed himself along the lines of an envoy sent by the divine king, Yahweh, whose primary task was to bring the message of the divine king to human beings. 'That is why he does not talk about his god but in the words of his god: the prophet bears, corresponding to the style of the diplomats, not his own message but that of his lord; this is kept in the first person which is typical of prophetic literature' (Lang, 1983: 71).

The close relationship between messengers and prophets is further reinforced by the use of a similar commissioning formula ('Go to . . . and say . . .') for both. This is found, for example, when Elisha dispatches Hazael with a message which he is to take back to his master Ben Hadad, king of Aram (2 Kings 8:10, cf. Gen. 32:3–4). The formula also occurs on a number of occasions in the prophetic literature. For example, Jeremiah is commissioned as part of his calling to 'go to all to whom I send you, and you shall speak whatever I command you' (Jer. 1:7; cf. 2:1–3). The fact that both God and important human figures commissioned their respective representatives with the same formula suggests that both prophets and messengers were conceived of as performing a similar role.

Given the importance of their role as envoys/messengers, it is interesting to consider how the prophets actually received the message they were required to pass on. In other words, how did the Lord reveal his word and will to the prophet? Unlike the priests who were able to consult the Urim and Thummim or ephod, there is no evidence to suggest that the prophets could discover the will of God by recourse to mechanical means or procedures. Instead, the prophet directly heard or perceived Yahweh's voice. This may have come unbidden or possibly following a period of preparation, including music, fasting or prayer.

Two modes of reception are emphasized in the prophetic literature.[17] The first is aural – the prophet hears the word of the Lord that he/she is required to pass on. This auditory dimension is suggested by the fact that 'many prophecies are presented in speech form, as if received through an audition' (Grabbe, 1995: 108). Furthermore, we find a reference in the Hebrew text of 1 Samuel 9:15 to the Lord revealing his message to the ear of Samuel (cf. Isa. 5:9; 22:14; Ezek. 9:1, 5 etc.). The second, possibly more dramatic, mode of reception is visual – the prophet is granted a vision which forms the basis for the message that he/she is required to communicate (cf. 1 Kings 22:19–22; Isa. 6:1–13; Amos 7). The importance of visions as a mode of divine revelation is suggested by the fact that numerous prophetic books (e.g. Amos, Micah and Habakkuk) open with a superscription which describes the subsequent contents of the book as what the prophet 'saw', and the fact that two of the major titles for the prophets, *rō'eh* and *ḥōzeh*, are active participle forms of Hebrew words for 'seeing'.

> **Going deeper:**
> **JOB 4:12–21 AND PROPHETIC REVELATION**
>
> A text which may help to shed light on the prophet's reception of revelation, and, in particular, the close relationship between auditions and visions, is Job 4:12–21. This describes a nocturnal experience of one of Job's 'friends', Eliphaz, and his encounter with a 'spirit' (*rûaḥ*). Even though Eliphaz is clearly not a prophet, his experience may well have been similar to one. Indeed, von Rad argues that 'This is easily our most comprehensive and detailed description of the outward circumstances which accompanied a revelation' (1968: 47). Note, in particular, the close linkage between what Eliphaz hears ('A word stole to me, my ear perceived a whisper of it') and what he sees ('amid visions of the night . . . I could not discern its appearance').

At the end of the day, however, it is not really possible to draw a hard-and-fast dividing line between the two modes of revelation, auditions and visions. Visions may include an auditory dimension; in fact, sometimes 'vision' is used with reference to a revelation which seems to have been given only in the form of speech (Grabbe, 1995: 108). As Miller concludes, 'There is enough interchange of word and vision, of "saw" and "heard" in prophetic book superscriptions (Isa. 2:2; Amos 1:1; Micah 1:1) that it is difficult to distinguish in any significant way between auditory and visual reception of the divine message' (2000: 184).

The spoken word was the most popular medium for communicating the divine message once this had been received. This is shown by the fact that the prophetic books are filled with oracles which the

## Have you considered?
## WERE THE PROPHETS ECSTATICS?

The place and significance of ecstasy or trance-like states in the experience of Israel's prophets remains a controversial topic. While it is clear that many ANE prophets exhibited some form of ecstatic behaviour (cf. the Egyptian story of Wen-Amon in which the very symbol translated as 'prophet' seems to be the image of a person in violent motion, and the use of the title *muḥḥûm* at Mari which literally means 'trancer or ecstatic' (Wilson, 1980: 103)),* there has been a greater reluctance in OT circles to associate such activity with the prophets of Yahweh.

Nevertheless, the evidence is clear that for some of Israel's prophets, especially the early ones, ecstasy was a genuine part of their experience. While this was not the norm, it appears that it was not uncommon. Key examples include Moses and the 70 elders (Num. 11:16–30); Saul's frenzy (1 Sam. 10:5–13; and 19:20–24) and Elisha (2 Kings 3:14–19). On a number of occasions music seems to have played a key role in stimulating such experiences (1 Sam. 10:5–6, 10–13). Perhaps the best example of this is 2 Kings 3:15 where Elisha calls for a musician before the 'hand of the LORD' comes on him and he delivers a prophecy. In terms of Israel's writing prophets, however, it is generally recognized that only Ezekiel has such experiences (Ezek. 2:2; 3:14, 22). The evidence for Jeremiah (e.g. Jer. 4:19; and 23:9) is less convincing and there is almost nothing to suggest that any of the other writing prophets were subject to such states.

How are we to account for the presence of ecstasy in the experience of some of Israel's prophets and its absence in others? Perhaps the answer lies within the diversity of the prophetic movement itself. The very label 'prophet' is given to a wide variety of people, operating within a wide variety of social contexts, performing a wide variety of roles. I think it is reasonable to assume, therefore, that certain elements within this movement will exhibit behaviour which is not manifested by all (just as certain roles are not performed by all, see the discussion of inter-cession, miracle working and healing below).

The *muḥḥûm* prophets of Mesopotamia seem to provide a good parallel (Wilson, 1980: 103–4). In some texts these prophets are described as engaging in trance behaviour that is considered irrational, incapacitating and potentially destructive. This reaches a point such that by the Neo-Assyrian period the activities of the *muḥḥûm* were seen as a form of insanity. (The references to the prophets as 'mad' (*mᵉsugga'*) in Jer. 29:26 and Hos. 9:7 perhaps suggest a similar perception within Israel.) Yet we have other texts that view the *muḥḥûm* in a very different light – the prophets are portrayed as delivering intelligible oracles in 'normal' situations. This example suggests that there was a great degree of variability of ecstatic experience and behaviour within prophetic circles of the ANE, and that we could therefore expect to see such diversity within Israel itself.

* It is also clear that the prophets of Baal demon-strated ecstatic behaviour which was brought on by self-laceration (1 Kings 18:26–29).

prophets proclaimed. Nevertheless, spoken discourse was not the only medium of communication that a prophet had at his/her disposal. A number of prophets, both writing and non-writing, engage in symbolic actions whereby the prophet 'acts out' in various, sometimes startling, ways the word he/she had received from the Lord.

**Going deeper:**
**SYMBOLIC ACTIONS IN THE OT**

The OT contains a number of instances of prophets engaging in some very strange (at least from a modern perspective) symbolic actions. Notable examples include the (false) prophet Zedekiah, son of Chenaanah, making for himself iron horns to symbolize the 'goring' (i.e. the coming defeat) of the Syrians (1 Kings 22:11), and Isaiah walking about naked and barefoot to symbolize the humiliating defeat of Egypt and Ethiopia by the Assyrians (Isa. 20). But it is the prophet Ezekiel who engages in the most frequent and unusual symbolic actions. For example, in chapter 12 the prophet breaks through the wall of his house, takes up his baggage and carries it out by night in order to represent the imminent defeat and exile of the citizens of Jerusalem. In chapter 24 he is forbidden from performing the customary mourning rites at the death of his wife, symbolizing the people's lack of grief when the Jerusalem temple is destroyed. In chapter 4 he carries out a series of symbolic actions (including lying on his side for 390 days, building brick models of attacking armies, and eating food cooked over human excrement) which are all connected in some way with the imminent siege of Jerusalem. One can only wonder what his contemporaries must have been thinking!

**Figure 3.3  Egyptian hieroglyph showing an individual in an ecstatic state, from the story of Wen-Amon**

Matthews and Benjamin (1993: 215–16) suggest that the symbolic actions of Israel's prophets belong to three main categories:

1  Single dramatic gestures: for example, when Jeremiah buries his loincloth in the bank of the Euphrates River as a sign of the imminent judgement of Judah (Jer. 13:1–11). Most of the prophetic symbolic actions belong to this category.

2  Austere practices or asceticism: for example, when Jeremiah refuses to marry or attend funerals or celebrations as a way of illustrating the widespread death and joylessness which is about to come on God's people (Jer. 16:1–13).

3  The prophet, like a docent, identifies the silent actions or crafts of another: for example, when Jeremiah draws the attention of his audience to vintners jugging their wine and connects this with the coming drunkenness and destruction of the inhabitants of Jerusalem (Jer. 13:12–14).

In each case, the action is initiated by Yahweh in exactly the same way as the spoken word was given to the prophet. Thus Lindblom (1962: 172) refers to such activities as '*verbum visibile*', a visible word.

We should not underestimate the provocative impact of such acts. A number of these public demonstrations would have caused a sensation within Israelite society and challenged the wider public to respond to the prophet's message. 'It is the street theatre itself which teaches us to understand the prophets not only as theologians of a meditative bent, but also as showmen, as experts in public agitation and propaganda. They reject violence it is true, but they retain all other possibilities of obtaining a hearing and giving weight to the word of their god' (Lang, 1983: 82).

While communicating the divine word and will was central to the role of Israel's prophets, it was not the sum and total of their work. The biblical text points to some of Israel's prophets performing a variety of additional, albeit less common, roles, including miracle working, healing and intercession.

### 3.4.2 MIRACLE WORKING

A number of Israel's early prophets are depicted as performing various miracles which manifest the power of God.[18] For example, Moses' staff turns into a snake, his

---

**Going deeper:**
**ELIJAH, ELISHA AND MIRACLES**

Elijah and Elisha are the two prophets most frequently connected with the miraculous in the OT. In addition to their involvement in healing miracles (see below), Elijah supplies a widow with a jar of meal and jug of oil which do not run out (1 Kings 17:14–16), and calls down fire from heaven on two occasions (1 Kings 18:38; 2 Kings 1:2–12). Elisha's miraculous exploits are even more numerous. These include 'healing' the bad land and water of a town (2 Kings 2:19–22), recovering an axe head which had been lost in the Jordan River by causing it to float to the surface (6:1–7), and feeding 100 people with 20 loaves of barley and some fresh grain (4:42–44), an act reminiscent of the Gospel accounts of Jesus feeding large crowds.

---

hand is covered with and healed from 'leprosy', and he heals and feeds the people during their wanderings in the wilderness (cf. Deut. 34:9–12). Samuel's prayers to God result in upheavals of nature (1 Sam. 7:8–11; 12:17–18), while Elijah and Elisha are both involved in reviving the dead and splitting the Jordan River, among many other miracles (see 'Going deeper: Elijah, Elisha and miracles').

It is unlikely, however, that this involvement with the miraculous was an essential element of the prophet's job description. While miracle working appears to be a key element of the portrayal of prophets in the Deuteronomistic History, Isaiah is the only classical prophet associated with such supernatural activities (e.g. the healing of Hezekiah and the moving backwards of the shadow of the sundial as narrated in Isa. 36—39).[19]

While such miracles were therefore not essential for someone to be recognized as a prophet (and as Deut. 13:1–5 recognizes their performance could, in fact, be misleading),[20] the presence of such divinely empowered activities would certainly have helped to validate the prophet's status and message within his/her society. For example, in the case of Moses these signs point to the fact that God has indeed appeared to him, and therefore that he should be believed and listened to (Exod. 4:1–9).

### 3.4.3 INTERCEDING

As with miracle working, intercessory prayer appears to have been a key role of some prophets but not all. Strong evidence for an association between intercession and the prophetic office is suggested by the reference to Abraham in Genesis 20:7 as a prophet who 'will pray for you (i.e. Abimelech) and you shall live'. In this text Abraham is

**Figure 3.4   Procession of worshippers with arms upraised in a gesture of prayer, from Kuntillet Ajrud**

explicitly identified as a prophet on the basis of his ability to intercede before God, suggesting that, at least in some circles, such activity was believed to be a characteristic part of a prophet's responsibilities (Wilson, 1980: 151).

Key prophets such as Moses, Samuel and Amos intercede on a number of occasions to avert divine wrath or judgement from coming upon the nation. For example, following the apostasy of the golden calf at Mount Sinai, God decides to destroy his people and start again with Moses (Exod. 32). Moses' prayer, however, results in the Lord changing his mind and the promised judgement is averted. For his part, Samuel commits to pray for the people so that they may not be judged for their wicked act in requesting a king (1 Sam. 12:19 and 23).

In terms of the writing prophets, Amos' role as intercessor is particularly prominent. Amos appeals to the Lord on two occasions and this results in the Lord relenting and not bringing about the judgement that he had threatened (Amos 7:1–6). In a similar vein, Jeremiah is requested by the king and people not simply to 'inquire' of the Lord,

but to 'intercede' for them and their wellbeing (Jer. 37:3; 42:2, 4; cf. 7:16; and 27:18).[21]

While these are the only named prophets who are recorded as engaging in acts of intercession, the book of Ezekiel suggests that holders of the prophetic office were clearly expected to pray for the people. This becomes obvious when we compare Ezekiel 22:30 with 13:4–5. In the former passage, Yahweh claims to have 'sought for anyone among them who would repair the wall and stand in the breach before me on behalf of the land, so that I would not destroy it; but I found no one'. In the latter passage, the Lord explicitly identifies the ones who were meant to be responsible for 'repairing the walls' and 'standing in the breach' as Israel's prophets. Thus, while intercessory activity was not limited to the prophets (e.g. priests could serve in this capacity, offering up prayers and sacrifices on the people's behalf), holders of this office were clearly expected, by both God and the people, to engage in this work.

### 3.4.4   HEALING

Given the general belief in ancient Israel in the supernatural cause of much illness, it is not surprising to find figures such as prophets, who stand between the divine and human realms, involved in healing activities. For example, Elisha treats the Syrian commander Naaman for his skin condition (2 Kings 5:1–19) and Isaiah administers a fig poultice which results in the recovery of the deathly ill Hezekiah (2 Kings 20:7//Isa. 38:21).

Even more remarkable is the involvement of Elijah and Elisha in reviving not only the sick but also the dead (1 Kings 17:17–24; 2 Kings 4:18–37; 13:21). The first of these texts, in particular, highlights the close link between healing and the prophetic office. Here, the widow of Zarephath explicitly recognizes that Elijah is a 'man of God', one of the titles for a prophet (see 3.1), on the basis of his healing activity. Following the resuscitation of her son, she declares, 'Now by *this* I know that you are a man of God' (1 Kings 17:24 – author's translation).[22]

Healing was a specific aspect of the prophet's broader roles of intercession and miracle working, and thus we should not draw a strict distinction between these three responsibilities. For example, in 1 Kings 13:1–6 Jeroboam appeals to the unnamed man of God from Judah to 'entreat now the favour of the LORD your God, and pray for me' so that his withered hand might be healed. In 1 Kings 17:20 we see Elijah interceding before God to heal the widow's son. Likewise, Elisha's prayer is a key element in the healing of the Shunammite woman's son (2 Kings 4:33). It is likely that prophets were expressly sought out at such times because it was believed their prayers to God were particularly efficacious.

## 3.5  SUMMARY

Israel's prophets were a remarkably diverse lot. They were found in various locations (religious centres, political centres or non-institutional contexts), underwent differing formational experiences and could perform a wide variety of roles, ranging from communicating the word of the Lord through to miracle working, intercession and healing. Nevertheless, they all held one thing in common. Whether cult, royal or 'non-aligned' prophet, each believed they were responsible for bringing a message from God to the Israelite people, bridging the gap between the divine and human realms.

## NOTES

1  Although the OT connects the origins of the prophetic movement in Israel with the figure of Moses (cf. Deut. 34:10–12; and Hos. 12:13), it only really emerges as a distinct and widespread social phenomenon from the time of Samuel onwards (1 Sam. 3:1—4:1).

2  One of the key features which demarcates the two periods is the nature of the literary texts that record the work of the prophets who were active during them. In the case of the former, we primarily have prophetic narratives (stories about the prophets) preserved in the so-called Deuteronomistic History (i.e. 1 and 2 Samuel; 1 and 2 Kings). In the case of the latter, however, we have distinct books filled with prophetic oracles (words from the prophets) that are attributed to various prophetic figures.

3  It is often suggested that during the former period prophecy was characterized by ecstasy and miracles and had as its primary audience the king. This is contrasted with the latter period where ecstasy and miracle working seem to be almost non-existent and the primary audience is the people as a whole.

4  Likewise, Blenkinsopp claims, 'There is therefore no essential discontinuity between the "school" of Elisha that supported the Jehu dynasty and Amos and Hosea who opposed it, between the representatives of "primitive" and "classical" prophecy. The impression of discontinuity, of distinct and discrete phases in the history of prophecy, can be explained by the inevitable but misleading tendency to periodize and also by the nature of the source material at our disposal' (1995a: 140).

5 Blenkinsopp goes on to suggest that in contrast to seer, there is no indication of a cultic connection for a man of God and that people who held such a title were probably itinerant (Blenkinsopp, 1995a: 125–6).

6 Other texts which suggest a close relationship between the titles *ḥōzeh* and *nābî'* include 2 Kings 17:13; Isaiah 29:10 and Micah 3:7.

7 Furthermore, in 1 Samuel 9—10 the same figure, Samuel, is referred to both as a *rō'eh* and *'îš 'ĕlōhîm*, suggesting the titles' synonymity.

8 I am using the label 'writing prophets' as a convenient way to refer to those prophets who have books associated with them, even though they were probably not responsible for actually writing these.

9 Further evidence for the 'overlap' of roles between that of prophet and priest is provided by the figure of Pashhur, an opponent of Jeremiah. This individual bears the title of priest (Jer. 20:1) while engaging in prophetic activity (20:6).

10 For example, certain elements may have been included primarily owing to the fact that they were a recognized part of the way in which such experiences were expected to be recorded and disseminated.

11 In fact, von Rad argues that the experience of the call and the writing down of the call served two different purposes. 'This makes clear that the writing down of a call was something secondary to the call itself, and that it served a different end from the latter. The call commissioned the prophet: the act of writing down an account of it was aimed at those sections of the public in whose eyes he had to justify himself' (1968: 34).

12 This also appears to be the case for Moses where the experience of being called and commissioned by God is to serve an important role in legitimating Moses before the captive Hebrews (Exod. 3:15–18).

13 In contrast, Verhoef suggests that Elisha 'could have taught them the history of God's revelation, the moral issues implied by the *tôrâ*, and, perhaps, pastoral care' (1997: 1073). Without clear evidence from the biblical text itself, we can only hypothesize on the basis of Elisha's prophetic activity elsewhere in the book of Kings.

14 In this chapter I have not devoted much time to the actual message of the various prophets. This is covered in most standard introductory texts on the OT prophets. See, for example, McConville (2002).

15 This practice of kings consulting their prophets before engaging in a military battle was not restricted to Israel. For example, the annals of the Assyrian kings Sargon and Sennacherib mention the receipt of oracles from Ashur which lead to the king fighting and defeating his opponent.

16 See also the example of David who 'consults' with Nathan about his desire to construct a temple for the Lord (2 Sam. 7:1–3).

17 For more details see von Rad, 1968: 30–49.

18 For a fuller discussion, see Meier, 2009: 120–6.

19 'The exceptional nature of the four chapters in Isaiah is explicable: they originate elsewhere, copied almost verbatim from the books of Kings in the Dtr history, a work where . . . it was important to depict prophets as wonder-workers' (Meier, 2009: 123).

20 Freedman concludes, 'Certainly they (i.e. wonders) were not obligatory, and such miracles seem to be attached to unusual charismatic individuals who were also prophets, but not necessarily to the role or office of prophet' (1997: 62).

21 As Hutton points out, 'Only by understanding the signal importance of the prophet's role as the community's chief intercessor can we appreciate . . . Jeremiah's pain at being disallowed by God to perform his intercessory role for a time (Jer. 7:16; 14:11; 15:1–2)' (1994: 123).

22 The identification of someone as a prophet on the basis of their healing activity is also found in the NT. In John 9:17 Jesus is declared to be a prophet following his healing of the man born blind.

## FOR FURTHER READING (IN ADDITION TO TEXTS CITED IN CHAPTER 2)

J. Blenkinsopp (1996), *A History of Prophecy in Israel: Revised and Enlarged*, Louisville: WJKP.

B. Lang (1983), *Monotheism and the Prophetic Minority: An Essay in Biblical History and Sociology*, SWBAS 1, Sheffield: Almond Press.

S. Meier (2009), *Themes and Transformations in Old Testament Prophecy*, Downers Grove: IVP.

R. Wilson (1980), *Prophecy and Society in Ancient Israel*, Philadelphia: Fortress Press.

Chapter 4

# THE WISE IN ANCIENT ISRAEL

## 4.1 INTRODUCTION

Jeremiah 18:18 points to the existence of three groups of religious leaders within ancient Israel: the priests (who provided instruction in the *tôrâ*), the prophets (who spoke the word of the Lord) and the wise (who gave counsel). The group that most people have the least familiarity with is probably the wise. While prophets and priests pop up relatively frequently in the OT narrative and have a number of books that are either attributed to them or describe the tasks they performed, references to the wise men and women of ancient Israel (with the exception of Solomon) are much fewer in number. Furthermore, the three OT books that are commonly associated with the wise (Job, Proverbs and Ecclesiastes) shed little insight on their social locations or roles, especially during the pre-exilic period.

A similar lack of recognition has also been present in much OT scholarship, which has traditionally focused on the Pentateuch and Prophets at the expense of the Wisdom Literature. Such literature was often downplayed or marginalized as a result of a focus on the historical, narrative nature of Israel's faith.[1] While there have been positive attempts to redress this imbalance since the 1970s,[2] it would be fair to say that we still know less about the sages of Israel than their prophetic and priestly counterparts. Thus, questions such as who the wise were, where they were found and what they did are much more difficult to answer, and much more likely to provoke debate.

Before we attempt to address these issues, however, it is necessary to develop some awareness of the way in which wisdom terminology is used in the OT. In the majority of cases, the term 'wise' is used in a generic sense to refer to a person or persons endowed with a particular skill or ability. Thus, we find it applied to those who performed any number of different occupations or trades, including the sailor (Ezek. 27:8–9), the farmer (Isa. 28:23–29), the mourner (Jer. 9:17–18) and even the magician (Isa. 3:3)! On some occasions, however, the term 'wise' is used in a more narrow sense to refer to a distinct class or group of people who were specifically known for their wisdom (and not another skill such as sailing, farming, mourning etc.) and who appear to have held a position of leadership within Israelite social, religious and political life. It is this group that I will focus on in this chapter.

## 4.2 WHERE WERE THE WISE TO BE FOUND?

Locating the wise within the social world of ancient Israel is no easy feat. 'The quest for the social setting of the sages has long been and continues to be a matter of considerable debate among scholars' (Lemaire, 1990: 165). On the basis of the scattered references we find in the OT and comparative ANE texts, however, it is possible to suggest some contexts in which people revered for their wisdom and who held positions of leadership within Israelite society would have been found.

### 4.2.1 THE ROYAL COURT

A professional group or class of wise men whose primary role involved advising the Israelite king was probably located in the royal court. Crenshaw (2010: 24) has suggested that the main supporting evidence for this proposal is of four kinds:

1  analogy with the situation in Egypt and Mesopotamia;
2  the presence of a literary corpus which reflects sapiential concerns and which would seem at home in the context of the royal court;
3  attacks upon the wise within prophetic texts; and
4  the likelihood that a royal court would need the particular talents that sages possessed.

Although each argument is hardly decisive in and of itself, when taken together they do provide a reasonable basis for suggesting that there did, in fact, exist such a special class of sages within ancient Israel. I shall

### ANE parallels: AHIQAR AS A COURT SAGE

One of the most famous wisdom figures from the ANE was Ahiqar. In an Aramaic text from Elephantine dated to the late fifth century BC but whose origins probably go back to the sixth century BC, he is described as a high official at the courts of the Assyrian kings Sennacherib (704–681) and Esarhaddon (680–669). He is referred to as 'the wise scribe, counsellor of all Assyria' and 'father of all Assyria, by whose counsel king Sennacherib and all the host of Assyria were guided' (*ANET*, 427, 428). This connection between Ahiqar and the royal court is further reinforced by his commitment to train up and present his nephew (Ahiqar is himself childless) to the king as his successor.

Kottsieper (2008: 124) has suggested that the focus on Assyria proves that the narrative is a work of fiction, since it is unlikely that there was a single man who was so influential in the great Assyrian Empire. Rather than being completely fabricated, however, he argues that the work probably reflects the situation of a smaller kingdom (perhaps similar to Israel or Judah?) where it was possible for a man who held the office of scribe and was well known for his wisdom to wield such influence.

focus on the first and third arguments as these are the most compelling.

Both biblical and ANE texts locate people who are characterized as wise within the context of the royal courts of Egypt and Mesopotamia. For example, in Genesis 41 Pharaoh summons all the magicians of Egypt and his 'wise men' to interpret his dreams (cf. Exod. 7:11) while in Isaiah

19:11 the sages of Egypt are described as 'wise counsellors of Pharaoh'. From Mesopotamia our strongest evidence for a link between the wise and royal court comes from the Neo-Assyrian period, and, in particular, the more than 350 letters written by various 'scholars' (*ummânu*, also translated as 'experts' or 'specialists') to kings Esarhaddon (680–669 BC) and Ashurbanipal (668–*c*.627 BC). These scholars included expert exorcists, lamentation singers, scribes, astronomers and diviners who were expected to provide the king with professional reports and advice upon which he could base his important decisions. Finally, the Aramaic wisdom document, *Ahiqar*, may point to the presence of 'wise men' within the context of the royal courts of smaller ANE kingdoms (see 'ANE parallels: Ahiqar as a court sage').

It should be recognized, however, that the validity of such analogies is a matter of debate. We need to be careful of simply transferring what we know about the social location of the wise in the great empires of Egypt or Assyria to Israel. As Hunter has cautioned:

Arguments from analogy have often been employed – Israel is compared with other ancient Near Eastern societies about which we know much more. The trouble is that the comparisons are usually made with large imperial regimes such as those of Egypt, Babylon and Assyria while Israel and Judah were arguably more like Moab, Edom and the like: small states with poorly developed infrastructures. We cannot simply transfer the known institutions of Egypt to the Israelite context as though we were comparing like with like. (2006: 42)

While Israelite society was clearly not of the same size and complexity as the great ANE

**Scholar focus:**
**GERHARD VON RAD (1901–71)**

The suggestion that there was a close association between the wisdom literature/the wise and Israel's royal court received major support from the work of Gerhard von Rad, the most significant OT theologian of the twentieth century. Von Rad argued that the wisdom literature was a product of the 'spiritual enlightenment' that took place in Israel during the reign of Solomon. According to von Rad, during this period the Israelite royal court closely modelled itself on that of Egypt. This resulted in a sudden, rapid cultural development which brought Israel into the mainstream of Near Eastern civilization, and which led to the production of much literature, including wisdom literature. 'The blossoming of economic life was naturally followed close behind by an intensive interchange of spiritual ideas . . . The court was a centre of international wisdom-lore, as the Egyptian courts had been in an earlier age . . . In short, the time of Solomon was a period of "enlightenment", of a sharp break with the ancient patriarchal code of living' (1984: 203).

While von Rad's reconstruction has met with some degree of scepticism (anyone hear overtones of the European Enlightenment?) and criticism (critical scholars, in particular, have challenged his more-or-less unquestioned acceptance of the historicity of the biblical narratives of David and Solomon), his work continues to be influential in some circles. More recent scholarship (e.g. Blenkinsopp, 1995a: 32–7), however, has tended to substitute the reign of Hezekiah (late eighth century BC) for that of Solomon, suggesting that any significant development which encouraged scribal activity within Israel's royal court would most likely have taken place at this later stage.

empires, the development of a monarchy and kingdom would have required the creation of an accompanying bureaucracy, albeit on a smaller scale, to service the royal court and run the nation. That such a development did take place is suggested by the list of David and Solomon's chief officials in 2 Samuel 8:16–18; 20:23–26; 1 Kings 4:1–6; 18:18, 37. There is no reason to suspect that this bureaucracy would not have included a group of wise men who were responsible for advising the king, if not during the reign of David or Solomon then certainly later.

The best evidence we have that such a group did, in fact, exist within ancient Israel is found in the prophetic literature. A number of the pre-exilic prophets, especially Isaiah and Jeremiah, attack a group labelled as 'wise' who were at work within the Israelite royal court. For example, Isaiah 29:14 seems to refer to royal counsellors whose diplomatic schemes consistently elevate human wisdom over Yahweh's plan as revealed by the prophet (van Leeuwen, 1990: 302). Likewise, Isaiah 30:1–5 and 31:1–3 appear to be targeting groups who view themselves as 'wise' (31:2) and who are responsible for 'counselling' (30:2) the king in the formation of foreign policy but who are, in reality, responsible for leading the nation to disaster. Finally, Jeremiah 18:18 points to the existence of a distinct group of royal counsellors who were responsible for providing advice to the king. Thus, McKane concludes, 'The wise against whom the pre-exilic Judahite prophets

**Plate 4.1    Relief of Horemheb's tomb depicting Egyptian scribes writing documents (eighteenth dynasty of Egypt, 1328–1298 BC)**

## Have you considered?
## THE RELATIONSHIP BETWEEN SCRIBES AND 'THE WISE'

A key element of the national and religious administrations of ANE kingdoms, including Israel, were scribes. Their importance in Israel is suggested by the fact that the head scribe appears on various lists of royal officials along with other prominent individuals such as the head of the army and the head of the priests (e.g. 2 Sam. 8:16–18; 20:23–26; 1 Kings 4:1–6; 18:18, 37). Although the specific duties of Israel's scribes are not well spelled out within the OT, they probably performed a variety of roles including drawing up official edicts, copying and preserving documents, functioning as secretaries and recorders, and travelling on important diplomatic missions (cf. 2 Kings 18; Isa. 36). They may have also assumed increasing responsibility for the preservation, transmission and interpretation of the law (cf. Jer. 8:8–9 which seems to associate the scribes with the law of the Lord). This is certainly the case by the post-exilic period (cf. Ezra who is described both as 'a scribe skilled in the law of Moses' (Ezra 7:6) and a 'scholar of the text of the commandments of the LORD' (7:11)), where scribes emerge as important figures due to the increasingly textual nature of Jewish religion.

So what was the relationship between the scribes and the wise? The lack of an explicit association between scribes and wisdom within the OT suggests that the two cannot simply be equated. Nevertheless, there was probably some overlap. Jeremiah 8:8–9 seems to imply a connection between 'the wise' and 'the lying pen of the scribes', while in Egypt 'the sage was inseparable from the scribal tradition' (Grabbe, 1995: 164). It is plausible, therefore, to suggest that at least some of the wise who were found within the context of the Israelite royal court would have been drawn from the ranks of the scribes.[*] Along similar lines Dell concludes: 'It seems likely that the "sages" were a subgroup of the scribes, i.e. most sages were also scribes (even if they didn't perform the formal tasks of a scribe), but not all scribes were sages. The sages were probably the elite of the scribes, having a function well beyond simple writing. It is possible that they had important administrative and political roles at the royal court (following Egyptian parallels again) and the likelihood that they would have been trained to a higher level, possibly in a court school, is high' (2008: 130). For more details see Dell, 2008.

[*] 'While some distinction must be maintained between the roles of 'wise' (ḥākām) and 'scribe' (sēper), there was significant overlap. Almost by definition, the scribe belonged to the learned and wise element of society and was so characterized' (Miller, 2000: 198).

conducted a polemic were statesmen in the service of the kings of Judah on whose expertise and sagacity (ʿēṣâ) the kings relied for advice and policy' (1995: 142).

So what would one of the court sages have looked like? Von Rad (1984: 292–300) has suggested that the figure of Joseph gives us a good image. In Genesis 39—50 we see Joseph engaging in public speaking, counselling the reigning monarch, constructing administrative programmes, and forward planning to help overcome potential problems for the nation. His interactions are marked by courtesy and a cool head (even in his dealings with his treacherous brothers) and his attributes include self-discipline and control, modesty, godly fear, patience, prudence and humility. In other words, he is an archetypal ANE wise man.[3]

## 4.2.2 SCHOOLS

Given the focus on teaching, learning and instruction in a wisdom text such as Proverbs, it would seem logical to locate the wise within an educational context. The presence of schools within ancient Israel, however, is a matter of significant scholarly debate.[4] While there is little clear archaeological or textual evidence which points to their existence, a number of circumstantial arguments have been martialled by scholars in support of their presence. The most significant of these include:

1  Hints in the book of Proverbs – Proverbs contains a number of passages which could imply the presence of schools. For example, it talks about teachers and instructors (5:13), tuition (17:16) and 'lodging among the wise' (15:31).
2  The presence of wisdom literature in the OT – 'the strongest argument for the existence of schools in Israel and Judah is the quality and quantity of the literature produced there' (Crenshaw, 2007: 198). On the basis of parallels with the Egyptian 'Instruction' genre, it has frequently been argued that a document such as Proverbs would have been used as a school text.
3  Archaeological – the significant increase in epigraphic material beginning in the eighth century BC may point to the existence of Israelite schools and the growth of the scribal profession (Lemaire 1990: 170; 1992: 308–9).
4  ANE Parallels – the widespread presence of schools in the neighbouring cultures of Egypt and Mesopotamia from as early as the third millennium BC is often put forward as a major argument for the presence of schools in ancient Israel.

Those who accept the presence of schools in ancient Israel usually locate important

### ANE parallels:
### EGYPTIAN INSTRUCTIONS AND THE BOOK OF PROVERBS

The closest ANE parallels to the book of Proverbs belong to the Egyptian genre of *Sebayit*, usually translated as 'teaching' or 'instruction'. About a dozen examples of such documents have been preserved and they usually record the teachings of an important, sometimes royal, figure to his son. It appears, however, that such instructions were primarily used as school texts, where they were repeatedly copied in order to educate young people in foundational social values and rules of proper conduct and behaviour. For example, the introduction to the *Instructions of Amenemope* reads: 'The beginning of the teaching of life, the testimony for prosperity, all precepts for intercourse with elders, the rules for courtiers . . . to know how to return an answer to him who said it, and to direct a report to one who has sent him, in order to direct him to the ways of life, to make him prosper upon earth' (*ANET*, 428).

*Amenemope* is well known in OT circles due to the presence of a number of close parallels with Proverbs 22:17—24:22. For example, *Amenemope* chapter 6 reads, 'Do not move the markers on the borders of fields', which resembles Proverbs 23:10: 'Do not remove an ancient landmark or encroach on the fields of orphans.' *Amenemope* chapter 9 declares, 'Do not befriend the heated man, nor approach him for conversation', which is similar to Proverbs 22:24: 'Make no friends with those given to anger, and do not associate with hotheads.' The presence of such *literary* parallels is often taken to imply some sort of *functional* parallel between the two documents. As G. Davies concludes, 'Thus it appears that the borrowing of this extract from an Egyptian Instruction was made with its original purpose still very much in mind, namely the instruction of would-be courtiers and officials' (1995: 203).

centres for learning in the royal court and temple.[5] Texts that may point to the existence of royal schools include 1 Kings 12:8–10 and 2 Kings 10:1, 5–6. Such schools would have been involved in training young, aristocratic men who were destined to hold important positions within the state bureaucracy, such as diplomats and royal advisers. Evidence for the presence of temple schools is less conclusive; however, proponents call attention to texts such as 2 Kings 12:2–3; Isaiah 28:7–13; and 2 Chronicles 17:7–9. Such schools may have played a key role in the development of priests, cultic functionaries and those involved in the administration of the temple, including the temple library. Some of the OT literature (esp. the Psalms) could be attributed to people who worked in such educational institutions.

At the end of the day, however, the presence of schools in ancient Israel must remain a (likely?) possibility, rather than an accepted fact. The use of analogies from the great Mesopotamian and Egyptian empires is not convincing. The relatively easy to learn Hebrew alphabet would not have required the same degree of education as Akkadian cuneiform or Egyptian hieroglyphs and therefore the need for formalized, institutionalized education may have been less. Likewise, the much smaller governmental bureaucracies of Israel and Judah would have required fewer formally educated individuals and therefore less need for schools. In fact, the better ANE parallels from kingdoms of a more comparable size to ancient Israel (e.g. *Ahiqar* and Ugarit) suggest that education took place almost entirely in a domestic context. There is no evidence for schools in a text such as *Ahiqar*; instead, Ahiqar himself is directly responsible for training his

### ANE parallels:
### SCHOOLS IN UGARIT?

In order to grasp the nature of education in ancient Israel, I believe we are better off considering the example of Ugarit rather than the great world empires of Mesopotamia and Egypt. Significantly, not a single document mentions the presence of schools in ancient Ugarit, nor has the word for 'school' ever been found in any of the recovered texts. Nevertheless, the presence of educational exercises and textbooks suggests that scribal instruction of some form did take place. What is particularly interesting, however, is *where* these texts were unearthed – rather than being located in centres of learning associated with the royal palace or large temples, the remains of such 'school' activity were found in rooms or sections of private buildings which belonged to people who held important positions in the state bureaucracy (Rowe, 2008: 106–7). This leaves Rowe (2008: 107) to conclude that teaching in Ugarit primarily took place in a familial milieu, and thus 'schools' were located within an essentially domestic context.

successor to stand before and answer the Assyrian king. Thus, we need to recognize that even *if* schools did exist in ancient Israel it is highly likely that they were a secondary rather than primary locus of education, with the majority of instruction taking place in the context of the family.

So far we have located the wise within the significant cities of ancient Israel, especially the royal courts and schools of the capitals. The vast majority of Israel's population, however, did not live in such cities, but instead resided on farms or in small villages. It is in these towns and villages that we can locate a third group known for their wisdom, the elders. These are the people that an 'average Israelite' would have sought out if he/she had wanted to consult a wise individual.

### 4.2.3 THE TOWN GATES

A third group in ancient Israel that was specifically known for their wisdom was the elders. The elders were significant, usually older, males who represented a distinct social group or community (village, city, tribe or the nation) and exercised a certain degree of influence over the people who belonged to this group.

The evidence for an association between wisdom and the elders is twofold. First, we have a number of wisdom texts which associate old age with wisdom in general. For example, Job 12:12 seems to be a popular proverb which locates wisdom with the aged and understanding with 'length of days' (cf. 15:7–10 and 32:7). 'This is in accord with the observation that in the ancient Near East wisdom teachers are often depicted as men of particularly great age' (Conrad, 1980: 124). Other texts such as Psalm 105:22; 119:100; Job 32:9 and Ecclesiastes 4:13 seem to play against this notion, but in so doing they imply

the belief that wisdom was the preserve of the aged was popular and widespread. While none of these passages contain an explicit reference to the class of elders per se, they do show that old age was expected to bring with it wisdom, and thus the elders (who were often marked out by their age) would have been viewed as wise virtually by default.

The second reason for associating wisdom with the elders is that they are often described as performing the characteristic tasks of the wise, including the provision of advice (ʿēṣâ). This is most clearly seen in Ezekiel 7:26. Here, the prophet describes the impending judgement that is about to fall upon Jerusalem in a way which resembles a similar declaration in Jeremiah 18:18. Comparing the two passages is instructive (see Table 4.1).

Both of these passages highlight the characteristic roles of Israel's leaders: instruction is brought by the priests, and divine revelation (in the form of a word or vision) by the prophets. The third role, the provision of counsel (ʿēṣâ), remains constant in both passages, but in Jeremiah 18 this is said to be the domain of the wise while in Ezekiel 7 it is associated with the elders, implying some sort of linkage between the two. While it would be too simplistic to set

**ANE parallels:**
**OLD AGE AND WISDOM**

In the ANE the link between old age and wisdom is not just found on the human plane. For example, in the texts from Ugarit all of the occurrences of the root ḥkm ('wise') are associated with the elderly father of the gods, El. In one passage Athirat explicitly connects El's advanced age and his wisdom: 'You are great, O El! The greyness of your beard does indeed make you wise' (KTU 1.4 v 3–4).*

* Translation from Wyatt, 1998.

**TABLE 4.1**

| Ezekiel 7:26 | Disaster comes upon disaster, rumour follows rumour; they shall keep seeking a vision from the prophet; instruction shall perish from the priest, and counsel (ʿēṣâ) from the elders. |
| --- | --- |
| Jeremiah 18:18 | Then they said, 'Come, let us make plots against Jeremiah – for instruction shall not perish from the priest, nor counsel (ʿēṣâ) from the wise, nor the word from the prophet.' |

up the equation 'elders' = 'wise', it seems likely that people who were known for their wisdom often belonged to this social group (just as people recognized for their wisdom in the royal court were often drawn from the scribes, see above) and thus it is appropriate and, in fact, necessary to discuss this group when considering the wise in ancient Israel.

So who were the elders? In most cases, the elders were probably drawn from the male heads of families, the leading citizens within the community, prominent men of rank and

influence.[6] Together they formed a sort of 'municipal council' which was responsible for representing and regulating the lives of the towns and villages of Judah and Israel (1 Sam. 16:4; 30:26–31; 1 Kings 21:8; 2 Kings 23:1). This group gained their authority from the confidence placed in them by the townspeople who recognized their wealth of experience, and hence wisdom, and its potential benefit to the community (Matthews and Benjamin, 1993: 122).

Perhaps the best image of an elder we have in the OT is the figure of Job.[7] In chapters 29 and 31 'Job describes himself as a man of means, whose opinion his neighbours hold in the highest esteem, and who regularly exhibits justice, mercy and righteousness in his dealings with others' (Willis, 2007: 233). He is the head of his household and is identified as a teacher (4:3; 27:11) and

**ANE parallels:**
**THE INSTITUTION OF ELDERS**

The institution of local elders was found throughout the ANE, with the possible exception of Egypt. Groups of elders are mentioned in Mesopotamian texts ranging from the eighteenth-century BC Mari documents, all the way through to the royal correspondence of Sargon II (late eighth century BC). References in Old Babylonian (c. nineteenth–sixteenth-centuries BC) texts are particularly informative. Here, the elders of the city form a judicial body that functions alongside the royal courts but which is more concerned with local legal issues. 'One passage clearly distinguishes the elders from the old men; they clearly constitute a distinct committee, probably composed of the wealthy and respected citizens, especially the heads of the important major families' (Conrad, 1980: 126). Although the ANE evidence does not present a uniform picture, it does suggest that such groups could exercise significant power, especially in the political realm, functioning as the representatives of their cities or tribes, overseeing the internal affairs of their group and, if needs be, advising the king.

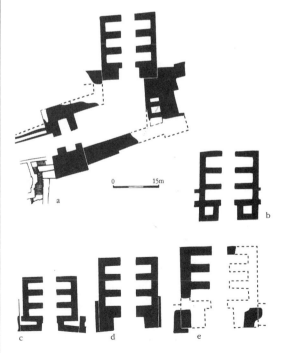

**Figure 4.1 Plans of city gates of Megiddo (a), Hazor (b), Gezer (c), Ashdod (d) and Lachish (e)**

counsellor who gives advice (29:21) – key roles of the wise. In short, Job is a wealthy, upper-class member of his society, who is viewed with a great deal of respect by his community and is thus able to speak into the life and affairs of his community.

Members of this group would often have been found sitting at the gate of the town (or, if the village did not have a gate, at the threshing floor where the grain was processed). Such locations served as the courthouses of ancient Israel and were where the community's significant political, religious and legal affairs were discussed. For example, the husband of the Proverbs 31 'capable wife' is described as 'known in the city gates, taking his seat among the elders of the land' while in Joshua 20:4 a person who has committed manslaughter is told to plead his case to the elders located at the gate of the city (cf. Gen. 23:10, 18; Deut. 21:18–21; 22:13–21; 25:5–10; Ruth 4; Prov. 24:7). There were very practical reasons for this choice of location.[8] The two sides of the main gate which faced one another created bays or semi-enclosed areas which were ideal for public meetings and trials (Matthews and Benjamin, 1993: 122). Furthermore, the choice of the gates had the effect of keeping any legal proceedings open since the deliberations took place in front of a steady flow of people (Matthews and Benjamin, 1993: 123).

## 4.3 WHAT DID THE WISE DO?

The obvious answer to this question would be that they shared their wisdom, that is, they engaged in teaching. Yet as we have seen with both the prophets and priests, such simplistic, one-dimensional answers are insufficient, for they fail to appreciate the diverse roles that holders of these offices were expected to perform. As a result of her analysis of the OT material, Fontaine (1990: 157) has helpfully suggested that the typical role set of Israel's sages included teaching, counselling, planning and settling disputes, and in a later work (2002: 14) she adds authorship and scribal duties (including copying, collecting and editing) among others. Using this as the basis for our discussion, I shall focus specifically on the roles of the wise as teachers, counsellors, arbiters and composers of literary works. It needs to be kept in mind, however, that this list does not exhaust the roles that a wise person could perform, nor was a specific wise person necessarily expected to perform all of these roles.

### 4.3.1 TEACHING

The wisdom literature clearly suggests that a primary role of Israel's sages involved teaching, or, as Blenkinsopp declares, 'the sages of Israel were primarily teachers' (1995b: 12). Such teaching may have included moral instruction, guidance for living, vocational training or theological reflection.

The teaching role of Israel's sages is implied, for example, in the rhetorical questions of Job 15:2–3: 'Should a wise man utter windy knowledge, and fill himself with the east wind? Should he instruct with unprofitable words, with speech that is useless?' (translation from Albertz, 1990: 244). In other words, a wise man *should* utter knowledge – but it should not be windy – and a wise man *should* instruct – but not with unprofitable words.[9] In the book of Proverbs we read, 'The tongue of the wise dispenses knowledge, but the mouths of fools pour out folly' (15:2, cf. v. 7) and 'The teaching of the wise is a fountain of life, so that one may avoid the snares of death' (13:14). Furthermore, the book of Proverbs as a whole, and chapters 1—9 in particular, is clearly instructional in nature (cf. 1:2–4), suggesting that a primary concern of the wise individuals who were responsible for collating such material involved education and teaching.

Israel's elders were also expected to perform an educative role. According to Deuteronomy 32:7 the elders were to tell the people of Yahweh's historic work with the nation. Other passages suggest that they could be involved in reciting and teaching the people the *tôrâ*, a role they shared with Israel's priests (cf. Deut. 27:1; 31:9–13). As Blenkinsopp concludes, 'the elders were also the depositaries, custodians, and transmitters of the group

ethos and the shared traditions that helped to constitute the group's identity' (1995a: 25).

### 4.3.2  ADVISING/COUNSELLING

The role of the wise in offering counsel and advice is closely related to their teaching responsibility, for both essentially involve instruction. The key difference, however, is the object of their activity: the wise teach their students but they offer guidance and advice to their peers or to someone who is of higher social standing (e.g. their employer, the king etc.).

Two key prophetic texts suggest that a characteristic role of the wise/elders was to offer counsel (*ʿēṣâ*): Jeremiah 18:18 and

## ANE parallels:
## ROYAL COUNSELLORS

Both the biblical text and comparative documents point to the role of wise counsellors in advising ANE monarchs.

In terms of Egypt, Isaiah 19:11–12 lampoons the supposedly wise sages of Pharaoh who give 'stupid counsel' and who, in spite of their claims to greatness, are unable to tell Pharaoh what Yahweh plans to do. While the Egyptian documents themselves are generally reluctant to name individuals as counsellors of the king (perhaps because of the dogma of Pharaoh's divinity), such a role is implied in a number of inscriptions (Williams, 1990a: 97). For example, from the reign of Osorkon II (ninth century BC), Nebneteru, the royal scribe, is variously described as 'an official of the outer chamber who guides the land by his counsel' and 'a mouth effective at privy speech . . . whose coming is awaited at the palace and whose sagacity has promoted his person' (cited in Williams, 1990a: 97–8).

From Mesopotamia, the first millennium wisdom text, *Advice to a Prince*, warns the ruler against dismissing the counsel of the wise: 'Should he not pay heed to the scholars, the land will rebel against him' (line 5) (cited in Beaulieu, 2007: 17).* The more than 350 letters written to the Neo-Assyrian kings Esarhaddon and Ashurbanipal show that they had access to a wide variety of specialists, including divination experts and astrologers, who could be called on to assist the king in making critical decisions. Finally, while Ahiqar may not reflect realities present within Assyria itself (see above), the various descriptions of his role ('the counsellor of all Assyria . . . father of all Assyria, by whose counsel king Sennacherib and all the host of Assyria were guided') may well point to the presence of royal counsellors within smaller kingdoms in Israel's vicinity.

* In fact, Nabonidus, the last king of the Neo-Babylonian Empire, is rebuked precisely because he did not listen to his scholars and advisers (Beaulieu, 2007: 16–17).

Ezekiel 7:26. As discussed above, in both passages we find reference to the key groups of leaders within Israelite society and their expected responsibility: the prophets bring a word/vision from God, the priests offer instruction, while the wise or elders furnish counsel. This link between wisdom and counsel is not restricted to the human plane; it is also true of God. For example, in Job 12:13 God is described as possessing 'wisdom and strength . . . counsel and understanding', while in Proverbs 8:14 personified Wisdom is said to have 'good advice', 'sound wisdom' and 'insight' (cf. Isa. 11:2). Such passages reflect a divine ideal which human sages were expected to embody.

The counselling role of the wise was particularly important in the context of the royal court. This was true both inside and outside of Israel. Within Israel, we see the elders functioning as advisers or counsellors for various kings. For example, in 1 Kings 12:6–11 they appear as counsellors to Rehoboam, unsuccessfully advising the young king to serve, rather than exploit, the people. Likewise, in 1 Kings 20:7–12 the elders offer advice to the unnamed king of Israel (possibly Ahab) when he is unsure how to respond to the messengers of the Aramean king Ben-hadad.

A trusted official within the Israelite king's entourage was the royal counsellor ($y\hat{o}$'$\bar{e}\d{s}$) whose role was to provide 'advice' ('$\bar{e}\d{s}\hat{a}$) to the monarch during the course of his reign. 'The task of the counsellor was to formulate plans to assist both rulers to succeed in their efforts to rule wisely and well and others to experience well-being' (Perdue, 2008b: 50).

**Plate 4.2 King Bar Rakab seated on his throne, with his scribe who is holding writing implements, from Zinjirli**

The best example of such a figure is Ahithophel, the counsellor of David (2 Sam. 15:12), whose advice was like an oracle from God (16:23). During the later monarchical period the royal counsellor probably headed up a larger body of counsellors. Proverbs, for example, points to the presence of a multiplicity of counsellors within the Israelite royal court (Prov. 11:14; 24:6; cf. Isa. 1:26, 3:1–4). While such individuals are never explicitly described as 'wise' in the biblical text, it seems reasonable to suggest that they would have been recognized by the king and wider population for their wisdom. In fact, Stähli (1997: 558) argues that the occurrence of the Hebrew roots $y$'$ṣ$ (from which we get 'counsellor') and '$ēṣâ$ (from which we get 'advice/counsel') in the context of roots such as $ḥkm$ ('wise') and $bîn$ ('understanding') suggests that such activity clearly belongs to the realm of wisdom (cf. Jer. 49:7 which explicitly associates counsel with wisdom: 'Is there no longer wisdom in Teman? Has counsel perished from the prudent? Has their wisdom vanished?').

It would be a mistake to think, however, that Israel's sages only offered advice or counsel within the context of the royal court. They could also provide guidance to others who sought their help, especially those undergoing difficulties, assisting them to experience success and wellbeing. For example, Job (sarcastically) declares of his three friends, 'How you have counselled one who has no wisdom, and given much good advice!' (26:3), and later goes on to describe the revered position he himself once held: 'They [i.e. the citizens of his local city] listened to me, and waited, and kept silence for my counsel' (29:21). Proverbs 15:22 also implies that the work of such counsellors was not restricted to the king.

### 4.3.3 ARBITRATING DISPUTES

Another role which the wise were expected to perform was to adjudicate between parties and settle disputes. This often involved making legal judgements. For example, Job hears and settles the complaints of his servants that are brought to him (31:13–15), and is also involved in establishing justice for the needy at the city gate (29:7–17). Proverbs, in contrast, does not explicitly associate this role with the wise, but the exhortation in 18:5 ('It is not right to be partial to the guilty, or to subvert the innocent in judgement') perhaps implies that they could perform this task (cf. v. 17 which also suggests some involvement in judicial decisions).

Both legal and narrative texts suggest that a primary task of the elders was to adjudicate and decide local legal matters (cf. Deut. 19; 21:1–9, 18–21; 22:13–21; 25:5–10). They conducted civil and criminal trials, settled disputes, imposed any penalties, and played a particularly important role in upholding and protecting the rights of those members

**Going deeper:**
### THE ELDERS IN THE BOOK OF RUTH

An example of the involvement of elders in a local legal matter is given in Ruth 4:1–12. After becoming aware of Ruth's situation, Boaz sits at the gate of the town, the normal place for Israelite legal proceedings (for more details, see 4.2.3), and hails the kinsman who has the right of redemption over Naomi's field. He then chooses ten elders who sit down beside him and are to serve as witnesses to the proceedings. The case is stated and discussed between the parties, the man renounces his right of redemption and Boaz calls the elders and all the people to witness his decision to take Ruth as his wife.

**Have you considered?**
## WHO WERE THE 'WISE WOMEN' AND WHAT DID THEY DO?

Second Samuel contains two references to individuals known as 'wise women': the wise woman of Tekoa (2 Sam. 14) and the wise woman of Abel (2 Sam. 20). Unfortunately, relatively little information is provided about either of these figures – we are not told of their place in society, nor is the nature of their wisdom ever explicitly described. Instead, the author appears to assume that his audience would be familiar with such figures. A close reading of the text, however, does allow us to shed some light on the nature and roles of such individuals.

In 2 Samuel 14 Joab, a commander in David's army, hatches a plan to effect a reconciliation between David and his estranged son, Absalom. He brings a wise woman from Tekoa and instructs her in what she is to wear, how she is to behave and what she is to say as she goes before the king. While it has been argued that in this passage the wisdom belongs to Joab and not the woman (cf. v. 3), as Fontaine has pointed out 'Clearly, this woman was known for her wisdom, and it is the good report of her efficacy in difficult diplomatic situations that causes Joab to fetch her to instigate his plan for returning Absalom to the king's favour . . . Whatever words David's general may have instructed her to say, it was her own experience, wisdom and ingenuity that allowed her to carry off her role' (2002: 192).

In 2 Samuel 20 Joab is involved in chasing down the Benjaminite Sheba who has led an attempted rebellion against David. Joab lays siege to the city of Abel where the rebel has sought sanctuary. A wise woman talks to him from the city wall and brings the siege to an end by

of the village who did not belong to a household, such as the widow, the orphan and the alien. According to Deuteronomy, the elders were to be involved in cases involving capital offences (21:1–9, 18–21; 22:13–21; cf. 1 Kings 21:8–14; and Jer. 26:17–19), levirate marriage (Deut. 25:5–10; cf. Ruth 4:1–12) and asylum (Deut. 19:11–12; cf. Josh. 20:1–6). This list is likely to be representative rather than exhaustive.

The role of the wise in settling disputes is also hinted at in 1 Kings 3. Here Solomon prays to the Lord for a 'listening heart' in order that he may be able to judge the people of God and 'distinguish right from wrong' (v. 9). He receives the gift of wisdom (vv. 10–14) and the famous episode of the two harlots is immediately narrated (vv. 16–28). Solomon's ability to resolve the dispute results in public recognition of the king's wisdom: 'All Israel heard of the judgement that the king had rendered; and they stood in awe of the king, because they perceived that the wisdom of God was in him, to execute justice' (v. 28). In this passage, wisdom is clearly linked with the ability to make sound legal judgement (cf. Deut. 16:18–19; 1:13–18).

### 4.3.4 COMPOSING DOCUMENTS
The presence of a body of wisdom literature within the OT clearly suggests that some of Israel's sages were responsible for composing texts. It needs to be acknowledged, however, that the OT contains few explicit references which connect the wise with writing or the production of literature (Prov. 22:17; and 24:23). Perhaps we should not read too much into this, however, as the OT is virtually silent regarding who was responsible for the formation of literature during the pre-exilic period full stop.

offering to hand over the head of Sheba. A number of things about this woman are worth noting:

1  She was obviously a significant and well respected figure – Joab treats the wise woman seriously and readily answers her (vv. 16–17).
2  The wise woman does not consult any of the male authorities in her town before deciding on a course of action – she concludes the arrangement with Joab and *then* tells the people of her plan (vv. 21–22).
3  The wise woman seems to function as an elder – she is able to represent and speak on behalf of her townspeople (Camp, 1990: 189).

In both passages the woman's ability to solve problems and resolve disputes through the use of persuasive speech is emphasized.* Both women use proverbs as part of their negotiating strategy (2 Sam. 14:14; and 20:18) suggesting a good knowledge of folk wisdom: they possess rhetorical skill, good sense and an ability to discern the appropriate course of action. These skills are brought to bear on significant personal and political problems, suggesting that a key role of such women was to mediate important disputes that involved individuals or the community of which they were a part. This may find a possible parallel in fragmentary Egyptian texts which mention a 'wise woman' who 'may have been a kind of intermediary for problematical affairs in the village community' (Borghouts, cited in Harris, 1990: 16).

* Fontaine, for example, speaks of 'their excellent and timely use of language in the resolution of conflicts' (2002: 65).

---

**Going deeper:**
## FEMALE COMPOSITION OF AN OT WISDOM TEXT

There is one passage in the biblical wisdom literature which is probably a result of female 'authorship': the teaching attributed to the queen mother of King Lemuel in Proverbs 31:1–9. These verses resemble the Egyptian Instruction genre where a king or high official sought to pass on his life's learning to his successor (for more details, see above). Here the king's mother warns her son to keep away from wicked women and excessive drinking, and calls on him to judge righteously and care for the poor and needy. Note that the mother feels free to offer a number of admonitions and make direct prohibitions, employing a number of imperatives, showing that she has the authority to speak and expects her words to be obeyed (Fontaine, 2002: 61). This text may give us some idea of the nature of the 'mother's teaching' that we find mentioned elsewhere in the book of Proverbs (1:8; 6:20).

---

On the basis of what little evidence we do have, however, OT scholars have generally argued that scribes were engaged in composing texts from the pre-exilic period. As suggested above, scribes were a key part of the national and religious administration of Israel, with oversight of the records and documentation which was required to keep a state-level bureaucracy functioning. It is highly likely that some of the members of this profession would have possessed the necessary time, ability and knowledge of literature and

**Plate 4.3  Diorite statue of a seated Egyptian scribe with a papyrus scroll (nineteenth–twentieth dynasty, 1295–1069 BC)**

## 4.4  HOW DID SOMEONE BECOME WISE?

While the OT may not provide much direct information about the social location and roles of the wise, it is easier to document the process by which an individual was believed to gain wisdom. Three main factors stand out: education, experience and divine revelation. In other words, both human effort (education and experience) and divine gifting (revelation) were essential in the gaining of wisdom.

### 4.4.1  EDUCATION

A primary way in which wisdom was acquired in ancient Israel was through education. In other words, wisdom was something that could be learned, a quality that could be acquired through diligent study and obedience to one's teachers. This perspective clearly underlies a text such as Proverbs 4 which repeatedly calls on its reader to 'get wisdom' (vv. 5 and 7) and Proverbs 8:5 in which personified Wisdom cries out to her hearers to 'learn prudence; (and) acquire intelligence'. While wisdom may not be dependent on education, 'those who are instinctively wise benefit from education; and some who are not at first wise become so through the educational process' (Hunter, 2006: 3).

literary conventions that were required to produce the biblical texts (Grabbe, 1995: 170).

Since the sages of the Israelite royal court were often drawn from the ranks of the scribes, we can expect that they would have been able to compose documents. In fact, Dell has argued that we should view the sages as 'the elite of the scribes' and that when it came to the compilation of writings they were involved at the 'more creative end of the procedure: authors and compilers rather than redactors and copyists' (2008: 137).

So how did education take place in ancient Israel? All Israelite children, male and female, would have received some form of initial instruction from their parents within the context of the home. Proverbs 6:20 declares 'My child, keep your father's commandment, and do not forsake your mother's teaching' (cf. 1:8; 10:1; 15:20; 20:20; 23:2, 25; 30:11 and 17). While such parental language could be used to refer to one's teacher (just as the title 'son' could refer to a student), it is quite clear from elsewhere in the OT that parents did, in fact, have a key role to play in the education of their children (e.g. Deut. 4:10; 6:4–9; 11:19; Ps. 78:5). 'The home may be regarded as perhaps the original site of wisdom teaching, before and after such teaching became professionalized among the sages' (Murphy, 2002: 4).

We can summarize the content of the teaching that would have been given within the household under four key headings: religious teaching, moral development, cultural expectations and vocational instruction. The OT repeatedly emphasizes that children were to receive *religious teaching* from their parents. For example, the *Shema* (Deut. 6:4–9) emphasizes the responsibility of all Israelite parents to teach their children the commandments of the Lord from morning until evening.[10] Parents were also to play a key role in the *moral development* of their children, helping them to discern right from wrong, and inculcating responsible behaviour and attitudes (e.g. the value of hard work, the proper conduct of relationships (especially sexual ones), self-control etc.). Mothers and fathers were also involved in passing on the *core values and norms of their society* (a process sometimes referred to as 'enculturation'), which would have included some instruction in normal gender roles, responsibilities and expectations.[11] Finally, parents were usually expected to provide some level of *vocational instruction* to their children, with fathers guiding their sons in the occupation or craft that they had pursued, while mothers taught their daughters the required tasks associated with being a wife and mother. In short, parents were expected to provide an education that shaped their children's character and skills, thereby placing them on the road to achieving success in life.

**Have you considered?**
**MOTHERS AS INSTRUCTORS IN WISDOM**

Although the book of Proverbs (and the OT as a whole) tends to emphasize the role of the father in instructing his children, it is highly likely that mothers also performed an educative role that was at least as important as her husband's, if not more so. Proverbs 1:8 and 6:20 both mention 'mother's teaching' which is set in parallel with 'father's instruction/commandment', clearly emphasizing its significance. Furthermore, the teaching role of the Israelite mother is suggested in Proverbs 31 where the 'capable wife' is portrayed as opening her mouth with wisdom and speaking the 'teaching of kindness' (v. 26).

Mothers were responsible for instructing children of both genders. Daughters were taught the various duties and skills required to perform their roles first as young women, and then as wives and mothers (cf. Ezek. 16:44). Mothers would have also been the primary educators of young boys until their father took a more direct hand. The exact age at which this transition took place is unclear; however, estimates range from the age of five to the approach of puberty (i.e. 12 to 14). It is likely, however, that motherly instruction of their sons would have continued well past this age: in Proverbs 31:1–2 the mother of King Lemuel instructs her adolescent son in the various responsibilities associated with rule, while 30:17 and 31:28 'anticipate compliance, deference and appreciation from her household, including her grown male children' (Fontaine, 2002: 27).

So far we have considered the kind of education that virtually any Israelite child received. Can we be more specific regarding the type of education that a wise man

**Going deeper:**
## HOW WERE ISRAELITE SCRIBES EDUCATED?

According to the available ANE and biblical evidence, two primary pedagogical tools were regularly employed: repetition and the rod. We have a number of school documents from Mesopotamia which suggest that students were expected to recite texts from memory (one document mentions performing a song ten or 20 times!), commit these to writing, and copy classical texts. Isaiah 28:9–10 and 13 may mock similar exercises. Poor performance on assignments could result in harsh punishment. For example, a Sumerian document from the Old Babylonian period (c.1900–1600 BC) reads, 'After the instructor has collected the tablets, he will inspect them. He will correct the places where the wedges are not right. If the student is found to be deficient and could not recite his exercise tablet and his word list, the instructor and the master will strike his face' (cited in Civil, 1992: 303). Proverbs 29:15 also points to the practice of such discipline: 'Rod and reproof give wisdom, but a mother is disgraced by a neglected child' (cf. 3:12 and 23:13–14).

destined for service in the royal court would have been given? It is likely that the initial training for such individuals would still have taken place within the context of the household. As suggested above, Israelite fathers were generally responsible for the vocational instruction of their sons and the scribal profession (from which many of the wise in the royal court were probably drawn) also seems to have been hereditary. For example, both Shaphan (2 Kings 22) and his son, Gemariah (Jer. 36:10), held important scribal positions within the Israelite bureaucracy (cf. 1 Chron. 2:55 which mentions 'the families . . . of the scribes that lived at Jabez').[12] Thus, Whybray (1995: 25) has argued that we should look to the home, rather than schools, as the primary training place for the majority of Israel's scribes.[13] Further evidence for the training of royal courtiers within the context of the household is provided by the example of Ahiqar who takes a direct hand in preparing his successor, his nephew Nadin, for service before the Assyrian king. At this stage, it is likely that the young boys would have received a general education in reading, writing and the scribal arts. There may also have been some basic instruction in the wisdom tradition.

Those who were destined for service in the royal court would have received further specialized training, perhaps in the context of a royal school. It must be emphasized, however, that formal education outside the home would have been extremely rare in ancient Israel. 'Widespread schooling was unlikely, given the demands of an agrarian culture, the disruption of life from invading armies, and the Deuteronomic injunction that religion be the subject of instruction and that it take place in homes' (Crenshaw, 2007: 198). At this more advanced level, students may have been taught Israelite law and literature, ANE geography and history, as well as a diplomatic language such as Aramaic (cf. 2 Kings 18:26) (Lemaire, 1992: 310). Proverbs implies that they would have also received some education in administration and how to succeed in their personal lives and in the king's service.

### 4.4.2 EXPERIENCE AND OBSERVATIONS OF LIFE

The second major way in which wisdom was developed in ancient Israel was through observation of the created order and reflection on one's own and others' life experiences. 'The *ʿēṣâ* of the sage was the product of observation and induction drawing on concrete experiences of nature and the human condition' (Hutton, 1994: 179).

On the basis of Job 28:27 ('(God) saw it and declared it; he established it, and searched it out'), Crenshaw (2007: 203) has argued that Israel's sages followed a four-stage intellectual process:

1 Observation – because Israel's sages believed that Yahweh had hidden universal truths deep within the created order (Prov. 25:2, cf. Eccl. 3:13), the task of human beings was to search diligently for these lessons through observation of the world around them. Such observations often focused on human nature and activity and were born out of one's own experiences or through reflecting on the situation of another. For example, both Job (13:1; and 21:17) and his friends (4:7–8; 15:17; 5:27) point to their own experiences as the basis for their teachings. While the attention of Israel's sages was often directed towards human beings, their work was not restricted to this. The author of 1 Kings describes the wisdom of Solomon as follows: 'He would speak of trees, from the cedar that is in the Lebanon to the hyssop that grows in the wall; he would speak of animals, and birds, and reptiles, and fish' (4:33). Proverbs draws a number of moral lessons from nature (30:15–33) and even holds out the prospect of becoming wise through paying attention to the ant (6:6)!

2 Discussion – such observations were then brought into dialogue with the work of other wisdom figures. This conversation had a vertical as well as a horizontal dimension, including not only the sage's contemporaries but also his/her forebears. For example, in Job 8:8–10 Bildad calls on Job to 'inquire now of bygone generations, and consider what their ancestors have found . . . Will they not teach you and tell you and utter words out of their understanding?' Likewise, in Job 15:17–19 Eliphaz explains that his teaching is based both on what he has seen (v. 17) and what the ancestors have revealed (vv. 18–19). Such discussion may have resulted in the individual confirming the received wisdom tradition (e.g. Job's friends) or led to attempts to subvert it (e.g. Job).

3 Establishing hypotheses and reaching provisional conclusions – on the basis of their observations and discussions, the wise sought to establish reliable principles that would enable them to make sense of reality and succeed in life. Insights from the natural realm were transferred to the human by way of analogy. For example, Proverbs 25:14 likens 'clouds and wind without rain' with 'one who boasts of a gift never given' while 27:8 sees similarities between a 'bird that strays from its nest' and 'one who strays from home'.

4 Analytic assessment – the various facets of the idea were critically assessed in order to determine potential flaws and weaknesses.

Such observations and life experience were often associated, rightly or wrongly, with Israel's elders, and would have provided a primary reason for their recognition as wise. As suggested above, members of this group were probably drawn from the older, male heads of prominent families whose 'length of days' was expected to bring with it wisdom (cf. Job 12:12; and 32:7).

### 4.4.3 DIVINE REVELATION

The third way in which wisdom could be gained was through direct divine revelation. Wisdom is a divine attribute (Isa. 31:2; Job 9:4; Jer. 10:6–8) and possession of God (Job 12:13), and the deity is able to give it to whom he chooses. Thus wisdom is said to derive ultimately from God, and can be explained as a gift from God. For example, Proverbs 2:6 declares, 'For the LORD gives wisdom; from his mouth come knowledge and understanding', while Job 35:11 describes God as the one who 'teaches us more than the animals of the earth, and makes us wiser than the birds of the air'. The nature of wisdom as a divine gift is particularly emphasized in the story of Solomon; following his ascent to the throne, the newly established king prays to God for wisdom, rather than power or wealth, and is granted all three as a reward (1 Kings 3; 4:29–34). Thus, Solomon's wisdom is described as 'divine wisdom' or 'the wisdom of God' in 1 Kings 3:28 (cf. 1 Kings 10:24 and 5:12).

To summarize, the OT recognizes a balance between human effort and divine giftedness in the acquisition of wisdom. Wisdom may in part be learned, but there is also an element of divine inspiration to it (Grabbe, 1995: 162). The balance between these two factors is highlighted by Proverbs 2:1–6;

verses 1–5 emphasize human endeavour (note the particular emphasis on 'seeking', 'searching' and 'finding' wisdom in vv. 4–5) while verse 6 recognizes the importance of divine revelation. Likewise, the wisdom of Daniel is a result of both formal education and training (1:5) and divine giftedness (1:17). Thus, we should not seek to draw a sharp distinction between these two formative elements; both reason and revelation were essential for the sages of ancient Israel. Crenshaw ties the two together well: 'In short, a sage needed a gift from the deity to grasp the full meaning of information processed by arduous intellectual effort and to put knowledge to effective use' (1998: 253).

## 4.5  SUMMARY

The wise of ancient Israel are a difficult group to pin down. People who were specifically recognized for their wisdom, who held positions of leadership and who performed wisdom-oriented roles (such as teaching, advising and arbitrating disputes) would have been found within the capital city of each kingdom, and more specifically within the royal court and key educational centres (if these existed). Yet such individuals would have been quite distant (geographically and socially) from the majority of the Israelite population. If an 'average Israelite' had wanted to track down a wise figure, he/she probably would have sought out one of the local elders who resided in the villages and towns that were spread throughout the kingdom. Such individuals played a key role in maintaining the unity and stability of the communities of which they were a part, and, on the basis of their wisdom and experience, could be called on to safeguard and foster the wellbeing (including the religious wellbeing) of its members.

## NOTES

1 For further discussion, see Crenshaw, 1976: 1–35.

2 Good examples include Gammie and Perdue, 1990, and Perdue, 2008a.

3 Crenshaw has questioned the identification of Joseph as a model sage, arguing that a number of factors (including the loss of control of his emotions and his cat-and-mouse treatment of his brothers) count against this interpretation (personal correspondence). In response, I would suggest that Joseph is described in ways which clearly evoke the court sages of the ANE, even if he is not a perfect example of this. Thus, he is the best 'model' we find in the OT, even if he is not the best model full stop.

4 For summaries of the various arguments for and against the presence of schools in ancient Israel, see Davies, 1995, and Crenshaw, 1998.

5 Lemaire (1990; 1992) argues for a much more widespread presence of schools in ancient Israel; however, his arguments generally remain unconvincing.

6 Willis (2001: 8–13) distinguishes between three general categories of elders in the OT: senior members of a group united primarily by vocation (e.g. elders of the priests), national or tribal elders, and local or city elders. I am primarily concerned with the third category.

7 It should be acknowledged, however, that the biblical author never uses the specific term 'elder' to describe Job.

8 For a discussion of the symbolic reasons why such places were used, see Matthews and Benjamin, 1993: 123.

9 The educational function of the sages is repeatedly emphasized throughout the book of Job: they are expected to teach

(6:24; 27:11; 33:33; 34:32), instruct (4:3) and transmit knowledge (15:17–19).

10 Parents were also expected to instruct their children about the 'mighty acts of God' in history (Exod. 12:26; 13:8; Deut. 32:7; Josh. 4:21–22).

11 For more details regarding education and enculturation in ancient Israel, see Carr, 2005: 126–34.

12 Note also the prominent role of another of Shaphan's sons, Elasah, who appears to function as a diplomat (Jer. 29:3).

13 There is also ANE evidence which suggests that the scribal office was hereditary and that fathers could be responsible for the education of their sons. For example, texts from Deir el-Medinah in Egypt indicate that an elite family held scribal office for six generations (Crenshaw, 2007: 197). In terms of Mesopotamia, a number of studies have concluded that scribal education in the Old Babylonian period 'was basically a private affair taking place in private houses, where a father, who was himself a scribe, taught his own son' (Alster, 2008: 50, note 8).

## FOR FURTHER READING (IN ADDITION TO TEXTS CITED IN CHAPTER 2)

J. Crenshaw (1998), *Education in Ancient Israel: Across the Deadening Silence*, ABRL, New York: Doubleday.

J. Day, R.P. Gordon and H.G.M. Williamson (eds) (1995), *Wisdom in Ancient Israel: Essays in Honour of J.A. Emerton*, Cambridge: Cambridge University Press.

J. Gammie and L. Perdue (eds) (1990), *The Sage in Israel and the Ancient Near East*, Winona Lake: Eisenbrauns.

L. Perdue (ed.) (2008a), *Scribes, Sages, and Seers: The Sage in the Eastern Mediterranean World*, FRLANT 219, Göttingen: Vandenhoeck & Ruprecht.

L. Perdue (2008b), *The Sword and the Stylus: An Introduction to Wisdom in the Age of Empires*, Grand Rapids: Eerdmans.

# EXCURSUS: THE ROLE OF KINGS IN THE RELIGIOUS LIFE OF ANCIENT ISRAEL

The king was the central and key figure in the life and affairs of the Israelite nation. He exercised some degree of power over virtually every aspect of the nation's existence, whether economic, political or social. Generally speaking, however, Western readers of the Bible have tended to neglect or downplay the role of the king in Israel's religious life. This is probably due to two key reasons.

First, we have emphasized a division between church and state, sacred and secular realms in the modern, Western world. Readers of the OT may unconsciously project this separation back into ancient Israel and thus view the king as a central element in the political, but not necessarily religious, life of the nation. Such a sharp ideological division, however, was not present in the ancient world. Kings were not only political figures: they also provided religious leadership for the nation and played an especially important role in the central cult (for more details, see below).

This lack of demarcation between political and religious roles is seen perhaps most clearly in Psalm 110:4, a royal coronation psalm which probably dates from the early monarchic period. Here the Davidic king is described as 'priest for ever according to the order of Melchizedek'.[1] In other words, the king combines in his person both 'political' and 'religious' (priestly) functions.

The second factor which has led to a diminished view of the role of the king in the nation's religious life is the tendency of the OT itself to downplay the religious responsibilities of Israel's kings. For example, the cultic regulations found in Leviticus give no special place to the king, suggesting that he was viewed as a standard member of the laity without any special or unique cultic prerogatives. Furthermore, in

## ANE parallels:
## PHOENICIAN PRIEST-KINGS

Examples of ANE kings holding priestly office come from the neighbouring region of Phoenicia. From the ninth century, we have Ethbaal, king of Tyre (and father-in-law of the Israelite King Ahab, 1 Kings 16:31) and, from the fifth century, Tabnit and Eshmunazzar, kings of Sidon, all of whom are heralded as priests of Astarte, goddess of war and sexuality and possible consort of Baal (Day, 1998: 75).

a number of passages where the king does perform some kind of cultic role he appears, at least at first glance, to be condemned for doing so. For example, in 1 Samuel 13 Saul offers a sacrifice rather than waiting for the priest Samuel and, as a consequence, has the kingdom taken from him. In 2 Chronicles 26:16–21 King Uzziah of Judah enters the Jerusalem temple in order to offer incense on the altar in the Holy Place and is subsequently struck down with leprosy. It should be noted, however, that in the former example Saul is not condemned for offering a sacrifice per se but rather because he refused to wait the allotted period of seven days as instructed by Samuel. In other words, his sin is not that he has performed a religious action that was restricted to Israel's priests but rather that he has disobeyed the word of Samuel, a prophet of the Lord. Therefore, this passage cannot be taken as proof that Israel's kings did not engage in cultic acts. In fact, it is only in a single, late, post-exilic text – 2 Chronicles 26 – that kings are explicitly disqualified from the offering of sacrifices.

While the OT's lack of explicit discussion may make it difficult to reconstruct the cultic roles of Israel's king, it is far from impossible. We will simply need to adopt a more indirect approach, reading between the lines, looking for hints within the text and considering comparative ANE documents and practices. The latter should be particularly valuable as the biblical text itself suggests that the Israelite monarchy was modelled along the lines of the surrounding ANE nations. The reference to the Israelite people coming to Samuel and requesting a king 'like the other nations' (1 Sam. 8:5) suggests a desire to establish a monarchy according to common cultural norms, and therefore we should expect some degree of overlap in terms of the institution and practices of kingship. As Wyatt has concluded:

> The accumulating evidence suggests that allowing for local variations and emphases, we should postulate a broadly similar ideology of kingship throughout the region. It would be most unusual if any particular social group had a radically different perception of kingship from its neighbours. Constant interaction in trade, diplomacy and warfare constantly reinforces the common elements. (2010: 65)

When we approach the biblical text in this fashion – reading between the lines, focusing on that which is implicit, and considering common ANE practice – it quickly becomes clear that the Israelite king was central to the religious life of the nation. We can categorize the king's cultic roles and responsibilities under two broad headings.

1 The kings established, maintained, and reformed the central cult – the kings had a key role to play in the official state cult, particularly in the operation of the central religious sanctuary of the nation. For example, they were involved in *building* and dedicating such sanctuaries when required. The obvious example of such building activity is the work of both David and Solomon in the planning and eventual construction of the temple at Jerusalem. But they were not the only Israelite kings to establish temples. When Jeroboam I led the secession of the north from the Davidic dynasty during the tenth century BC one of his first tasks was to build temples at Bethel and Dan, thereby establishing these sites as key, independent religious centres for the northern kingdom (1 Kings 12). The close connection

**ANE parallels:**
**KINGS AND THE CONSTRUCTION OF TEMPLES**

One of the most important responsibilities of an ANE king was to provide a temple for the god or gods of the state. Meyers' extended explanation is worth considering in full: 'One of the tasks of the king, as representative of a centralized community that depended upon the official administration for its welfare, was to erect an earthly home for the deity who was the source of the bounty and stability that the populace hoped would prevail. Without the deity's presence in a temple building, where he or she was accessible to the public (or at least the priestly leadership) and available to receive the offerings that were meant to help secure divine favour, the authority of the king to rule his people was not clearly established. Conversely, the decay or disrepair of a temple was seen as evidence of divine anger; and kings were as anxious to set about the restoration of existing temple buildings as they were to initiate the construction of new ones' (Meyers, 1987: 364).

**ANE parallels:**
**KINGS AND CULT ORGANIZATION**

It is clear that many ANE kings played an important role in organizing the cult that was practised within their realm. Much of the relevant material has been gathered together in Ahlström, 1982. For example, in his famous law code the Babylonian king Hammurabi describes himself in ways that suggest he was 'caretaker, restorer and organizer of the temples and their cults' (Ahlström, 1982: 7). The texts from Mari suggest that the king was responsible for regulating religious practice by deciding dates for festivals and sacrifices in the provinces. A later, Babylonian inscription states that Marduk, the chief god of the Babylonian pantheon, 'entrusted Nabu-apla-iddina with organization of the cult, its rites and sacrifices' (Ahlström, 1982: 8).

between the monarchy of the northern kingdom and the important cultic centre at Bethel is suggested by its description as 'the king's sanctuary' in Amos 7:13.

Israel's kings could also be involved in building places of worship that were not connected with the veneration of Yahweh. In addition to the temple in Jerusalem, Solomon is said to have built multiple sanctuaries for the gods of the surrounding nations and his foreign wives (1 Kings 11:7–8). Likewise, King Ahab built a temple in Samaria for his wife Jezebel which was dedicated to the Tyrian Baal (1 Kings 16:32).

In addition to constructing the temple buildings, some kings were involved in staffing and *organizing* their cultic establishments. This is certainly the case for Jeroboam I. After establishing Dan and Bethel as his key religious centres, he installs new, loyal priests to serve within them and arranges a new calendar of festivals.[2] There is also evidence elsewhere in the OT which indicates that important cultic functionaries, such as the chief priest, were public officials who could be nominated and dismissed by the king.[3] For example, 2 Samuel 8:17 suggests that David appointed Abimelech and Zadok as priests, while Solomon removed Abiathar from his position (1 Kings 2:26–27) and set up Zadok (and his line) as his sole chief priest (2:35; cf. 4:2). By this means, the king continued to exercise authority over the nation's religious establishments, mediated, as it were, through the priests whom he appointed to office.

**ANE parallels:**
## THE MAINTENANCE OF TEMPLES IN THE HITTITE EMPIRE

The kings of the Hittite empire were also concerned with the maintenance of any religious sanctuaries that were found within their borders. This is clearly suggested in an official text addressed to the commander of the border guards (see *ANET*, 210–11). Here, the king instructs the commander to inspect the local temples, to check that the cult of the country was being performed correctly and to ensure that the temple buildings themselves were kept in good condition. The king directs his commanders to restore or rebuild the temples if necessary (Ahlström, 1982: 12).

While only a few of Israel's kings could be responsible for the construction of new sanctuaries, subsequent kings were expected to look after the *upkeep and maintenance* of the ones they had inherited. For example, 2 Kings 12:1–16 describes how Jehoash initiated a programme of repairs for the House of the Lord, while Josiah is also depicted as being proactive in this regard (2 Kings 22:3–7). These passages suggest that the king (along with the priests) was responsible for maintaining the temple building itself and had the final say in how temple revenues would be spent (Miller, 2000: 193).

Kings could also play a key role in *reforming* the state cult should they so desire. A number of such reforms are

**Plate Ex.1** Limestone plaque depicting Ur-Nanshe of Lagash bearing a basket on his head, possibly containing the first brick for the foundation of a temple (c.2500 BC)

## Going deeper:
## WHAT WAS NEHUSHTAN?

Nehushtan was the name of the bronze serpent that Moses had constructed and placed on a pole while Israel travelled from Sinai to the promised land. Numbers 21:4–9 describes how God provided the serpent as a means of curing those who had been bitten by poisonous snakes. According to this text, the emblem was originally a symbol of Yahweh's power to heal (Hendel, 1999: 616). By the time of Hezekiah, however, it appears that the image had developed a life of its own – it had become an idol with people making offerings to it (2 Kings 18:4), and thus needed to be destroyed. An alternative suggestion, however, has been proposed by Handy (1992: 1117). He argues that Nehushtan was not originally associated with Yahweh but represented a distinct deity within the Judahite pantheon, a god of healing. Although this deity was subservient to Yahweh, the image was destroyed by Hezekiah as it was viewed as being incompatible with the call to worship Yahweh alone.

mentioned in the biblical text, including those led by Asa (1 Kings 15:9–24), Jehoshaphat (1 Kings 22:41–51), Athaliah (2 Kings 11), Joash (2 Kings 12:1–17), Hezekiah (2 Kings 18) and Josiah (2 Kings 23).[4] These often involved the king removing so-called 'Canaanite' influences and re-establishing 'orthodox', Yahwistic beliefs and practices.[5] For example, Hezekiah's eighth-century cult reforms involved the destruction of the high places, pillars, sacred poles and the bronze serpent Nehushtan (2 Kings 18:4), moves designed to bring Israel's worship

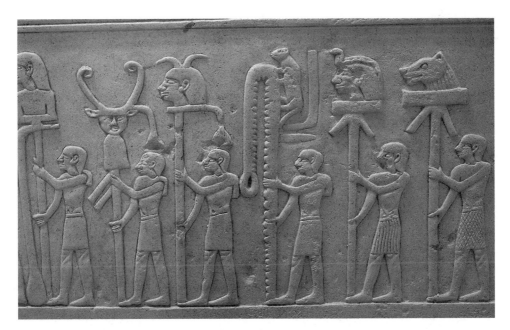

**Plate Ex.2  Egyptian stele showing six individuals carrying various standards. Note the two animals (eleventh dynasty, c.2000 BC)**

**Have you considered?**
## WHY DID MANASSEH DO WHAT HE DID?

Manasseh, son of Hezekiah, is viewed in the biblical text as Judah's worst king with his reign singled out as responsible for the exile of the nation (2 Kings 21). Manasseh not only abandoned but reversed the reforms that his father had implemented – he rebuilt the high places, erected altars for Baal and set up a sacred asherah pole (v. 3). So why did he adopt this course of action? A key reason would have been the perceived consequences of Hezekiah's policies. Rather than securing divine blessing and favour, Hezekiah's actions had led the country to the brink of disaster: most of the territory of Judah had been given over to the Philistines by the invading Assyrian army and only Jerusalem and perhaps also part of the Judean desert was left for Hezekiah and his son to rule (Ahlström, 1982: 68). The reforms of Hezekiah would have been an unmitigated disaster in Manasseh's eyes. Something needed to change!

Manasseh, therefore, sought to return the nation to the religious situation that had existed prior to Hezekiah's 'innovations'. In particular, he reinstated practices that had long been observed (e.g. worship at the various high places throughout the nation) with the hope that these would win back the support and blessing of the gods. From a purely political perspective, Manasseh seems to have got it right. The biblical and archaeological records suggest that Manasseh was able to recover some, if not all, of the territory that his father had lost. From the perspective of the biblical authors, however, Manasseh couldn't have got it more wrong, for his actions ultimately stirred God to act in judgement against the nation.

practices into line with the exclusive veneration of Yahweh and the rejection of divine images. Likewise, in the late seventh century Josiah is recorded as engaging in a similar, albeit more wide-scale, reform, targeting Assyrian-influenced practices (e.g. the horses and chariots of the sun) among other things (2 Kings 23). Such texts indicate the significant role the king could play in the religious life of the nation should he decide to get involved.

2 Kings could function as leaders of cultic activity – while we may be inclined to think of the priests as providing leadership for Israel's religious ceremonies, it is clear that the king himself would occasionally officiate during major cultic events. In particular, the king's role could include the offering of sacrifices, prayer and blessing the people.

Israel's early kings are repeatedly depicted as presenting offerings and making sacrifices. David offers sacrifices while the ark is being brought to Jerusalem (2 Sam. 6:13), when it finally arrives (2 Sam. 6:17–18), and following the construction of an altar on the threshing floor of Araunah, the site of the future Jerusalem temple (2 Sam. 24:25). Solomon engages in sacrificial activity at Gibeon (1 Kings 3:4) and is involved with the numerous sacrifices that accompany the dedication of the temple (1 Kings 8:5, 62–64). Jeroboam I performs sacrifices and offers incense on the altar he had constructed in Bethel (1 Kings 12:32; and 13:1). While some of these texts are ambiguous and could possibly be

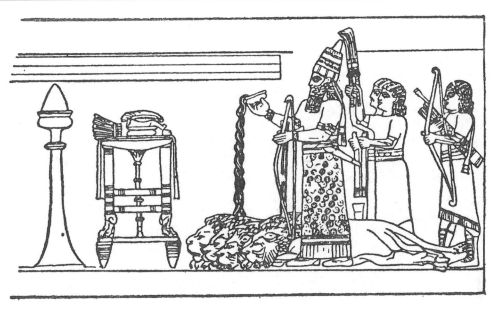

**Figure Ex.1   The Assyrian king Ashurbanipal pouring a libation over four dead lions before an offering table and incense stand**

interpreted to mean only that the king brought the animal(s) for the priests to sacrifice, in others it is quite clear that the kings themselves actually carried out the sacrificial ceremonies at the altar (e.g. 2 Sam. 24:25; 1 Kings 12:32; and 13:1) (Grabbe, 1995: 40).

While these examples suggest that Israel's kings could directly engage in acts of sacrifice if they chose to do so, this was probably not a frequent or common occurrence. Unlike the priests, kings would not have been involved in sacrificial rites on a day-to-day basis; they had other things

**Going deeper:**
**AHAZ'S ALTAR AND SACRIFICE**

A good example of the king's involvement in sacrifice is found in 2 Kings 16. This chapter describes the reign of the Judahite king Ahaz (c.735–715 BC) who called on the Assyrians for help against an attack by a coalition of forces, including the northern kingdom of Israel. Following the intervention of the Assyrian military, Ahaz travelled to Damascus to meet the Assyrian king, Tiglath Pileser III. He was so impressed by the altar of Damascus that he ordered a copy be constructed in the Jerusalem temple. When he

returned to Jerusalem, Ahaz offered various sacrifices and offerings on the altar (v. 13), probably to dedicate it. He then told the priest Uriah to offer the regular, daily sacrifices at the new altar – in other words, to continue the routine, ongoing sacrificial activity. This passage reinforces the picture that we find elsewhere in the OT. While kings *could* be involved in sacrifice, this was usually restricted to special occasions with priests being responsible for the standard daily operations of the cult.

with which to concern themselves. As Miller concludes, 'It cannot be inferred from these texts, however, that administering the sacrificial system was regularly a part of the royal responsibilities. In most of the cases . . . the sacrifice went on in the context of the building of a new altar or a new sanctuary and thus was a one-time service of dedication and consecration' (2000: 194). Nevertheless, it would be incorrect to suggest that the king's involvement in sacrifice was restricted to such 'once-off', initiatory events. For example, 1 Kings 9:25 describes how Solomon offered sacrifices at the three great feasts of the year, suggesting that Israel's king may have officiated at the significant national festivals and great public sacrifices (Wyatt, 2010: 66).[6] The king's involvement on such occasions would make sense given that the national interest was at stake.

Israel's kings could also be responsible for blessing the people. This activity is particularly associated with David and Solomon. For example, David 'blessed the people in the name of the LORD of hosts' following the arrival of the ark in Jerusalem (2 Sam. 6:17–18), and Solomon blessed the people as part of the dedication of the temple (1 Kings 8:14). While these activities – sacrifice, prayer and blessing – were usually the special domain of the priests (for more details see 2.3 'What did a priest do?'), 'neither the prophets nor the historical books before the exile make any protests against these intrusions by the king into liturgical worship' (de Vaux, 1965: 114). In other words, the king's participation in these rites seems to have been viewed as completely legitimate, perhaps even necessary. This was probably a result of the king's unique position before and in relation to Yahweh. As Yahweh's

adopted son (cf. Ps. 2:7), the monarch was the deity's delegated representative on earth, ruling over and responsible for Yahweh's people; and as such was authorized to perform various religious rites, especially those which pertained to the wellbeing of the nation as a whole (Rooke, 1998: 193).

Although the king's involvement in the religious life of the nation does not receive significant, explicit treatment in the OT, it is clear that the monarch could play a very important role if he chose to do so. Israel's kings were responsible for establishing, maintaining and, if needs be, reforming the national cult, especially the central sanctuary. Furthermore, as a result of their unique position between Yahweh and the people, the kings could engage in various ritual activities such as sacrifice, prayer and blessing, particularly when the wellbeing of the nation as a whole was believed to be at stake. Thus, the Israelite king was not a peripheral figure to the religious life of the nation; he instead stood at its heart.

## NOTES

1 Melchizedek is the enigmatic pre-Israelite, priest-king of Jerusalem who encounters Abraham in Genesis 14. He is recognized as both 'king of Salem' and priest of God Most High who blesses Abraham.
2 According to the Chronicler, David had a key role to play in the organization of the cult within the Jerusalem temple (cf. 1 Chron. 22—26 where he organizes the Levites, priests, musicians, gatekeepers, treasurers and judges).
3 The ability of the king to nominate and dismiss priests may have diminished over time as this office became a more fixed and established institution.

4 It should be recognized that the historicity of these reforms, even that of Josiah, is not accepted by all scholars. For a discussion of these issues from a critical perspective, see Davies (2007), Albertz (2007) and Uehlinger (2007).

5 While descriptors such as 'Canaanite' and 'orthodox' are commonly employed in the secondary literature, it should be recognized that their use is problematic. For example, it is highly likely that many Israelites would have viewed the high places that Hezekiah destroyed as a legitimate and acceptable element within their faith. The reason I have continued to use such terminology, however, is that the biblical text itself views these things in this light.

6 The king's involvement in regular sacrifices may also be suggested by Ps. 20:3. When read in context (cf. vv. 6 and 9), this seems to be a description of the king's cultic activities.

## FOR FURTHER READING

G. Ahlström (1982), *Royal Administration and National Religion in Ancient Palestine*, SHANE 1, Leiden: E.J. Brill.

J. Day (1998a), 'The Canaanite Inheritance of the Israelite Monarchy', in Day (1998b: 72–90).

J. Day (ed.) (1998b), *King and Messiah in Israel and the Ancient Near East: Proceedings of the Oxford Old Testament Seminar*, JSOTSS 270, Sheffield: Sheffield Academic Press.

D. Rooke (1998), 'Kingship as Priesthood: The Relationship between the High Priesthood and the Monarchy', in Day (1998b: 187–208).

N. Wyatt (2012), 'Royal Religion in Ancient Judah', in F. Stavrakopolou and J. Barton (eds), *Religious Diversity in Ancient Israel and Judah*, London: T&T Clark, pp. 61–81.

# Chapter 5

# THE COMMON PEOPLE IN ANCIENT ISRAEL

## 5.1  INTRODUCTION

So far in this book we have focused on those individuals who held key leadership roles within Israelite religion.[1] We need to be aware, however, that such people only ever comprised a very small percentage of ancient Israel's total population. The census data provided in the book of Numbers suggests that descendants of Levi accounted for only 3 per cent of Israel's adult male population.[2] Even if we add to this 1,500 or so prophets at work at any given time[3] and a similar number of sages, it is clear that the VAST majority of Israel's population (at least 98 per cent) did not hold a recognized position of leadership in Israel's religion. So what did these people believe? Who did they worship? When and where did their religious practices take place? How were these people involved in the religious life of ancient Israel? This chapter will answer these questions.

Before we get underway, however, we need to clarify an important misconception: the religion of the common people of ancient Israel was not identical to the form of religion that we find enshrined in the OT and, in particular, its legal sections. It is generally recognized that the OT was produced by, and thus reflects the perspective of, urban-dwelling, male elites. Yet such people, who account for no more than 5 per cent of Israel's population, are hardly representative of the broader reality of popular belief and practice.[4] Furthermore, the OT itself, and in particular the prophetic books, clearly highlights the fact that the religion which much of the population practised did not line up with what was laid out in the law.

Overall, the value of the Bible for reconstructing the religious beliefs and practices of the common people is somewhat limited. In addition to the fact that it reflects the perspective of only a small percentage of the population, the OT is essentially a 'national' document, focusing on the theology and cult that was present at the top of Israel's socio-political pyramid. The everyday religious practices of the common people, on the other hand, receive little explicit treatment. So, for example, the OT provides us with copious details regarding the construction, dimensions and practices of the key sites of the nation's worship life – the Tabernacle and Jerusalem temple – but offers almost no insight into the nature of domestic sacred space and no specific guidelines for religious practices that may have been carried out within this.

Yet the OT is not completely without use. A number of its narratives (esp. those found in Gen. 12—50 and Josh.—2 Sam.) provide occasional allusions and incidental references to religion as it was experienced and practised at the level of the family. Furthermore, OT laws and prophetic texts may also shed indirect light on common beliefs and practices (the fact that such a belief or practice had to be condemned implies that it was present in the first place!). And the good news is that we have another major source of evidence – archaeology – which is in a unique position to contribute to our discussion. As Dever has argued, archaeological discoveries

> can 'flesh out' a history of ancient Israel, precisely because of archaeology's unique ability . . . to supplement the elitist approach of the 'great tradition' of the classic literature. Archaeology at its best provides a graphic illustration of the everyday masses, the vast majority of ordinary folk, their brief lives forgotten by the biblical writers in their obsession with eternity, their voices long muted until modern archaeology allows them to speak again to us. (2001: 173)

Archaeologists have unearthed literally thousands of items over the past century that appear to have been associated with domestic religious practices, including cult stands, figurines and amulets. These provide an unparalleled glimpse into ancient Israelite religion as it was actually experienced on the ground by the common people.

**Going deeper:**
**THE FOUR TIERS OF ISRAELITE SOCIETY**

A good example of the structure of Israelite society is found in the story of Achan's sin and punishment (Josh. 7:14–18). A key condition for the capture of Jericho was that the Israelites were to devote all of the precious metals (silver, gold, the vessels of bronze and iron) to the treasury of the Lord (Josh. 6:19). Following the nation's subsequent defeat at Ai, however, Joshua is informed by the Lord that this has not taken place. A process of identification is established in order to determine who has stolen the items that were supposed to be devoted to the Lord. This begins with the people coming forward tribe by tribe, clan by clan, household by household followed by the individual members within this until only Achan is left.

In order to discuss the religious beliefs and practices of the common people, we need to develop some understanding of the way in which Israelite society was structured. Biblical scholars have long recognized that ancient Israel essentially consisted of four socio-political levels, which can be arranged in decreasing order of size: the nation, the tribe, the clan (sometimes referred to as the village) and the household. This chapter will focus on the last two as they form the immediate context for understanding popular religious beliefs and practices.

The household (*bêt 'āb*, literally 'house of the father') was the foundational component of Israelite society. Although the smallest in size, this primary social unit exerted the greatest influence over the lives of its members. People may have been aware of the larger social structures of which they were a part but

## Going deeper:
## WHO WERE THE 'RESIDENT ALIENS'?

Resident aliens or sojourners (*gērîm*) were foreigners who lived within Israel on a more or less permanent basis. They were usually poor but enjoyed the same level of protection as an Israelite under the law. Like Israelites, they were expected to observe the Sabbath, fast on the day of Atonement and obey the regulations regarding clean and unclean (with the possible exception of eating food that had not been properly slaughtered, Deut. 14:21; but cf. Lev. 17:15). They could offer sacrifices, and take part in religious festivals, including the Passover (Exod. 12:48–49; cf. Num. 9:14). Resident aliens are to be distinguished from foreigners whose participation in Israelite religious activities was more restricted. Foreigners were prohibited from eating the Passover meal (Exod. 12:43) and their admittance in 'the assembly of the LORD' was curtailed (Deut. 23:3–7; cf. Ezek. 44:5–9).

their daily lives took place within and were directly shaped by their household (Meyers, 2010: 119). 'It was the focus of the religious, social, and economic spheres of Israelite life and was at the center of Israel's history, faith and traditions' (King and Stager, 2001: 39).

So what did an Israelite household (*bêt 'āb*) look like? Usually it involved a multi-generational, extended family led by a *paterfamilias* (male head) living at a single site. In addition to parents and their unmarried children, members of a *bêt 'āb*

**Figure 5.1    Artist's reconstruction showing a large residence in a provincial town with people performing various everyday activities**

may have included grandparents, married adult male children and their wives (and children), and widowed and divorced adult children. The household could also incorporate members who were not connected directly via either blood or marriage, such as debt servants, slaves, concubines, resident aliens, day labourers, orphans and Levites. In terms of size, Gerstenberger (2002: 20) has suggested that households in the rural areas may have consisted of up to 30 or 50 people, however, Dever's (2005: 18) more conservative figure of from 15 to 20 is probably closer to the mark.

This extended family (or perhaps better, families) usually lived together, either in a single, large house or in two or three smaller houses which were structurally connected or closely adjacent, and which may have shared a common courtyard and some facilities.[5] If located within a larger village, such 'multi-building compounds' were separated from each other by streets, paths or stone enclosure walls (Ackerman,

---

**Going deeper:**
**THE INHERITANCE OF THE *BÊT 'ĀB***

A good example of the inalienable nature of the family's land inheritance is provided by the story of Naboth's vineyard (1 Kings 21). Here King Ahab attempts to purchase Naboth's ancestral land so that he can turn it into a vegetable garden. Naboth, however, emphatically refuses the king's request, a decision that Ahab initially respects (even if he does not like it). The seriousness with which ancient Israelites approached the requirement to maintain their family's inheritance (*naḥălâ*) is clearly shown by the fact that Naboth is willing to defy the desires of the reigning monarch – a decision that would ultimately cost him his life.

---

2008: 128). Central to the identity of each *bêt 'āb* was the possession of its own land inheritance (*naḥălâ*), which the members were expected to maintain for the next generation. This land was inalienable (i.e. it could not be sold or transferred to another party) as it was believed to be the deity's gift to the family, and was usually the place of the family's tomb.

Each household was nested within a larger clan (*mišpāḥâ*). A clan consisted of a group of related households, often joined by perceived kinship and/or marriage. Clans were important because they provided members with a greater level of military protection and agricultural production than an individual household could achieve on its own. They were also the locus for a number of religious celebrations, including the annual clan sacrifice (for more details, see below).

A clan appears to be equated with the inhabitants of a village in much of the OT. In fact, Meyers defines a clan as 'related farm families sharing common settled space and earning their livelihoods in the fields, orchards, and vineyards surrounding the village site' (1997: 13). The approximate population of a clan/village is hard to estimate, but the average probably ranged from 50 to 100 in the early monarchic period increasing up to 300 during the period of the divided monarchy.

The social structures of households and clans provide the essential context within which we are to understand the religious beliefs and practices of the common people. These guided and regulated virtually every aspect of an Israelite's existence – economic, social and religious – determining who, how, where and when they worshipped.

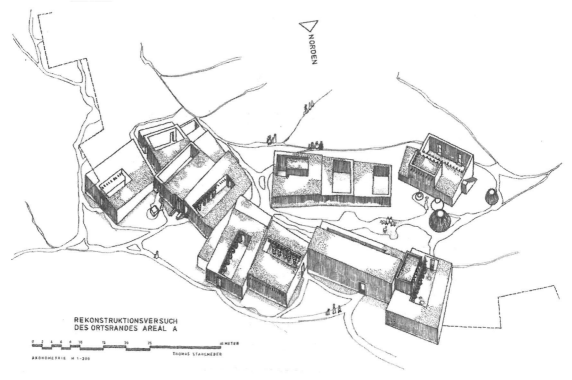

**Figure 5.2   Artist's reconstruction showing several multi-house compounds within a typical Israelite village**

## 5.2   WHOM DID THE COMMON PEOPLE WORSHIP?

At first glance, the answer to this question would seem to be straightforward: as Israelites, the common people worshipped Yahweh. The reality on the ground, however, appears to have been much more complex.

### 5.2.1   THE GOD OF THE FAMILY

The key god that the majority of Israelites venerated was determined by the household of which they were a part. It is generally accepted in the modern, Western world that religion is a matter of individual choice and personal commitment. This is reflective of the individualistic nature of our society which prizes personal autonomy and freedom of expression. Such individualistic autonomy, however, simply was not present in ancient Israel where everyone was dependent on others, especially other family members, for their survival. Just as individualism would have been a foreign concept to the ancient Israelites, so too was the notion of individual belief systems (Meyers, 1997: 39).[6] Rather, a person's 'choice' of and relationship to a particular deity was a result of their membership within a certain family (*bêt 'āb*). 'The Israelite family was a community which shared life, dwelling place and belief to an extent and with an intensity that we in our atomized little remnant families can no longer imagine' (Gerstenberger, 2002: 25).

## Scholar focus:
## ALBRECHT ALT (1883–1956)

Alt was a leading twentieth-century German OT scholar whose extensive knowledge of the geography, history and religions of the ANE world resulted in the production of a number of highly influential works on the history of Israelite religion. Unlike Wellhausen, who had argued that the ancestral narratives contained in Genesis 12—50 and the religion they described held little historical value, Alt believed that the biblical text could be used to reconstruct 'patriarchal religion'. He suggested that Israel's ancestors practised a nomadic type of religion that centred on the worship of the 'god of the fathers'. This type of god had three main characteristics: (1) they lacked any local geographical association – unlike the many Canaanite gods, the gods of the fathers were not originally related to specific localities (i.e. they were not 'local numina'); (2) they were closely tied to a particular group or family; and (3) they were primarily concerned with the fortunes of their group of worshippers (Albertz, 1994: 27). While Alt's hypotheses have been developed and critiqued (e.g., his suggestion that the 'god of the fathers' indicates a nomadic type of religion has been shown to be incorrect as it is also found in some sedentary cultures), much of his basic outline still remains influential.

The corporate, familial nature of Israelite life and religion meant that the personal god of the *paterfamilias* (or a prominent ancestor) was also the god of the collective entity, the family or clan, of which he was the head. Thus, we find numerous references, especially in Genesis, to people invoking 'the God of my/your father' or the God of a prominent ancestor such as Abraham or Isaac. Women who married into the family or servants who joined the family were also expected to worship the personal god of the *paterfamilias*. For example, Eliezer, Abraham's servant, addresses the Lord as 'the God of my master Abraham' (Gen. 24:27) while Ruth adopts the God of her mother-in-law when she decides to return with her to Judah (Ruth 1:16).

The family god was believed to be heavily involved in the daily life and workings of the household. 'The family god was a personal and social god who provided protection and guidance for the family as well as the blessings of fertility and the continuity of life' (Miller, 2000: 63). This concern for the wellbeing of the family and its individual members is perhaps shown most clearly in the personal names that were given to Israelite children.

Israelite names (like personal names throughout the ANE) commonly consisted of two elements: the name of a deity linked with a verb or predicate describing the deity's nature or activity. For example, the name Ezekiel consists of the divine name El and a form of the verb meaning 'to strengthen' (El strengthens) while Isaiah contains an abbreviated form of the divine name Yahweh (Yah spelt in English as Iah) and a form of the word meaning 'salvation' (Yahweh is salvation). These names functioned as mini confessions of faith and thus provide a good insight into the personal beliefs of ancient Israelites.

Rainer Albertz (1994: 95–9; 2010: 137–9) has conducted a comprehensive study of 675 Hebrew names found outside the OT (i.e. those found on inscriptions, ancient seals etc.) and the approximately 1,000 names found within the OT. He suggests that with the possible exception of Ikabod (1 Sam. 4:21), not a single Hebrew name from the pre-exilic period commemorates any occasion in the salvation history of Israel, including those 'mighty acts of God' which are central to the OT narrative, for example, exodus, Sinai, conquest/settlement etc. He concludes, therefore, that these traditions were of minor importance in the day-to-day religious life of the people. Instead, personal names focused on the religious experience of the name giver and, in particular, events associated with the life and fortunes of the family. For example, 'birthing names' (i.e. names connected with the process of childbearing, from conception through to birth) account for almost 30 per cent of all names, suggesting that this event was of central importance to family piety. There is also a large group of thanksgiving and confession names which appear to reflect concrete experiences of divine rescue, help, blessing and prosperity. It appears, therefore, that the family god was seen as the one who was responsible for helping and protecting the family in times of trouble, and the source of blessing and prosperity in the good times.

### 5.2.2   EL AND BAAL

So who actually were the family gods of ancient Israel? Can we be any more specific regarding their identity? It is clear that in addition to the generic title 'god of my father' the deity possessed a specific personal name. As Miller has argued, 'The family god, however, was not a nameless deity; nor was it willy-nilly any of the gods of Syria-Palestine' (2000: 63). The evidence provided by Hebrew personal names suggests that in the early period (i.e. the period before the establishment of the monarchy) the most common family god was El (who is identified with Yahweh in

> **ANE parallels:**
> **THE GOD OF THE FAMILY**
>
> Walton (2006: 1423) argues than in the ANE the god of the family was often not the same as the god of the state/nation. The national god was connected to the major temple in the city, and the majority of the common people would have had little access to this temple and its god. Furthermore, the national god was primarily concerned with the fortune of the state and thus was unlikely to be interested in the affairs of the common people or respond to their requests. Consequently, while it was possible that the national god could be the family god, in practice the common people often turned to more minor gods within the pantheon. These gods were more likely to take an interest in them and could be petitioned to influence the national god when needed. This broader ANE pattern is significantly different from the situation in Israel where the God of the nation (Yahweh) was also regularly worshipped as the god of the family.

the OT but who was also venerated within the Canaanite pantheon as head of the gods, see below). From the period of the monarchy onwards, the family god appears to have been Yahweh in the vast majority of instances;[7] however, there is also some evidence that suggests that Baal was venerated, especially during the ninth and eighth centuries, and particularly in the north.[8]

The texts from Ugarit (c. fourteenth–thirteenth centuries) provide us with the greatest insight into the nature and characteristics of both El and Baal. These documents portray El as the transcendent and high god of the Canaanite pantheon, an aged patriarchal figure, head of the

Figure 5.3 Drawing of a bronze and gold statuette from Ugarit of a seated god, probably El. 'The face is delicately carved to portray an old and worn expression' (Pritchard, *ANEP*, p. 378)

Figure 5.4 Stele from Ugarit depicting an individual (perhaps a king or chief priest) presenting an offering to an enthroned god, probably El (1400–1300 BC)

Plate 5.1 Limestone stele from Ugarit depicting Baal with thunderbolt (1900–1500 BC). Note the small human figure located beside the god's leg which may represent a deity or person under the protection of the god

divine assembly, and creator of the gods and human beings. At the same time, however, El could also be venerated as a much more intimate, personal god. 'He frequently played the role of "god of the father/ancestor," the social deity bound to tribe or king with kinship or covenant ties, guiding or leading them' (Miller, 2000: 24). For example, in a number of narrative texts (*Keret* and *Aqhat*) we see El answering,

## Going deeper:
## THE RELATIONSHIP BETWEEN EL AND YAHWEH

The OT points to a close association between Yahweh and El, with the majority of texts clearly equating the two. For example, Yahweh is often referred to as El in the Psalms and Deutero-Isaiah while in Exodus 6:2–3 Yahweh declares to Moses that he had previously revealed himself to the patriarchs as El Shaddai. The historical development of the relationship between El and Yahweh, however, remains a matter of dispute in the scholarly literature. Two main options have been proposed.

The first is that Yahweh was identified with El from the beginning. In other words, Yahweh and El are the same deity, who was simply known by two different names. The most forceful advocate of this perspective is F.M. Cross. Cross has argued that Yahweh was originally part of a cultic title for El as he was worshipped in southern Canaan (‘*El ḏū yahwêh tsᵉbā'ōth*, ‘El who creates hosts’).

The second possibility is that Yahweh and El were originally separate deities who only became equated at a later stage. Scholars who support this perspective (such as J. Day and M. Smith) point to the fact that Yahweh has traits that were not traditionally associated with El (e.g. Yahweh has a fierce as well as a kind side, whereas in the Ugaritic texts El is revealed as a wholly benevolent deity), and that in early Hebrew poetry the home of Yahweh is located in the south, whereas El's is usually located to the north of Israel.

Whether the two started out as separate gods or not, their equation in the biblical text is clear, early and widespread. ‘El's names, iconography, and characteristics were always freely associated with Yahweh and without condemnation, a fact that seems not to have been true with regard to any other northwest Semitic god’ (Miller, 2000: 2–3). Major points of similarity include their portrayal as aged, patriarchal, wise figures, their role as creator of the cosmos and humanity, their position as head of a heavenly court, the sons of God, and their basic disposition towards humanity as compassionate (the description of Yahweh as a ‘God merciful and gracious, slow to anger, and abounding in steadfast love and faithfulness’ (Exod. 34:6) resembles El's epithet as ‘the benevolent, good natured’ one).

For further details see Smith, 2002: 32–42; and Day, 2000: 13–41.

helping, healing and blessing human beings with descendants. In fact, one of his most common epithets is 'the benevolent, good-natured El'.

Baal was clearly the most active and prominent of all the Canaanite deities even though he was not the head of the pantheon. He is mentioned more than five hundred times in the texts from Ugarit, and is the central character in a key mythological cycle (see below). Essentially, Baal was a great storm god who possessed power over the weather and was responsible for bringing the seasonal rains. By extension, he was considered to be in control of the fertility of the fields as this was dependent on the rain he supplied (cf. Hos. 2:8 where the Israelites attribute the production of grain, wine and oil to Baal and not Yahweh).

The reason for the popularity of Baal worship among the Israelite people is not hard to discern.

**ANE parallels:**
**THE UGARITIC BAAL CYCLE**

Our best source of evidence outside the biblical text for determining the profile of Baal is the mythological Baal cycle from Ugarit. This cycle is essentially broken into three 'chapters': the first describes the battle between Baal and Yam (god of the sea) for kingship, the second focuses on the building of a palace for Baal, and the third the conflict between Baal and Mot (god of death).

The last is particularly important for the study of the OT. Here Baal becomes afraid of Mot, travels to the underworld and is thought to be dead. His consort, Anat, however, wild with grief, confronts and defeats Mot. This allows Baal to return from Mot's realm, bringing with him the fertility of the land.

Scholars have long recognized that the conflict between Baal and Mot is a mythological expression of the cycle of the seasons as they are experienced in the Levant and impact on agricultural production

(van der Toorn, 2006: 368). Baal's disappearance in the underworld equates to the period of intense summer heat, a time of death, when the soil is parched and all fertility seems gone. As the god returns in autumn, however, so too do the rains, which, in turn, give life to the crops and vegetation.

First Kings 17—19, particularly the contest at Mount Carmel between Elijah and the 450 prophets of Baal (1 Kings 18), should be understood against this mythological backdrop. In fact, Elijah's mocking suggestion that Baal is 'on a journey, or perhaps he is asleep' (1 Kings 18:27) may be an allusion to Baal's descent to the underworld, with sleep commonly used as a metaphor for death (van der Toorn, 2006: 368). These chapters stress Yahweh's – and not Baal's – power over nature, including the storm (1 Kings 17:1–17; 18:41–46), and thus confirm that it is Yahweh alone who has the ability to produce rain, and hence to grant fertility to the fields.

The fact that the Israelites were settled among the Canaanites, for whom the worship of Baal was so important, and that Palestine is utterly dependent for its fertility upon the rain, which was held to be Baal's special realm of influence, accounts for the tempting nature of his cult as well as the strength of the OT polemic against it. (Day, 1992: 547)

A god who offered success and prosperity in the agricultural realm was always going to be attractive given the subsistence and agrarian nature of ancient Israelite society.

### 5.2.3 ASHERAH AND THE QUEEN OF HEAVEN
The biblical text and the findings of archaeology suggest a number of other

deities, including two female gods, Asherah and the Queen of Heaven, enjoyed relatively widespread devotion in ancient Israel.

The Hebrew term *'ăšērâ* appears approximately forty times in the OT with two different (albeit related) nuances. In the majority of instances, this word refers to a cult object (an asherah), perhaps a stylized wooden tree or pole (eg. Judg. 6:25–26 mentions 'cutting down' the *'ăšērâ* as well as using its wood for a burnt offering; for more details, see 2.4 Where were priests located?). In other passages, however, it is likely that a goddess (Asherah) is being spoken about. For example, Judges 3:7 declares 'The Israelites did what was evil in

## Archaeological insight:
## a/ASHERAH INSCRIPTIONS FROM ANCIENT ISRAEL

A number of important references to Asherah have been discovered in inscriptions from ancient Israel. The best known of these come from Kuntillet Ajrud, probably an ancient caravanserai (similar to a modern-day motel) located about 50 kilometres south of Kadesh Barnea, and dated to the late ninth or early eighth centuries.* Inscribed on two large storage vessels ('pithoi') were the following blessings: 'I bless you by Yahweh of Samaria and his a/Asherah' and 'I bless you by Yahweh of Teman and his a/Asherah'. Much scholarly debate has focused on the nature and function of 'a/Asherah' in these two passages. Two suggestions are particularly popular: that Asherah is a reference to a female deity, possibly Yahweh's consort, or that asherah is a reference to a (wooden) cult object or an image of the goddess. The second option is more likely from a purely grammatical perspective as there are no examples of a possessive suffix ('his') ever being attached to a proper noun in ancient Hebrew. Such an interpretation, however, does not exclude the possibility that the goddess Asherah was worshipped in Israel. As Dever has argued, 'whether a/Asherah at 'Ajrud means the goddess herself or merely her symbol as an "agent of blessing" that could be invoked alongside Yahweh, it was the widespread perception of the goddess's reality in ancient Israel that gave the symbolism its efficacy' (2001: 185–6).**

* Another inscription invoking Yahweh and his a/Asherah for protection and blessing is found in a burial cave from Khirbet el-Qôm.
** As Wyatt suggests 'Her reality is not in question, and the distinction between deity and cult object is ultimately not an ancient, but a modern one' (1999: 103).

**Plate 5.2   An ivory panel depicting an Ugaritic goddess, possibly Asherah, nursing two children (1400–1350 BC)**

the sight of the LORD, forgetting the LORD their God, and worshipping the Baals and the Asherahs',[9] and in 2 Kings 23:4 Josiah orders the high priest Hilkiah to remove from the Jerusalem temple 'all the vessels made for Baal, for Asherah, and for all the host of heaven' (cf. 1 Kings 18: 19). Evidence for the worship of Asherah is also found in inscriptional remains from ancient Israel (see 'Archaeological insight: a/Asherah inscriptions').

**Plate 5.3  Judean female terracotta figurine from the eighth century, possibly Asherah (for further discussion of female figurines see p. 125)**

So what do we know about this goddess? From the texts from Ugarit we learn that Asherah (here referred to as Athirat) was a significant goddess in the Canaanite pantheon, the consort of El and the mother of the gods (in fact, the gods can be referred to as 'the seventy sons of Athirat'). This position as El's consort may help to explain why some Israelites chose to worship her. As I have suggested above, Yahweh was identified with El, a god with whom he shared many traits in common.

Indeed, El traditions were so heavily appropriated that at least some ancient Israelites seem to have assumed they should appropriate for Yahweh the traditions concerning El's consort Asherah. For these ancient Israelites, then, Asherah is worshipped as Yahweh's consort; for as Yahweh supplants El as an object of worship, Yahweh lays claim to El's wife. (Ackerman, 2006: 299)

Furthermore, as El/Yahweh's consort, Asherah was in a privileged position to bring petitions and requests to her husband to grant. This is seen in the Baal cycle where Baal and his consort approach Asherah in anticipation that she might intercede with El to grant Baal a palace. In a similar fashion, Israelites may have appealed to Asherah in the hope that she herself would be able to respond to their prayers or, if not, present these to El/Yahweh to be answered.

Various other gods and goddesses could be called on by the people in order to bring about help in times of need and blessing and provision when the worship of Yahweh seemed inadequate for such purposes (Miller, 2000: 59). The most significant example found in the OT is the Queen of Heaven who is mentioned in two passages from the book of Jeremiah (7:16–20; and 44:15–30). The second passage, in particular, emphasizes the traditional and widespread nature of her worship. Here, Jeremiah rebukes the Judean refugees who have fled to Egypt for their persistent idolatry. The people, however, respond by declaring, 'we will do everything that we have vowed, make offerings to the queen of heaven and pour out libations to her, *just as we and our ancestors, our kings and our officials, used to do in the towns of Judah and in the streets of Jerusalem*' (44:17). In other words, veneration of this goddess was a long-standing and far-reaching practice.

Jeremiah 44 gives the impression that the worship of the Queen of Heaven was

## ANE parallels:
## CAKES (*KAWWĀNÎM*) FOR THE QUEEN OF HEAVEN

The worship of the Queen of Heaven involved a number of standard cultic activities including the pouring out of libations, the making of offerings and the performance of vows. Yet both texts from Jeremiah also suggest a rather distinctive activity – the baking of cakes (*kawwānîm*) marked with her image (7:18; 44:19). King and Stager (2001: 52) have suggested that this is a reference to cakes that were used in the cult of the goddess Ishtar as it was practised in Syria and Mesopotamia. These cakes were shaped in the image of the nude goddess, with particular emphasis on her sexual features. They were probably made of flour and sweetened with honey or figs (King and Stager, 2001: 65).

particularly associated with women (v. 15), however, the involvement of men is also accepted (v. 19). In fact, Jeremiah 7:18 emphasizes the familial nature of this activity – '*the children* gather wood, *the fathers* kindle fire, and *the women* knead dough, to make cakes for the queen of heaven'. The popularity of this particular goddess seems to have been connected with the blessings she was believed to bestow on her worshippers. Jeremiah 44:17 links her worship with the provision of plenty of food, prosperity and fortune, things that seemed to be in short supply when her worship was halted. Albertz concludes, 'In the goddess they (i.e. the female members of the family) had a direct partner to address, to whom they turned in the minor distresses of everyday life, when it was important for everyone to have enough to eat, to secure prosperity and ward off ill-fortune from the family' (1994: 194).

Determining the exact identity of this goddess, however, is not easy. The title 'Queen of Heaven' indicates that we are dealing with a powerful, significant and leading goddess, yet a number of deities fit this bill. Scholars have thus proposed a number of options,

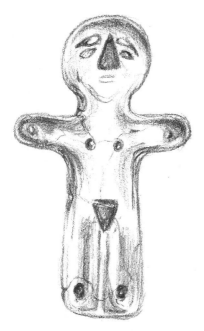

**Figure 5.5    A Cypriot terracotta cake mould, probably representing the Queen of Heaven (*c.* Iron II)**

**Figure 5.6    Seal from Shechem depicting an Assyrian king bringing a burnt offering to Ishtar. Note the portrayal of the goddess in a shining wreath or nimbus of stars**

including Astarte (or her Mesopotamian equivalent Ishtar), Asherah or Anat.[10] Yet, as Houtman points out:

> The question of her identity appears, however, not to be of considerable importance. In the syncretistic world of the first millennium BCE Near East, the title Queen of Heaven was evidently a designation for the universal mother goddess, who according to the time and the place of her worship could have a different character. The use of the goddess' title without mentioning her proper name may be considered as a symptom of a religious atmosphere in which the qualities of a deity are held to be of more importance than her name. (1999: 679)

### 5.2.4 THE HOST OF HEAVEN

The final god, or perhaps better group of gods, that appears to have been popular with the people was the 'host of heaven'. We have a number of narrative (2 Kings 17:16; 21:3; 23:4–5), prophetic (Jer. 19:13; Zeph. 1:5) and legal (Deut. 4:19; 17:3–4) texts which suggest that their worship was widespread, especially from the seventh

**Archaeological insight:**
**HORSE AND RIDER FIGURINES**

These figurines were common in Israel and Judah during the eighth–seventh centuries, with one cave from Jerusalem alone containing twenty-one examples. A number of specimens include an item, possibly a sun disk, between the ears on the horse's head, perhaps suggesting a connection with the 'horses' and 'chariots of the sun[god]' mentioned in 2 Kings 23:11–12. Keel and Uehlinger (1998: 343–7), however, propose a different interpretation. They suggest that the statuettes 'could possibly be understood as popular, anthropomorphic representations of the "Host of Heaven"', members of Yahweh's heavenly army and intermediaries between the sphere of the Most High God and the realm of humanity. Because of the statuettes' location in similar archaeological contexts (i.e. houses, graves and cultic sites) to the female figurines (see below), Keel and Uehlinger conclude that they 'belong in the context of family piety where they, like the pillar figurines, would have transmitted divine protection or blessing'.

**Figure 5.7  Terracotta figurine of horse and rider from Lachish (Iron II)**

**Figure 5.8  Close-up of head of horse figurine from Jerusalem with (solar?) disk between ears**

century onwards. For example, Jeremiah 8:1–2 suggests that, in a future day of judgement, 'the bones of the kings of Judah, the bones of its officials, the bones of the priests, the bones of the prophets, and the bones of the inhabitants of Jerusalem shall be brought out of their tombs; and they shall be spread before the sun and the moon and all the host of heaven, which they have loved and served, which they have followed, and which they have inquired of and worshipped'.

In the OT, the 'host of heaven' commonly refers to the group of heavenly beings, members of Yahweh's court, that surround Yahweh and carry out his will (cf. 1 Kings 22:1–28). In some texts (e.g. Josh. 5:14–15; 2 Kings 6:17) they clearly have a martial aspect and together constitute Yahweh's heavenly army. Over time, these beings became associated with the heavenly bodies, including the sun, moon and stars. While clearly of inferior rank to Yahweh, given their intermediary location between God and humanity it is not surprising that they were assigned a special status and became an object of worship for some.

**Plate 5.4  Two silver statuettes, possibly teraphim, found in a jar, from Ugarit (c.2000–1800 BC). The height of the larger figure is 28 cm. The height of the smaller is 16 cm**

Both the archaeological and biblical evidence suggests that a variety of gods alongside Yahweh were worshipped in ancient Israel and that the veneration of these was widespread and enduring. In fact, Jeremiah's accusation that the people have as many gods as they have towns (2:28; 11:13) doesn't seem to have been too far off the mark! The basic reason for the veneration of these gods, however, remained the same: they were believed to be concerned with the wellbeing of the household (*bêt 'āb*). Evidence for this is again provided by Hebrew personal names. Here we find the same divine predicates (i.e. actions) related to

different divine name elements (e.g. the verbal element *nātan* meaning 'has given (a child)' is applied to both Yahweh (Jonathan) and El (Elnathan)). Thus, Albertz (1994: 32) concludes that at the level of family piety the gods lose any specific characterization (in other words, whatever they are called they all do the same basic things, for example, provide offspring, protection, harvest etc.) and that more precise cultic, local and functional differentiations are really only found at higher political and social levels.

## Have you considered?
## WHO OR WHAT WERE THE TERAPHIM (TĔRAPÎM)?

Teraphim (often translated as 'household gods' or 'idols') are mentioned 15 times in the OT and are frequently associated with the religious practices of the people. For example, in Hosea 3:4 they are listed alongside other (legitimate) cultic activities and objects, including sacrifice, pillar (maṣṣēbâ) and ephod, while in 2 Kings 23:24 they are part of the illicit religious practices that Josiah sought to remove. Unfortunately, however, much about the teraphim – including their precise size and shape – remains elusive. In 1 Samuel 19 the teraphim appear to approximate human form and size as Michal was able to hide one in a bed as a substitute for David. Yet the examples in Genesis 31 must have been much smaller (no longer than approx. 30–5 cm) in order to fit under the saddlebag of Rachel's camel.

The identity of the teraphim is also uncertain. Traditionally, they have been viewed as household gods. This interpretation is suggested by three narratives in which teraphim are found in household or family contexts: Genesis 31:19–54 (where they are specifically referred to as ʾĕlōhîm, 'gods'); Judges 17—18 (where the teraphim is a key part of the cultic equipment of a household shrine); and 1 Samuel 19:11–17 (where it appears as a normal element within David's house, probably kept in the bedroom). It is clear, however, that the teraphim were not the same as the personal deity of the family, 'the god of the father'. Any identification of the two seems to be disproven by Genesis 31 where the loss of the teraphim does not jeopardize the possibility of Laban calling on the 'God of [his ancestor] Nahor' to conclude a treaty (v. 53)

(Albertz, 1994: 38). The references in Judges 17—18 suggest that more lowly 'deities' were represented by the teraphim – here the teraphim is distinguished from the pesel, a cultic image of the god proper (cf. Judg. 18:14). On the basis of their analysis of possible ANE parallels, van der Toorn and Lewis (2006: 783) have suggested that teraphim may have been representations of departed ancestors or images of deified ancestors. These images marked 'their [i.e. the ancestors] continuing "presence" in the family group' (Dever, 2005: 182) and thus 'served to secure the continuity of the family and the solidarity between one generation and the next' (Albertz, 1994: 37).

Can we say anything more specific about the teraphim's function? Along with household gods throughout the ANE, teraphim may have played an apotropaic (i.e. protective, evil-averting) role; however, this is not clearly attested in the OT literature. In contrast, the teraphim are explicitly connected with divinatory practices on a number of occasions. For example, in Zechariah 10:2 they are portrayed as oracular devices that 'utter nonsense' and are set in parallel with 'diviners' (cf. Ezek. 21:21). Although this text comes from the post-exilic period, it clearly points to realities which were present at an earlier stage in Israel's history (cf. 1 Sam. 15:23 where tĕrapîm, translated as 'idolatry', is linked with divination). The use of such images (perhaps as a means of consulting the dead ancestors) stood outside the boundaries of acceptable Yahwistic faith for the majority of the OT authors and, thus, was repeatedly condemned.

**Going deeper:**
## MONOTHEISM IN ANCIENT ISRAEL

As a result of the influence of traditional Christian and Jewish belief, people with little knowledge of the OT may assume that the ancient Israelites were monotheistic. A careful reading of the OT, however, suggests that this was not the case. As shown above, during the pre-exilic period many Israelites not only accepted the presence of but also worshipped a variety of gods alongside Yahweh. Such polytheism, however, was not universal. The authors of much of the OT themselves appear to embody a view of the divine realm that scholars refer to as monolotary or henotheism. Essentially, this perspective, while acknowledging the presence of other gods, suggests that Yahweh was both unique (incomparable) and supreme (greater than the other 'gods') and thus was to be exclusively worshipped by Israel. An interesting text in this regard is the first commandment: 'You shall have no other gods before me' (Exod. 20:3). This command does not deny the existence of 'other gods' per se, but it does relativize their position vis-à-vis Yahweh.

So how and when did the monotheism that Christians and Jews embrace emerge? This is a question that has provoked much debate in OT scholarship. While earlier developments (e.g. the establishment of the monarchy) may have begun the process, it is likely that the Babylonian exile was of crucial importance. It is from this period that we encounter texts that articulate a consistent and clearly defined monotheistic perspective (e.g. Isa. 45:6b–7).* In this context, monotheism would have provided an important source of comfort to the displaced and defeated Israelites, affirming that it was they who stood in relationship to the only deity, and were thus connected to a power that was greater than the mighty Babylonian empire and its so-called gods. For a nuanced discussion of the descriptors 'monotheism', 'monolotary' and 'henotheism', see Heiser, 2008.

* It should be acknowledged that this is based on the assumption that Isaiah 40—66 is to be dated to the Babylonian exile (or later), a view which is disputed by some evangelical scholars.

## 5.3 WHERE DID THE COMMON PEOPLE WORSHIP?

A cursory reading of the OT may leave us with the impression that the majority of Israelites regularly worshipped at the temple in Jerusalem.[11] It is conceivable that the average (male) Israelite visited the central sanctuary (whether at Jerusalem in the south or Bethel in the north) on some occasions.[12] For example, Deuteronomy identifies three key celebrations – Passover, Weeks and Booths (or Tents) – as pilgrimage festivals that all Israelites were expected to observe in Jerusalem.[13] It is likely, however, that this represents more of an ideal than reality and that an average Israelite's participation in such events was irregular at best.[14] Thus, the majority of the religious activity of the common people took place outside of this venue. So where did the common people worship instead? On the basis of the biblical text and the findings of archaeology, it is possible to identify three key loci/contexts where religious performance took place: within the household, within the village or town, and outside the village or town. It was in these more local and personal spaces that the Israelite people regularly carried out their cultic activities and worshipped their various deities.

### 5.3.1 WITHIN THE HOUSEHOLD

Because of the familial nature of Israelite religion it is almost certain that the household itself provided a primary context for religious practice. Given the relatively modest size of Israelite houses, however, it is unlikely that many contained a dedicated sacred space. In fact, Meyers (2010: 122) has argued that Israelite houses did not have areas that were solely used for one purpose at all. Instead, the use of household space shifted during the course of the day or from season to season depending on the tasks that needed to be performed. For example, a single room could be used as a workplace, a social place or a meal place at different times of the day. Analysing the archaeological remains of Israelite houses, therefore, is not likely to reveal a specific area for religious activities.

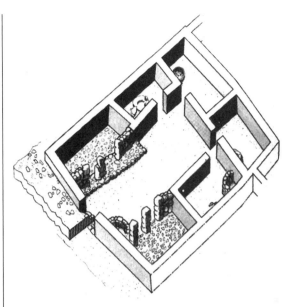

**Figure 5.9 Isometric drawing of a typical 'four-room house' at Tell el-Far'ah (north). A number of the rooms, including the broad room at the back, have been divided in two. The average size of a four-room house in rural areas was 110–30 m²**

#### Archaeological insight:
#### TELL HALIF AND THE USE OF DOMESTIC SPACE

An Iron II dwelling from Tell Halif provides an excellent insight into the multi-use nature of Israelite domestic space. Here artefacts of food preparation (cooking pots), food consumption (cups and bowls) and ritual/religious activity (incl. a fenestrated stand, two *maṣṣēbôt* and the head of a pillar figurine, see below) were all found in one room, suggesting that multiple activities took place within this single space (Hardin, 2004: 76–7). Hardin concludes that this 'living room' was well suited for 'group food consumption, sleeping, domestic ritual activity and the entertaining of guests and other social activities' (2004: 79). Furthermore, the presence of figurine fragments in other areas of the house suggests that cultic activity was not restricted to one room or locale.

Unfortunately, the biblical text does not shed much light on domestic sacred space either. Van der Toorn and Lewis (2006: 783) have suggested that the dark bedchamber (*ḥeder*) at the rear of the house may have been used as a sanctum of sorts. They argue that the relative isolation and privacy of this room would have made it an ideal place for performing religious activities. It should be recognized, however, that the identification of the bedchamber (*ḥeder*) with the rear ground-floor room of an Israelite house is far from certain; sleeping appears to have been a first-, rather than ground-, floor activity. (The rear ground-floor room was probably used for various daily activities and/or the storage of food, tools and even the occasional animal.) Alternatively, some Israelite houses may have had a cultic niche which contained the images of the household god/s, perhaps the teraphim, located near the door of the home (van der Toorn and Lewis, 2006: 783). This is suggested by the reference in Exodus 21:6 to a master bringing his slave before 'God' (NRSV) to make his vow. Such a suggestion, however, must remain in the realm of conjecture given the lack of further evidence both biblical and archaeological.

On the other hand, it is quite clear that the rooftops of houses were used as cult places from the seventh century BC onwards. We know from studies of the remains of houses at Beersheba that the roof could be used for a variety of storage and seasonal activities (such as weaving and drying), the collection of rainwater, and sleeping (Borowski, 2003: 18). Evidence for cultic practices, however, is also found in the biblical text. For example, both Jeremiah (19:13; and 32:29) and Zephaniah (1:5) announce judgement on those who worship and make offerings on rooftops. 'And the houses of Jerusalem and the houses of the kings of Judah shall be defiled like the

---

**ANE parallels:**
## ROOFTOPS AS A LOCATION FOR CULTIC PRACTICE

The Israelites were not the only ANE people to offer sacrifices on rooftops. Evidence for this practice among the Philistines was discovered by Stager who excavated the Babylonian destruction levels of Ashkelon dating to 604 BC. He unearthed the remains of a stone altar used for burning incense among the destruction debris that rested on top of a collapsed roof (King and Stager, 2001: 339). The story of Keret suggests that sacrifice on rooftops also took place at Ugarit. Here El comes to Keret in a dream and, after providing him with details about what is to be sacrificed, instructs him: 'Go up on to the tower, and mount the shoulder of the wall; lift up your hands (to) heaven, (and) sacrifice to the bull El your father, make Baal to come down with your sacrifice, the son of Dagon with your game. Then let Keret come down from the roof' (Gibson, 1978: 84). From Assyria, the Gilgamesh Epic describes how Ninsun, the mother of Gilgamesh, 'cl[imbed the stairs], mounted to the parapet, ascended the [roof], to Shamash offered incense' and then prayed for her son (ANET, 81).

---

**Archaeological insight:**
## CULT ROOM 65 FROM AI

Another possible example of a family cult room/ building has been unearthed at the early twelfth– mid-eleventh-century village of Ai, located approximately two kilometres east of Bethel. This room was associated with a complex of clustered-together houses and possessed a number of features which suggest that it was dedicated for religious purposes. From a structural perspective, two of the walls of the room (the western and southern) had narrow benches where worshippers could place their offerings (a common feature of religious sites). The presence of a 10-cm-deep channel that appears to have drained part of the floor area would have been suitable for the removal of poured-out libations. The room also contained a number of religious objects including a tall, fenestrated offering stand with feet (probably human but perhaps leonine) encircling its base, a large chalice-shaped stand, one or two animal figurines and jewellery. Dever (2005: 121) has suggested that the unique cult stand is meant to represent a temple of Yahweh with the feet symbolically representing the Lord's presence in the sanctuary.

place of Topheth – all the houses upon whose roofs offerings have been made to the whole host of heaven, and libations have been poured out to other gods' (Jer. 19:13). Corroboration for this practice is also found in narrative texts. For example, part of Josiah's widespread religious reforms included the destruction of 'the altars on the roof of the upper chamber of Ahaz' (2 Kings 23:12). These spaces were particularly associated with the worship of the host of heaven and other astral deities. Such practices may have become increasingly common during the seventh century as a result of greater Assyrian, and later Babylonian, influence over Judah. This location was often

preferred for Mesopotamian prayer and religious ceremonies because of the astral character of their religion, in which the gods were directly identified with particular stars (Albertz, 1994: 189).

While it is unlikely that the majority of people had any form of dedicated sacred space within their household, there is some evidence to suggest that wealthier Israelite families may have had their own cultic room or structure. For example, Judges 17 tells the story of the establishment of a family cult centre, a 'shrine' (*bêt 'ĕlōhîm*, literally 'a house of God', v. 5), in the household of Micah, the Ephraimite. This shrine,

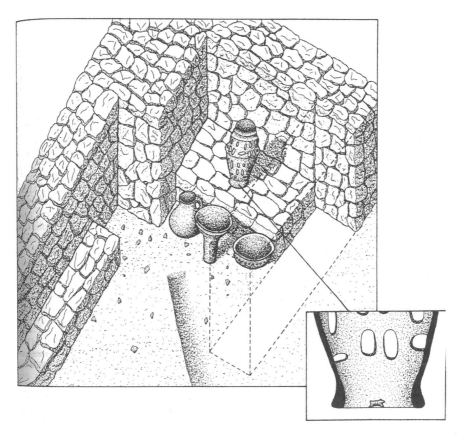

**Figure 5.10   Partial reconstruction of cult room 65 from Ai, including its distinctive fenestrated offering stand (on podium)**

*117*

complete with its own cultic assemblage of idol, ephod and teraphim, was probably a distinct structure (it is referred to as a 'house' (*bêt*) and 18:15 speaks of the 'house of the young Levite, at the home of Micah') but must have been located near the other buildings of the household.[15] This example, however, appears to constitute an exceptional case. Micah's family is obviously well off (note the reference to the eleven hundred pieces of silver and the use of two hundred of these to create the idol, Judg. 17:3–4) and therefore we need to be careful of viewing the presence of such structures as normative or common.

The final location for religious activities within the household was the family tomb, which was usually located on the family's ancestral land. This would have been the primary locus for burial rites and any practices associated with the deceased ancestors. For further discussion of the nature of such tombs see 5.4 'When did they worship?'

### 5.3.2  WITHIN TOWNS OR VILLAGES

Outside the household, people could visit dedicated cultic spaces within their town or village to perform religious activities. Archaeologists have unearthed a number of cult rooms and corners[16] from Lachish (second half of the tenth century), Megiddo (second half of the tenth century) and Dan (eighth century).[17]

These spaces are usually marked out by the presence of distinct architectural features (e.g. benches along the walls on which various offerings and gifts to the god/s could be placed, and niches or alcoves in which sacred objects could be displayed) and various cultic artefacts. These commonly include:[18]

- standing stones (*maṣṣēbôt*), which may have served as aniconic representations of the deity, marking the god's presence at the site (for a fuller discussion of these, see 2.4 'Where were priests located?');
- various animal and human, especially female, figurines (for a discussion of these, see 5.4 'When did they worship?');
- cult or offering stands, which were usually relatively small (from one to two feet high) and tapered to the top, with either a platform or socket for holding an attachable offering bowl. Various offerings, including incense or foodstuffs, could be placed in the platform or bowl;
- altars, ranging from large, fixed stone constructions which were used for animal sacrifices and other food offerings, through to smaller, portable limestone examples which were probably employed for incense offerings;
- sheep/goat astragali (knucklebones), which may have served a divinatory purpose. 'The bones were shaken like dice, then thrown onto a table or onto the ground to see whether they formed a telling pattern and thus revealed something of divine intent. If they did, the gods had spoken, whether a good omen or a bad one' (Dever, 2005: 125);
- various ceramic vessels, including bowls and jars. Some examples, including pitchers, juglets and small 'trick bowls' (bowls with hollow rims and animal heads for spouts) could have been used for pouring out oil or wine as libation offerings. Others may have been used for cooking and feasting, providing additional, non-textual evidence for the centrality of these activities to household worship (for further details see below).

Biblical evidence for public religious sites within or closely associated with a town is found in Judges 6. This tells of Gideon's establishment of a shrine for Yahweh, including an altar for sacrifice, at the family settlement of Ophrah (but probably outside the village itself, located near the oak in Joash's field, v. 19). While the narrator suggests that 'all Israel' prostituted itself before the ephod Gideon set there (Judg. 8:27), Miller (2000: 66) has argued that this was a cult centre for the Abiezrite clan to which Gideon belonged. (The family nature of the site is suggested by the fact that the Baal altar which it replaced was explicitly said to belong to Gideon's father, v. 25). Such sites may have been the venue for significant clan gatherings, including feasts, sacrifices and festival celebrations.

### 5.3.3 OUTSIDE TOWNS OR VILLAGES

Clan shrines could also be located outside villages, between the various settlements of clan members. The best example of this appears to be a small, open-air, hilltop cult place in the tribal territory of Manasseh

dated to the twelfth century BC. Significantly, there is no major tell (a mound created by continuous human occupation indicating permanent settlement) nearby. Instead, the cult place is located in the middle of a cluster of small agricultural villages all within a few hours' walking distance. It has been suggested, therefore, that this is a 'high place' erected by a farmer and used as the local shrine by members of the clan who lived in the surrounding villages (Miller, 2000: 66).

This site features a central paved area with a large standing stone (*maṣṣēbâ*) and an altar-like installation. It is surrounded by an enclosure wall, a common feature of cultic sites. Downhill from the wall, there is evidence for a building of at least three rooms, with possible tenting, sleeping and dining areas for visitors to the site. Zevit suggests that these rooms 'may have designated plots or camping sites for seasonal, local clergy or for pilgrims from

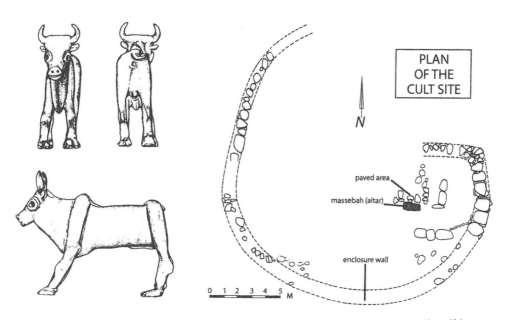

**Figure 5.11** **Plan of hilltop cult place from the territory of Manasseh with bull statue (twelfth century BC)**

119

any of the surrounding villages' (2001: 180). Significant small finds from the site include the remains of a terracotta offering stand, some bronze and silver jewellery, a few bowls and a beautifully preserved bronze zebu bull statue. The significance of the bull, possibly a votive, has provoked much debate. There have been various attempts to relate it to El, Yahweh and even Baal, with El, whose principal epithet in the Ugaritic texts is 'Bull', the most likely candidate.

The identification of the 'bull site' from Manasseh as a possible 'high place' (*bāmâ*) highlights the importance of such sites as places of worship for the common people. *bāmôt* are repeatedly mentioned in the biblical text and I have discussed these in some detail in 2.4 'Where were priests located?'

## 5.4 WHEN DID THE COMMON PEOPLE WORSHIP?

Religious practices tend to accumulate around certain types of events or occasions. For example, in the Judeo-Christian tradition key religious activities are connected with significant transitional events throughout an individual's life (e.g. baptism, bar mitzvah, wedding, death etc.) or are associated with important events in the religious calendar (e.g. Purim, Hanukah, Easter, Christmas etc.) The same was true in ancient Israel. Meyers (2010: 123–30) has helpfully placed the religious practices of the common people into three categories: regular religious activities related to the seasons or calendar, recurring activities related to the human life cycle (esp. birth and death), and occasional activities related to a crisis or concern for the household (such as impurity or sickness). This taxonomy provides an excellent framework for answering our question.[19]

### 5.4.1 REGULAR RELIGIOUS ACTIVITIES (ANNUALLY, MONTHLY, WEEKLY)

At its heart, ancient Israel was essentially an agrarian society. Meyers (2010: 120) has suggested that as many as 90 per cent of

**Going deeper:**
**THE PRE-HISTORY OF PASSOVER**

The primary significance of Passover in the OT is as a commemoration and celebration of the Israelites' deliverance from slavery in Egypt. It has frequently been suggested, however, that this historical association with the exodus is a secondary development, and that the festival may have originally begun life as a primarily agricultural rite or ceremony. Two main proposals have been put forward: (1) given its celebration in the spring, the festival and sacrifice was designed to celebrate and/or secure the fertility and safety of the flock; and (2) the event marked the nomadic or semi-nomadic tribe striking camp before setting out for their summer pasture (note the reference to staff and sandals in Exod. 12:11), and was practised to ensure the successful movement of the group and their flock. Hess (2007: 114–18) has recently sought to highlight parallels between the Passover and the *zukru* festival celebrated at Emar (c. thirteenth century BC). Key examples include: the roasting of a lamb, the recognition of twilight as a critical time, their celebration on the fifteenth day of the first month and inclusion within a seven-day cultic sequence of activities, and the fact that for both the primary focus of the celebration was the family. While the possible pre-biblical origins of the celebration are debated, the widespread nature of similar celebrations in the Middle East suggests that we are dealing with a pre-existing practice that went on to acquire a quite unique meaning within Israel (de Vaux, 1965: 489–90).

Israelites lived in agricultural settlements, the majority of which were less than 2.5 acres in size. Although this percentage may have decreased following the establishment of the monarchy and the accompanying growth in some key population centres, it is clear that the majority of Israelites continued to live in a non-urban context throughout the pre-exilic period.[20] Like virtually all agricultural peoples, ancient Israel celebrated a number of festivals that were associated with the seasons, the cycles of harvesting, and the raising of farm animals.

The most significant agricultural festival in ancient Israel was Passover. This was associated with the barley harvest and took place in the spring.[21] Both Leviticus and Deuteronomy depict Passover as a pilgrimage festival in which the people were required to bring the appropriate offerings to the central (Jerusalem) sanctuary. It is likely, however, that this festival began life in Israel as a household celebration and probably continued to be celebrated within households throughout Israel's history (cf. the regulations associated with the first Passover in Exodus 12 which locate the celebration within the context of the household (vv. 3–4) and the family house (v. 7)).

Exodus 12 indicates that the celebration of Passover consisted of three key elements: a sacrificial lamb was slaughtered, its blood was put around the door of the houses in order to protect the family against the entrance of the 'destroyer' (v. 23), and its flesh cooked and eaten along with unleavened bread and bitter herbs as a reminder of Israel's time in Egypt. Every member of the household could be involved in this celebration, with each receiving a portion of the lamb (v. 4, cf. Num. 9:14).[22]

Another key annual event was the clan sacrifice (*zebaḥ hayyāmîm*, literally 'the sacrifice of the days'). The OT provides few explicit details about this celebration; however, it appears to have been a significant occasion with all adult male members of the clan (*mišpāḥâ*), even those who no longer resided within a local village, expected to attend.[23] The actual ceremony probably involved the offering of a sacrifice and the sharing of a meal and drink (cf. 1 Sam. 1:7–9 and 21) and, if 1 Samuel 1 refers to a similar event, the sacrifice was probably offered within a cultic context. One of the primary functions of this celebration may have been to strengthen the cohesion of the clan and to define clan membership. Because of its clan orientation, the event had no inter-tribal or national significance and thus no fixed date (1 Sam. 20:5–6 suggests that Saul's clan did not celebrate at the same time as

## Going deeper:
## WHO WAS 'THE DESTROYER'?

'"Destroyer" is the designation of a supernatural envoy from God assigned the task of annihilating large numbers of people, typically by means of a plague' (Meier, 1999: 240). In Exodus 12 the destroyer is involved in the death of the Egyptian first-born, while in 2 Samuel 24:16 he is associated with a plague which ravages the people of Jerusalem (cf. 1 Chron. 21). In both instances, the destroyer is an agent of God who executes the deity's judgement. Parallels can be drawn with the angel of the Lord who destroyed 185,000 soldiers of Sennacherib's army in one night (2 Kings 19:35) even though this being is not explicitly referred to as the destroyer in the biblical text.

David's). The exact timing of its celebration probably varied from clan to clan.

Other regular religious activities took place on a monthly basis. The most significant of these was associated with the new moon. The lunar cycle was the basis for the reckoning of time in the ANE (which followed a lunar rather than a solar calendar) and this celebration marked the dramatic re-emergence of the moon after weeks of its waning. Unfortunately, the biblical text does not shed much direct light

### ANE parallels:
### A BABYLONIAN SABBATH?

A number of early twentieth-century scholars suggested that the origins of Sabbath observance were to be found in Babylonian practices. Certain Babylonian texts prescribe the seventh, fourteenth, twenty-first and twenty-eighth days of a month as 'evil' days, and declare that on these days "the shepherd of the people (i.e. the king) must not eat cooked meat or baked bread, must not change his clothes or put on clean clothes, must not offer sacrifice, must not go out in his chariot or exercise his sovereign power. The priest must not deliver oracles, and the physician must not touch the sick. It is an unsuitable day for any desirable action' (cited in de Vaux, 1965: 476). Such suggestions, however, have proved unconvincing. The Israelite Sabbath was an event that took place every seventh day and was not linked to a specific monthly cycle. Furthermore, there is no evidence to suggest that the Israelites ever thought of the Sabbath as an 'evil' day or day of ill omen (if anything it was the reverse, a day hallowed to the Lord!). Thus, it would seem more prudent to view the Sabbath as a unique Israelite development, rather than the borrowing of a Babylonian practice.

on the nature of this festival. In 1 Samuel 20 the new moon seems to be marked out by a meal, which was linked with a feast on the following day. The religious character of this meal is indicated by the fact that guests had to be pure to take part (cf. v. 26, de Vaux, 1965: 470). The primary locus for this celebration was clearly the household as it is nowhere referred to as a *ḥag* ('(sanctuary) festival'), the standard descriptor for events requiring the Israelite people to gather at the central shrine. Amos 8:5 suggests that the new moon was a day of rest from ordinary work, similar to the Sabbath (the similarity between the new moon and Sabbath is also suggested by their close linkage in 2 Kings 4:23; Isa. 1:13; 66:23; Ezek. 45:17; 46:1, 3).

The Sabbath was the key weekly religious event. This day was set aside as sacred to Yahweh and most forms of work were prohibited. According to Exodus 20:8–10 (cf. Deut. 5:12–14), the benefits of the Sabbath were to be enjoyed by the entire *bêt 'āb*, including any male and female slaves and 'the alien resident in your towns'. In addition to the fundamental element of rest, a special meal may have marked the occasion (Meyers, 2010: 125–6). There is little evidence to suggest, however, that any unique cultic activity or observances took place on this day, at least at the level of the common people. 'It would seem as if the ordinary Israelites knew of no specific religious practices peculiar to the Sabbath and that rest was the only, or [at] least the predominant Sabbath prescription they adhered to' (Bosman, 1997: 1160).

### 5.4.2 REGULAR RELIGIOUS ACTIVITIES RELATED TO THE HUMAN LIFE CYCLE

Religious activities in ancient Israel also clustered around key events in the human life cycle, especially birth and death.[24] These significant occasions were of profound importance to the functioning of the *bêt 'āb* as a whole and thus were marked by considerable ritual activity within the household.

As with many agrarian societies throughout history, having children in ancient Israel was not an issue of choice but of necessity. Children were a valuable asset; they could perform some of the agricultural work on which the family relied for its survival and care for elderly relatives. (There was no ancient social welfare system!) Without the benefits of modern science and technology, however, reproduction was a difficult and dangerous activity. Infertility, infant mortality (estimates suggest that as many as one in two children did not survive to the age of five) and childbirth complications leading to the death of the mother were ever present realities.[25] Divine power and protection, therefore, was believed to be essential to aid conception, safe pregnancy and birth and it is highly likely that some form of religious activity accompanied each stage of the childbearing process (Meyers, 2010: 126–7).

Common practices to help achieve conception included the offering of sacrifices and prayer either within the home or at a shrine. Prayer, in particular, was a trusted means for overcoming infertility as God was believed to be responsible for both closing and opening the womb. Thus, in Genesis 25:21 Isaac prays to Yahweh on behalf of his barren wife Rebekah and she

## Going deeper:
## THE SIGNIFICANCE OF VOWS

The OT contains numerous references to vow-making, suggesting that it was a widespread practice among the Israelites (as it was among other ANE peoples).

A vow refers to 'a person's explicit commitment to perform a favour for a deity if the deity will respond to his or her request for a favour' (Floyd, 2009: 793). Vows could be made by either men or women and were typically motivated by a desire for divine help, particularly during times of distress (such as mortal danger from enemies, travel, illness or human or agricultural infertility).

Vows could be initiated by anyone at any time and in any place but sanctuaries may have been preferred, as God was believed to be especially present at such sites. Vows usually accompanied prayers and de Vaux suggests that the purpose of such a vow 'was to add force to a prayer by making a kind of contract with God' (1965: 465). Hence, vows were taken with utmost seriousness – no one was obliged to make a vow, but once spoken, a vow was irrevocably in force and failure to fulfil it could result in serious, negative consequences (Deut. 23:21–23; and Eccl. 5:4–5) (Floyd, 2009: 793).

Once the deity had fulfilled his/her side of the agreement, the individual was obliged to offer the required payment or favour. The usual payment for a vow was some sort of sacrifice to the deity; however, sometimes a person could choose to bind themselves to a particular way of life for a period of time or perpetually (Kaiser, 1998: 244). The best example of this practice is the Nazirite vow by which one dedicated oneself (or another) to Yahweh and was forbidden to enjoy any produce of the grapevine (Num. 6:3–4), to shave the hair of the head (v. 5) or to have any contact with the dead or dying (vv. 6–7).

subsequently conceives (cf. Gen. 20:17) and in 1 Samuel 1:9–20 the childless Hannah herself prays at the shrine of Shiloh for the Lord to give her a son. The case of Hannah is particularly informative for her prayer was accompanied by the making of a vow – in this instance, Hannah swore that if Yahweh granted her a son she would dedicate him to the Lord as a Nazirite (1 Sam. 1:12).

Archaeological remains suggest additional practices associated with conception and pregnancy. Archaeologists have discovered hundreds of small, terracotta pillar figurines often showing a naked woman supporting her breasts with her hands. These are usually found within the debris of private homes, suggesting a connection with domestic religion. Although the exact significance and 'meaning' of these figurines remains debated (see below), Meyers has forcefully argued that they 'were likely votive figurines used in household rituals to assure successful reproduction' (2010: 127).

(A votive is an object presented to the deity, symbolizing and accompanied by a wish or a vow (Dever, 2005: 189).) Along similar lines, Zevit (2001: 274) has referred to these figurines as 'prayers in clay' (perhaps to the goddess Asherah), embodying (quite literally) the desires of the individual.

The archaeological data also suggest that Israelites employed a variety of devices to protect women against malevolent and harmful forces once they had become pregnant. These included amulets and small statues depicting the Egyptian dwarf god Bes or the eye of the god Horus. Lamplight was also utilized as this was believed to keep away the demonic powers associated with darkness. Textual and iconographical remains from the surrounding nations indicate that lamps were used to ward off Lamashtu, Lilith and other demonic beings thought to be particularly dangerous to pregnant or nursing women and to infants (Meyers, 2010: 44–5; Willett, 2002: 37).

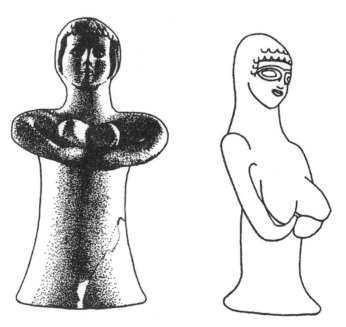

**Figure 5.12  Female figurines from Lachish and Jerusalem (eighth–seventh centuries BC)**

**Going deeper:**
## WHO DID THESE FEMALE FIGURINES REPRESENT AND HOW DID THEY FUNCTION?

Two main interpretations of the nature and significance of these figurines are commonly put forward. The first suggests that they represent a goddess (usually identified as Asherah) to whom women (and men) prayed (Dever). The second proposes that the figurines represent a human woman in prayer (Meyers).

Significant arguments can be marshalled for both possibilities. For example, Dever (2005: 185–95) points to the fact that the majority of Mesopotamian and Canaanite figurines are images of goddesses and not humans, and that the focus on the figurine's breasts suggest that we are dealing with the great Canaanite mother goddess. On the other hand, Meyers (2005: 27–31) points to their relatively crude construction and lack of any insignia or other decorations typically used to denote deities (e.g. they wear no crowns and carry no objects which could symbolize divine power) as proof that we are dealing with human depictions. Unless further evidence comes to light (e.g. a figurine is found with either the name of the deity or its owner inscribed on it), it is unlikely that the argument will be settled one way or the other.

There is broader agreement, however, on the function of these figurines. Whether viewed as an image of a goddess or human worshipper, the figurines are usually connected with rites associated with fertility and reproduction. Thus, Meyers suggests that they were 'vehicles of magical practice . . . typically used in rituals intended to deal with specific family situations, such as increasing fertility or producing healthy children' (2005: 29), while Dever views these as talismans (which he defines as a charm that is supposed to work 'magic' and bring some desired benefit) 'connected principally though not exclusively with reproduction' (2005: 188, 194). It should be recognized, however, that Dever adopts a broader perspective than Meyers, suggesting that the focus on the deity's breasts implies the overall notion of 'plenty', and thus a concern not just with human fertility and fecundity, but also that of the animals and fields.

The popularity of these figurines, particularly during the late eighth and seventh centuries BC, may be attributed to the need to produce offspring during this period. 'These figurines provided a visible means of maintaining and enhancing a population that was threatened with destruction by Sennacherib's campaign in 701 BC and by subsequent and ongoing pressures from the Assyrian (and later Babylonian) state in the seventh century BC' (Hess, 2007: 310).

For a fuller treatment of these figurines, including a detailed catalogue and summary of the history of research, see Kletter, 1996.

---

Following the birth of the child, he/she was named and, if male, circumcised on the eighth day. These acts could be carried out by either the mother or father.[26] Naming is often portrayed in the biblical text as an act of thanksgiving or a confession of the parent's faith. For example, Leah names one of her sons Simeon (meaning 'God has heard') because of the Lord hearing and responding to her plight (Gen. 29:33). Circumcision may have begun as a rite of passage, either from puberty to young manhood or in preparation for marriage (Miller, 2000: 70). In the biblical text, however, it is viewed as a mark of identity, a sign of incorporation and belonging to the covenant community of Israel (Gen. 17:9–14; 34:14–16; Exod. 12:47–48;

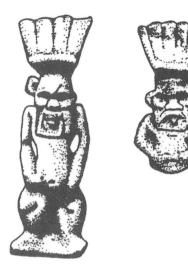

**Figure 5.13    Amulets from Lachish depicting the Egyptian dwarf god, Bes (Iron II)**

Lev. 12:3). The location of this practice within the context of family religion is suggested by the fact that it was usually performed by the father (or occasionally the mother, cf. Exod. 4:24–26) not by a priest in a sanctuary.

At the other end of a person's life, the biblical text points to the existence of a variety of mourning, funerary and burial rites and customs that were practised within ancient Israel. It is often hard to tell, however, whether such actions had direct religious associations.

Burial took place shortly after a person's death, perhaps even on the same day. The deceased's body was interred in the family's tomb, where possible (see 'Archaeological insight: ancient Israelite tombs'). This was probably located on the family's property inheritance (naḥălâ),[27] and was reused for multiple generations.[28] For example, the cave of Machpelah, which Abraham bought for the burial of Sarah (Gen. 23), also eventually served as the tomb of Abraham himself, Isaac and Rebekah, and Jacob and Leah. The deceased were buried fully clothed (cf. the description of Samuel coming up from Sheol with his cloak around him in 1 Sam. 28:14) and, in some cases, adorned with jewellery, but we have no other information for how the body was prepared. The embalming of Jacob's body in Genesis 50:2–3 was standard Egyptian, not Israelite, practice.

A variety of licit and illicit mourning practices could accompany the family member's death. These might include the rending of garments, donning of mourners' garb (usually sackcloth, a coarse material woven from camel or goat hair), putting earth on one's head, rolling in dust or ashes, the singing of laments, especially by women (Jer. 9:16–20 suggests that professional mourners, generally women, were paid to lament during a funeral), fasting for a period of up to seven days, and erecting a memorial stele. 2 Samuel 18:18 implies that such stela were usually

## Archaeological insight:
## ANCIENT ISRAELITE TOMBS

Richer Israelites were buried in rock-cut or cave tombs during the Iron II period (c.1000–600 BC). Borowski provides a good description of one of these:

> The common Israelite burial cave during the Iron Age was entered through a small, rectangular entrance that could be blocked with one large, flat stone. Two to three steps led into the burial chamber, where one to three benches lined the walls . . . The body of the deceased was placed on one of the benches, which sometimes had a depression for the head and a raised lip along the edge of the bench . . . Some tombs had niches in the walls or depressions in the benches for the placement of oil lamps. Special pits – repositories – carved in the room corners across from the entrance or under the benches were used for the collection of bones and other funerary objects. These include clay vessels, figurines, jewelry, weaponry and such. (See Figure 5.14.)

This tomb type was for multiple burials and was used as a family burial plot. Even when all benches were occupied, they were reused whenever a new burial had to take place. The remains from a previous burial (bones, objects) were placed in the repository, and a new burial was performed on the cleared bench. This explains the expression so often used in the Bible: 'he slept/was laid with his fathers'.

Some tombs belonging to well-to-do families were large, contained more than one chamber, and had carved decorations and grave markers. Some burials had inscriptions outside or inside the tomb warning against break-ins or asking the deity for blessing. (2003: 84)

A good example of an Israelite burial inscription was discovered over an eighth-century rock-cut tomb from Siloam, just outside Jerusalem. This reads: 'This is [the sepulchre of . . .] yahu who is over the house. There is no silver and no gold here but [his bones] and the bones of his slave-wife with him. Cursed be the man who will open this!' (Dever, 2001: 219). It has been suggested that this sepulchre belonged to the royal steward Shebna (a shortened form of the name Shebnayahu) who was condemned for his ostentatious tomb in Isaiah 22:15–19.

The preference for rock-cut or cave burials which could be reused by multiple generations was probably the result of a number of practical and social considerations. For example, it conserved labour in tomb construction (once the tomb had been built, little work was required from succeeding generations); it avoided a proliferation of individual tombs throughout the land; it helped to maintain family solidarity and provided an ongoing monument, even to an extinct family (Johnston, 2002: 61).

For more details regarding ancient Israelite tombs and burial practices see Bloch-Smith, 1992.

set up by the deceased's son and were designed to keep his/her name in remembrance (cf. the reference to a 'pillar' (*maṣṣēbâ*) also marking Rachel's grave, Gen. 35:20). This may have been one way in which ancient Israelites sought to honour their mother and father, even after their death!

A funerary feast (*marzēaḥ*) may also have been held to console the mourners. There are only two occurrences of this word in the OT: Amos 6:4–7 and Jeremiah 16:5–9. In the former passage it describes a luxurious banquet accompanied by revelry and excess. In the latter, it is used with reference to a house where mourning rites, including

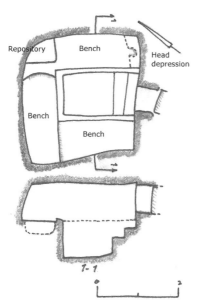

**Figure 5.14** **Plan of a typical Israelite burial cave from the pre-exilic period, from north of Jerusalem**

eating and drinking, take place. Some light may be shed on the nature of this practice by other occurrences of the term in comparative ANE texts. These suggest that 'the *marzēaḥ* was a widespread social phenomenon of gathering to celebrate, commemorate or simply consume alcohol' (Johnston, 2002: 49).[29] Unfortunately, the lack of further textual evidence makes it difficult to determine how common the practice was in ancient Israel.

Other mourning practices, including the gashing of the mourner's body or the shaving of one's head and beard, were viewed with a certain degree of suspicion in some circles. While numerous texts (e.g. Job 1:20; Isa. 15:2; 22:12; Jer. 16:6; 41:5; 47:5; 48:37; Ezek. 7:18; 27:31; Amos 8:10; Mic. 1:16) suggest that such activities were a common and acceptable element of the

**Plate 5.5** **Relief showing an Egyptian funeral procession from the tomb of Mermery (c. fourteenth century BC)**

## Going deeper:
## OFFERINGS FOR THE DEAD

There are two main sources of evidence, apart from the biblical text, which suggest that some ancient Israelites provided offerings for the dead. The first is archaeological, with excavations regularly uncovering a variety of grave goods, including an assortment of vessels for food and drink offerings, alongside bodies interred in the family tomb.* Our other source of evidence is comparative, ANE texts. These suggest that the practice of offering food to the deceased was common throughout the ANE. For example, from Mesopotamia we have numerous references to the *kispu*, a monthly rite in which the family shared their food with the ancestors and which took place in conjunction with the meals of the living (van der Toorn, 2008: 26). This rite provided the dead with ongoing sustenance, and reaffirmed their status as members of the family community (Walton, 2006: 322).

* It should be acknowledged, however, that it is unclear whether these vessels were used by the living as part of the burial rite itself or as a means of providing provisions for the deceased.

mourning process, others (e.g. Lev. 19:27; and Deut. 14:1) clearly state that such customs stood outside the boundaries of acceptable Yahwistic practice. A specific justification for their outlawing is never given: however, the most probable reason is that they were considered to be closely associated with foreign religions and/or the worship of the dead, and thus inappropriate for the children of the Lord (Deut. 14:1).

Another practice that appears to have been relatively widespread, even though it was frowned upon in Deuteronomistic circles, was the provision of offerings for the dead. The evidence for this practice, although not numerous, is suggestive.[30] According to Deuteronomy 26:14 an Israelite who had given his tithe to the marginalized members of Israel's society was required to declare before the Lord, 'I have not eaten of it (i.e. the tithe) while in mourning; I have not removed any of it while I was unclean; *and I have not offered any of it to the dead*.' Two things about this law are worth noting.

**Plate 5.6 A funerary stele depicting an elaborately dressed woman (perhaps a queen) with offerings for the deceased, from Zinjirli**

**Have you considered?**
## WAS NECROMANCY PRACTISED IN ANCIENT ISRAEL?

Necromancy, the raising and consultation of the dead, was practised throughout the ANE, including Israel. The clearest example of this is found in 1 Samuel 28, where King Saul approaches a female medium in order to raise the spirit of the deceased prophet Samuel. Further evidence for this practice is found in the numerous laws that warn against attempting to raise the dead or consult them by means of spirit mediums (e.g. Deut. 18:11; Lev. 19:31; and 20:6). So why was necromancy performed? The basic reason was that some Israelites believed that the dead could provide guidance for the living and answer questions they had. For example, Saul approaches the medium to raise Samuel because he wants the prophet's counsel regarding the impending battle with the Philistines. Similarly, in Isaiah 8:19–20 the prophet condemns those who consult ghosts, familiar spirits and the dead for 'teaching and instruction'. Such practices were diametrically opposed to the vision of Yahwism advocated both by Isaiah and by the authors of the book of Deuteronomy (cf. Deut. 18:11), who located supernatural revelation and teaching with Israel's prophets and priests.

polemicizes against the pouring out of libations and the bringing of offerings for the 'smooth stones', which is probably a reference to the dead.[31] Much clearer is Sirach 30:18 which likens 'good things poured out upon a mouth that is closed' with 'offerings of food placed upon a grave'.[32]

Why were such offerings made? This is a difficult question to answer as it requires us to 'get inside the head' of people who lived within a culture vastly different from our own. Undergirding the practice, however, seems to be the belief that death did not mean the end of an individual's existence – he/she continued to survive, albeit in diminished form. In fact, the dominant picture we find in the OT is of the departed person descending to the underworld (commonly referred to as Sheol) where he/she endures in a sleep-like, shadowy state. Thus, 'death is not extinction but transition to another kind of existence' (King and Stager, 2001: 374).

Within this basic intellectual framework, gifts could have been given for any number of reasons. For example, such activities may have been a way of children honouring their deceased parents and perpetuating their memory (as suggested above, expectations connected with the fifth commandment may have continued even after the parent's death). Another possibility is that food offerings were believed to serve as sustenance for the departed as they made the journey to Sheol. Alternatively, the provision of gifts may have been a way of placating potentially hostile deceased family members or of obtaining the assistance of potentially helpful ones. In some circles, the living may have attributed a kind of divinity to the dead (cf. 1 Sam. 28:13 and Isa. 8:19 where the word *'ĕlōhîm*,

First, the injunction specifically refers only to food that has been tithed and is thus not a general law against feeding the dead (Bloch-Smith, 1992: 123). Second, the fact that such a prohibition was required at all suggests that the practice of offering food to the dead was well known and possibly widespread in ancient Israel. Other texts point to the continuation of this custom during the post-exilic period. Isaiah 57:6

usually translated as 'god', is applied to the deceased) and thus viewed such practices as an appropriate form of veneration. Thus, rather than proposing a single, uniform answer, I think that the motivation for such offerings probably varied from person to person, and may have even changed depending on the circumstances they faced. Such gift giving, like sacrifice in general, was a 'thick' activity, the significance of which could be perceived on a number of different levels.

### 5.4.3 OCCASIONAL RELIGIOUS ACTIVITIES RELATED TO A SPECIFIC CRISIS OR CONCERN

In addition to regular activities connected with the seasons, calendar and human life cycle, there was a whole host of religious practices that occurred on a sporadic or ad hoc basis. These were often connected to an issue of immediate concern for the wellbeing of the household, the most noticeable example of which was the sickness of a family member.

The biblical text and comparative ANE practices give us a relatively good insight into the various religious activities that were undertaken to bring about the recovery of a sick individual. Initially, the family, probably led by the father or mother, offered 'informal, everyday' prayers. These would have been accompanied by traditional household remedies, such as poultices, herbs (Isa. 38:21) and healing drinks. If the sickness worsened, a family member, often the mother, would be sent to enquire of the deity as to whether the sick person would recover or not. This process of divine consultation could take a number of different forms, but the biblical text suggests that one common practice was to consult a prophet. For example, in 1 Kings

14 Jeroboam I instructs his wife to enquire of the Lord via a prophet to determine whether their son Abijah would recover.

> Jeroboam said to his wife, 'Go, disguise yourself, so that it will not be known that you are the wife of Jeroboam, and go to Shiloh; for the prophet Ahijah is there, who said of me that I should be king over this people. Take with you ten loaves, some cakes, and a jar of honey, and go to him; *he will tell you what shall happen to the child.*' (vv. 2–3) (my italics)

A similar practice is found in the story of Elisha and the Shunammite woman's son recorded in 2 Kings 4:18–37 (esp. vv. 22–23). Consulting a religious specialist, however, was obviously a costly exercise (note the numerous items that Jeroboam's wife is required to take with her), and thus may not have been affordable for the majority of the population.[33]

Once a prognosis had been received, further prayers would have been offered. These may have been spoken by the sick individual him/herself (cf. the example of Hezekiah in 2 Kings 20:1–3). Alternatively, intercession could have been sought from other members of the family and/or a well-known member of the community who was experienced in healing rituals and prayers. If more specialized help was required (and the household was relatively well off), the family may have chosen to employ an outside specialist such as a prophet (cf. 1 Kings 13:6; 17:19–21; and 2 Kings 4:33–35) or priest.

Once (if!) the sick person recovered, the family arranged a thanksgiving ceremony.[34] This began with the healed person inviting the members of his/her family, relatives and neighbours from the village to the celebration. A sacrifice was slaughtered in the presence of a priest and the meat (with the exception of the portions dedicated to God) was eaten. The final key element involved the healed person offering a song of thanksgiving to God, in which he/she spoke of his/her distress, lamentation and rescue by God, before the gathered community. This shared feast was particularly significant, for it possessed both a religious and social dimension. From a religious perspective, it involved the individual offering thanks and praise to God for healing him/her. From a social perspective, this event marked the re-integration of the healed individual back into the life of the village community, thus indicating the conclusion to this serious life crisis.

## 5.5 SUMMARY

The religion of the common people of ancient Israel was an incredibly complex phenomenon. Multiple gods, both male (El, Yahweh and Baal) and female (Asherah, the Queen of Heaven) and intermediary beings (the host of heaven, the dead?), were venerated. Multiple places of worship, including the household (esp. the roof), domestic shrines and local sanctuaries, were utilized. Multiple and diverse religious activities were practised according to the time of the year, human life cycle and pressing need. The religion of the common people was a dynamic, organic and living reality that changed and developed throughout the nation's history. At its heart, however, lay a close and strong relationship between the worshippers and their god/s, and a belief that the god/s were intimately and fundamentally concerned with the wellbeing and success of the people and families who venerated them.

When I work through this material in class, some of my students are initially uncomfortable. They struggle to reconcile certain elements of this reconstruction of popular belief and practice (especially its polytheism and veneration of the dead) with the kind of faith which we find prescribed in the biblical text, and which, by extension, forms the basis for Christian belief today.

But this is exactly the point. We *shouldn't* expect the faith of the common people to match exactly what we find advocated in the Bible. The biblical text repeatedly points out that Israel did not, in fact, practise the kind of faith that it should have. For example, after confronting the prophets of Baal on Mount Carmel and fleeing for his life, Elijah can declare, 'I have been very zealous for the LORD, the God of hosts; for the Israelites have forsaken your covenant, thrown down your altars, and killed your prophets with the sword. I alone am left, and they are seeking my life, to take it away' (1 Kings 19:10). Likewise, the frequent prophetic critique of Canaanite religious practices suggests that this was a large-scale problem which the people genuinely struggled with.

The reconstruction which I am advocating, therefore, should not make us feel uncomfortable – ultimately, it undergirds rather than subverts the biblical portrayal of Israel's religious life. In fact, it would be more problematic if this were *not* the kind of religion we encountered. If this were the case, then the frequent critique of the prophets and the laws outlawing such illicit practices wouldn't make sense! The above analysis thus provides the backdrop against which we can appreciate the distinctive claims of the authors of the OT.

This raises a further important point for members of the contemporary community of faith. In our discussion of the religion of ancient Israel, we need to distinguish between the ideal and the actual, between what was prescribed and what was practised, between what should have been normative and what actually was. In the above discussion, I have tended to focus on the latter, attempting to describe the religion of ancient Israel as it was actually practised on the ground. For the community of faith today, however, it is the former which dominates the canonical witness and thus

has primary ongoing significance as we seek to live as genuine and faithful 'people of the book'.

## NOTES

1 A note on terminology: I am well aware of the various titles scholars have used to label the level of Israelite religion that I am focusing on in this chapter (e.g. 'domestic cult', 'popular religion', 'folk religion', 'family religion', 'household religion'). Unfortunately, each of these is problematic in its own way. I have decided, therefore, to talk about 'the religion of the common people'; 'common' not in a derogatory sense but rather with the nuance of majority, general, average. Thus I am focusing on religion as it would have been experienced and practised by your typical, ordinary, everyday Israelite, in other words, beliefs and practices that were prevalent throughout ancient Israel. I will, however, employ some of the other labels throughout the discussion from time to time.

2 It should be recognized that the accuracy of these figures is questioned by many scholars as they suggest an Israelite population far in excess of what the land of Israel (let alone the wilderness!) could have sustained. For example, Borowski (2003: 8) has suggested that Israel's population at its height (i.e. during the eighth century BC) may have been approximately 460,000, well short of the more than 2,000,000 people required by the census data. My concern, however, is not the specific numbers themselves but rather the general picture they suggest regarding the relative sizes of the various Israelite tribes. I have derived the 3 per cent figure as follows. Exodus 38:26 indicates there were 603,550 men

over 20 years of age who departed from Egypt (this figure does not include the women, children and mixed multitude who accompanied them). Numbers 3:39 suggests that there were 22,000 Levites over one month old. From this we may subtract 25 per cent for infant mortality (I have based this 25 per cent on the suggestion that 50 per cent of children did not make it to the age of 5 but that at least half of these deaths would have occurred in childbirth or shortly after), yielding a maximum total of 16,500 who would have been 20 years of age or over (this figure seems to be on the generous side given that Numbers 4:48 suggests that there were 8,580 Levites between the ages of 30 and 50 years). Hence, Levites accounted for approximately 2.7 per cent of the adult male population. We can compare this with the second census figures found in the book of Numbers which suggest that there were 601,730 non-Levite, Israelite males over the age of 20 on the plains of Moab (Num. 26:5–51). Levites would have totalled an additional 17,250 people at the absolute maximum (Num. 26:62 suggests that there were 23,000 Levites over one month old from which we can subtract 25 per cent). This suggests that Levites accounted for approximately 2.8 per cent of the adult male population.

3 This figure is based on the mention of 850 prophets of Baal and Asherah in the royal court (1 Kings 18:19) plus a similar number spread throughout the rest of the country.

4 This figure is based on Meyers' (2010: 120) suggestion that only 10 per cent of Israel's population was truly urbanized, and that only half of these were males.

5 Faust and Bunimovitz (2003: 25–6) have argued that in rural areas the four-room houses tended to be larger (avg. 110–30 m²) and would have accommodated an extended family (*bêt 'āb*). In urban areas, however, the houses tended to be smaller (40–80 m²) and thus would have suited a nuclear family.

6 In fact, Meyers (1997: 39) has argued that there was probably no such thing as personal religion in Israel or in the ANE as a whole. In my opinion, however, this seems to be going too far. See, for example, the work of Albertz (2010: 135–48) who argues that 'the personal piety of family members constituted a specific stratum of beliefs and ritual practices within the religion of ancient Israel and Judah'.

7 Further evidence for Yahweh as the key Israelite family god during this period is provided in tomb and cave inscriptions. As Miller (2000: 243, endnote 93) has argued, one might naturally expect these to invoke or thank the inscriber's family god. The deity that is always named in ancient Israel is Yahweh.

8 It needs to be kept in mind, however, that the evidence of personal names is not conclusive in this regard for it is clear that during Israel's early history (up to the time of Hosea in the eighth century) 'baal' could be used as an epithet or alternative name for Yahweh. Such a practice, for example, seems to lie behind Hosea 2:16. Thus, the use of a baal element in personal names need not necessarily imply veneration of a deity distinct from Yahweh. Nevertheless, the evidence from the OT narrative (e.g. Judg. 2:13; 8:33; 1 Kings 18:18; 2 Kings 17:16) and prophetic (Hos. 2:8; 11:2; Zeph. 1:4; Jer. 2:23; 9:13–14) texts does emphatically point to the worship of Baal in ancient Israel.

9 It needs to be acknowledged, however, that a number of scholars (e.g. Miller) view this passage as textually suspect, suggesting that it should instead read 'the Baals and Ashtaroth' ('Ashtaroth' being a plural form of the well-known Canaanite goddess Astarte).

10 By the first millennium BC these goddesses held many traits in common (e.g. they could all be associated with fertility, love and war) and bore similar epithets, thus making it difficult to differentiate clearly between them.

11 The attentive reader will note that I have not discussed synagogues as a place of worship. The reason for this is that synagogues did not emerge until the exilic period (or later) and thus fall outside the bounds of this study.

12 The Psalms of Ascent (esp. Ps. 121) point to the fact that pilgrimages to Jerusalem did occur.

13 Even though wives are not explicitly mentioned in the list of those who were expected to participate in the pilgrimage festivals at the central sanctuary (Deut. 12:12), it is likely that they are included in the generic address 'you and your house' in v. 7.

14 Pilgrimage to Jerusalem would have involved significant time and financial costs and few farmers would have been able to regularly afford this, let alone three times in a single year.

15 For further elaboration on the presence of a distinct shrine within Micah's household compound see Ackerman, 2008: 128–36.

16 A cult corner was a smaller space, usually part of a room or courtyard, which has been designated for cultic purposes. Zevit (2001: 123) distinguishes cult rooms from cult corners on the basis that the former were built specifically for cultic purposes and had their own entrances, whereas the latter appear to be secondary appropriations of particular spaces.

17 For a discussion of each of these see Zevit, 2001, and Dever, 2005.

18 The cultic artefacts are discussed in more detail in Dever, 2005: 117–25. My discussion essentially represents a summary of Dever's work.

19 Much of the following is indebted to the work of Carol Meyers, esp. 2010: 123–30.

20 Borowski (2003: 9) proposes a smaller percentage, suggesting that only 66 per cent resided in small villages with the rest in settlements (towns, cities) larger than 12 acres. The majority of scholars (including Ackerman, Dever, King and Stager), however, follow Meyers' figures. Faust (2003) has recently argued on the basis of the archaeological evidence that there was a significant period of urbanization (and an accompanying abandonment of rural settlements) during the tenth century, a shift of population which is probably to be associated with the establishment of the Israelite monarchy. This seems to have been a relatively short-lived development, however, for between the ninth and seventh centuries we see the establishment of a number of rural settlements and increased growth in the rural areas. Thus, Faust concludes that rural settlements 'comprised the majority of settlement during the later Iron Age II as well' (2003: 149).

21 The other two key feasts were Weeks, which marked the completion of the wheat harvest in the early summer, and Tabernacles/Booths, which took place in autumn and celebrated the completion of agricultural work.

22 Male members of the household needed to be circumcised before they could participate in the celebration.

23 The importance of this event is suggested by the fact that David could use it as a reasonable excuse to absent himself from King Saul's table (1 Sam. 20:5–6).

24 Some readers may be surprised to see that I have not included marriage as a key religious event associated with the human life cycle. It appears, however, that marriage in ancient Israel was primarily viewed as a secular rather than religious affair. For more details, see King and Stager, 2001: 54–8.

25 Maternal mortality rates are difficult to calculate given the lack of data from the ancient world. Figures range from 2.5 per cent to 10 per cent.

26 According to Meyers (2005: 42), in the OT women are depicted as pronouncing the newborn's name on 62 per cent of occasions.

27 The location of the family tomb on the family's nahălâ is suggested in the book of Joshua by the burial of Joshua (24:30), Joseph (24:32) and Eleazar (24:33) on their family's land. For more details see Stager, 1985: 22–3.

28 There may have been common burial fields for (poorer) people who lived in larger urban centres. This was the case for Jerusalem (2 Kings 23:6).

29 Johnston comments that the marzēaḥ combined 'elements of a pub, a drinking club, a London Gentlemen's Club, a Masonic Lodge, an annual fete and an Irish wake!' (2002: 49).

30 Psalm 106:28 also speaks of the Israelites eating 'sacrifices offered to the dead' as they journeyed from Sinai to the promised land. This refers to a once-off, historical event, however, and thus does not provide evidence for the continuance of such practices once the people had entered the land.

31 Even Johnston, who adopts a conservative interpretation of the data regarding the veneration of the dead in ancient Israel, concludes that Isaiah 57:6 'probably criticizes a cult of the dead' (2002: 176).

32 See also the Epistle of Jeremiah 6:27 which speaks of 'gifts placed before the dead'.

33 In 2 Kings 8:7–15 King Ben-hadad of Aram sends Hazael to Elisha to determine whether he will recover from his illness or not. The king instructs Hazael to take a present with him to pay for the prophet's services.

34 This reconstruction of a thanksgiving ceremony is based on Albertz, 1994: 101.

## FOR FURTHER READING

S. Ackerman (2008), 'Household Religion, Family Religion, and Women's Religion in Ancient Israel', in Bodel and Olyan (2008: 127–58).

R. Albertz (1994), *A History of Israelite Religion in the Old Testament Period, Vol. 1: From the Beginnings to the End of the Exile*, trans. J. Bowden, OTL, London: SCM Press.

R. Albertz (2008), 'Family Religion in Ancient Israel and Its Surroundings', in Bodel and Olyan (2008: 89–112).

R. Albertz (2010), 'Personal Piety', in Stavrakopolou and Barton (2010: 135–46).

J. Bodel and S. Olyan (eds) (2008), *Household and Family Religion in Antiquity*, Malden: Blackwell Publishing.

W. Dever (2005), *Did God Have a Wife? Archaeology and Folk Religion in Ancient Israel*, Grand Rapids: Eerdmans.

C. Meyers (2005), *Households and Holiness: The Religious Culture of Israelite Women*, Minneapolis: Fortress Press.

C. Meyers (2010), 'Household Religion', in Stavrakopolou and Barton (2010: 118–34).

S. Olyan (2008), 'Family Religion in Israel and the Wider Levant of the First Millennium BCE', in Bodel and Olyan (2008: 113–26).

L. Perdue, J. Blenkinsopp, J. Collins and C. Meyers (eds) (1997), *Families in Ancient Israel*, Louisville: WJKP.

F. Stavrakopolou and J. Barton (eds) (2010), *Religious Diversity in Ancient Israel and Judah*, London: T&T Clark.

Z. Zevit (2001), *The Religions of Ancient Israel: A Synthesis of Parallactic Approaches*, London: Continuum.

# CONCLUSION

In the first part of this book we focused on the key religious specialists of ancient Israel: the priests, prophets, sages (and kings). Such individuals lay at the heart of ancient Israel's religious life and practice, at least at a national level. For the sake of clarity, I have discussed each group within their own distinct chapter. This has the potential to be misleading, however, for there was not always a clear demarcating line between holders of the various offices. As Grabbe declares, 'the neat, watertight categories we so often work with exist only in our own minds, not in society' (1995: 221). The overlap between the various specialists is particularly noticeable with regards to their shared status and roles, with the priests occupying a central position.

The lack of a clear dividing line between the various religious specialists is seen in the way that certain individuals could hold multiple offices. For example, we have two clear examples of priests, or potential priests, functioning as prophets: Ezekiel (who is explicitly described as a priest in Ezek. 1:3) and Jeremiah (who is said to be a member of the priestly families who lived in Anathoth, Jer. 1:1). There is also good reason to think that at least some of Israel's

> **Going deeper:**
> **RELIGIOUS SPECIALISTS IN AFRICAN SOCIETIES**
>
> Anthropological studies of modern African societies have shown that often there is little clear separation between religious specialists. For the Nuer of Sudan, the roles of prophet and priest overlap, with the most famous prophets generally coming from priestly families. There is also a tendency for priests to take on prophetic functions and prophets to take on priestly as a means of strengthening their authority (Grabbe, 1995: 187). For the Kiganda of Uganda, 'the very profusion and variety of terminology for Baganda priests, prophets, mediums, diviners, healers, and medicine men . . . and the constant manipulation of them, is structurally consistent with the ease with which an individual may perform several of these roles simultaneously. It is also consistent with the ability of a person to transform himself from one role to another during the course of his professional life' (Rigby, cited in Grabbe, 1995: 189).

sages were drawn from priestly circles. Note, for example, the reference to the priest Jehoiada instructing the king of Judah, Jehoash, in 2 Kings 12:2, while in

**Have you considered?**
**PROPHETS, PRIESTS AND SAGES OUTSIDE THE CAPITALS**

It seems likely that outside the significant cities, especially Jerusalem, certain individuals would have functioned as prophet, priest and sage. The significant overlap between the three offices which is suggested by the biblical text points in this direction, as does the recognition that in non-urban, lower population density areas we find less well-developed role differentiations. While there is little explicit evidence to support this theory, perhaps one could point to the precedent of Samuel who was recognized as both a prophet (1 Sam. 3:20), priest (1 Sam. 3:1) and judge (1 Sam. 7:15–16).

the post-exilic period Ezra is hailed as both priest and scribe (Ezra 7:11). Finally, it is likely that the Israelite king also held priestly status (cf. Ps. 110:4, where the king is hailed as 'priest for ever according to the order of Melchizedek').

Overlap between the various religious specialists is also suggested by the fact that they could perform virtually identical roles. Both prophets and priests were involved in intercession and revealing the will of the Lord (in the case of the priests, by ephod or Urim and Thummim, in the case of the prophets, by more direct divine encounter). Israel's kings could perform various priestly roles, including blessing the people (cf. 2 Sam. 6:18, where David 'blessed the people in the name of the LORD of hosts' following the arrival of the ark in Jerusalem). While sacrifice is often viewed as the unique domain of the priests, we have at least one example where a prophet officiates

(Elijah in 1 Kings 18), and it appears that kings could also be involved in this activity (cf. the sacrifices of Saul in 1 Sam. 13, David in 2 Sam. 6 and Solomon in 1 Kings 3). (It should be recognized, however, that the participation of Israel's kings in this kind of cultic activity was probably restricted to special occasions, such as the dedication of a new place of worship or altar.) This overlap in the performance of priestly roles extends to the realm of the wise, with both priests and elders capable of performing a judicial role (cf. Deut. 17:8–13). Furthermore, priests, like scribes, were probably responsible for the production of literature, with a text such as Leviticus clearly reflecting priestly concerns. Finally, we can see that certain tasks, such as counselling and teaching, could be performed by all three classes of religious specialist – prophet, priest and sage. This overlap of role responsibilities was probably a potential source of conflict between holders of such offices. One only needs to think, for example, of the clash between Israel's prophets and court sages regarding their advice to the king as to the direction the nation should take.

The involvement of such figures in the religious lives of an 'average Israelite' life, however, would have been relatively minimal. Priests may have been engaged during significant, ritual occasions, while prophets could have been approached if a member of the household was ill. Sages, in the form of village elders, may have been called on to settle legal disputes and if teaching was required. The involvement of such specialists (with the possible exception of the elders), however, would have come at a cost (their services required some form of payment), and thus may only have been employed for important events or times of crisis. Instead, the majority of religious activity for an ancient Israelite would have taken place within the context of the household and have been led by the significant male or female figures of the family.

The religious life of an ancient Israelite household shares little similarity to what Christians practise today. Multiple gods may have been venerated (Yahweh, but also El, Baal, Asherah and the Queen of Heaven, to name a few). Multiple places of worship were utilized, both within and outside the home. Multiple religious rites and rituals were practised. But perhaps the most significant difference was that religion was not a distinct or separate element of their existence; it pervaded virtually every aspect of daily life in ancient Israel.

> It [i.e. religion] was never limited to a single day or prayer before eating and sleeping. Biblical people used religion to explain and to manage their natural surroundings. Every hour of the day had its religious significance, every season of the year had its sacred feast days, and the ordinary and extraordinary chores of every household were celebrated with ritual. The religion of the ancient world inspired its culture, and handed it on from one generation to the next. Every art and science was sacred, and had a different motivation from the art and science of today. In the biblical world the arts and sciences were a profession of faith. (Matthews and Benjamin, 1993: xix–xx.)

This 'embeddedness' of religion provides an important balance to much modern Western Christianity, which has essentially embraced a dualistic view of reality, separating the sacred from the profane, and hence resulting in a faith which is often not engaged with, but instead seems to escape from, life and the world around it.

# COPYRIGHT ACKNOWLEDGEMENTS

## PLATES

2.1 Terracotta figurine of a woman holding a drum from the Iron II period. © Israeli National Maritime Museum, Haifa/Wikimedia.

2.2 Faience die which may have been used in divination, found in the sacred precinct at Tel Dan. Courtesy David Ilan, Tel Dan Excavations, Hebrew Union College.

2.3 Man bringing an offering, from Zinjirli (F. von Lushcan, *Ausgrabungen in Sendschirli*, vol. 4. Berlin: Georg Reimer, 1911).

2.4 Assemblage of four-horned incense altars, from Ekron. Photograph by Ilan Sztulman. Courtesy the Tel Miqne Ekron Excavation and Publication Project.

2.5 The inner sanctum of the temple at Arad complete with two *maṣṣēbôt* (rear) and altars (front). © Acer11/Wikimedia Commons.

2.6 Stone stele depicting a warrior god from Moab (possibly Chemosh) (Louvre). © Marie-Lan Nguyen/ Wikimedia Commons.

4.1 Relief of Horemheb's tomb depicting Egyptian scribes writing documents (eighteenth dynasty of Egypt, 1328–1298 BC). © Neithsabes/Wikimedia Commons.

4.2 King Bar Rakab seated on his throne, with his scribe who is holding writing implements, from Zinjirli. (F. von Lushcan, *Ausgrabungen in Sendschirli*, vol. 4. Berlin: Georg Reimer, 1911).

4.3 Diorite statue of a seated Egyptian scribe with a papyrus scroll (nineteenth–twentieth dynasty, 1295–1069 BC) (Louvre). © Janmad/Wikimedia Commons.

Ex.1 Limestone plaque depicting Ur-Nanshe of Lagash bearing a basket on his head, possibly containing the first brick for the foundation of a temple (*c.*2500 BC) (Louvre). © Marie-Lan Nguyen/ Wikimedia Commons.

Ex.2 Egyptian stele showing six individuals carrying various standards (Louvre). © Guillaume Blanchard/Wikimedia Commons.

5.1 Limestone stele from Ugarit depicting Baal with thunderbolt (1900–1500 BC)

(Louvre). © Marie-Lan Nguyen/ Wikimedia Commons.

5.2 An ivory panel depicting an Ugaritic goddess, possibly Asherah, nursing two children (1400–1350 BC). Courtesy *Syria* 31:1 (1954), pp. 48–9, pl. 8.

5.3 Judean female terracotta figurine from the eighth century, possibly Asherah. © Hanay/Wikimedia Commons.

5.4 Two silver statuettes, possibly teraphim, found in a jar, from Ugarit (*c.*2000– 1800 BC). Courtesy *Syria* 14:2 (1933), pp. 124–5.

5.5 Relief showing an Egyptian funeral procession from the tomb of Mermery (*c.* fourteenth century BC). © Rob Koopman/Wikimedia Commons.

5.6 A funerary stele depicting an elaborately dressed woman (perhaps a queen) with offerings for the deceased, from Zinjirli (F. von Lushcan, *Ausgrabungen in Sendschirli*, vol. 4. Berlin: Georg Reimer, 1911).

## FIGURES

1.1 Female lyre player from Kuntillet Ajrud. Courtesy the Institute of Archaeology, Tel Aviv University.

2.1 The large four-horned altar from Beersheba, as reassembled. Adapted from photo: Israel Antiquities Authority. Courtesy William Dever.

2.2 Artist's reconstruction of a gate shrine from Dan, complete with set of five *maṣṣēbôt* (top corner) and basin structure (from Z. Zevit, *The Religions of Ancient Israel: A Synthesis of Parallactic Approaches*. London: Continuum, 2001, p. 194).

3.1 Two seals depicting winged serpents (from O. Keel and C. Uehlinger,

*Gods, Goddesses and Images of God in Ancient Israel*. Minneapolis: Fortress Press, 1998). Courtesy Fortress Press.

3.2 Detail from the Lachish reliefs showing the Assyrian army attacking the gate area of Lachish. Courtesy David Ussishkin, Tel Aviv University. Artist: Judith Dekel.

3.3 Egyptian hieroglyph showing an individual in an ecstatic state, from the story of Wen-Amon. Courtesy Aaron Chalmers.

3.4 Procession of worshippers with arms upraised in a gesture of prayer, from Kuntillet Ajrud. Courtesy the Institute of Archaeology, Tel Aviv University.

4.1 Plans of city gates of Megiddo (a), Hazor (b), Gezer (c), Ashdod (d) and Lachish (e). Courtesy Ze'ev Herzog, Tel Aviv University.

Ex.1 The Assyrian king Ashurbanipal pouring a libation over four dead lions before an offering table and incense stand (from A. Parrot, *Nineveh and the Old Testament*. London: SCM Press, 1955). Courtesy SCM Press.

5.1 Artist's reconstruction showing a large residence in a provincial town with people performing various everyday activities (from E. Heaton, *Everyday Life in Old Testament Times*. London: B.T. Batsford Ltd., 1956).

5.2 Artist's reconstruction showing several multi-house compounds within a typical Israelite village. Courtesy Harrassowitz Verlag.

5.3 Drawing of a bronze and gold statuette from Ugarit of a seated god, probably

# SELECT BIBLIOGRAPHY

S. Ackerman (2006), 'Asherah', in K.D. Sakenfeld (ed.), *New Interpreters Dictionary of the Bible*, vol. 1. Nashville: Abingdon, pp. 297–9.

S. Ackerman (2008), 'Household Religion, Family Religion, and Women's Religion in Ancient Israel', in J. Bodel and S. Olyan (eds), *Household and Family Religion in Antiquity*. Malden: Blackwell Publishing, pp. 127–58.

G. Ahlström (1982), *Royal Administration and National Religion in Ancient Palestine*, SHANE 1. Leiden: E.J. Brill.

R. Albertz (1990), 'The Sage and Pious Wisdom in the Book of Job: The Friends' Perspective', in J. Gammie and L. Perdue (eds), *The Sage in Israel and the Ancient Near East*. Winona Lake: Eisenbrauns, pp. 243–62.

R. Albertz (1994), *A History of Israelite Religion in the Old Testament Period, Vol. 1: From the Beginnings to the End of the Exile*, trans. J. Bowden, OTL. London: SCM Press.

R. Albertz (2007), 'Why a Reform like Josiah's Must Have Happened', in L. Grabbe (ed.), *Good Kings and Bad Kings: The Kingdom of Judah in the Seventh Century BCE*. London: T&T Clark, pp. 27–46.

R. Albertz (2008), 'Family Religion in Ancient Israel and Its Surroundings', in J. Bodel and S. Olyan (eds), *Household and Family Religion in Antiquity*. Malden: Blackwell Publishing, pp. 89–112.

R. Albertz (2010), 'Personal Piety', in F. Stavrakopolou and J. Barton (eds), *Religious Diversity in Ancient Israel and Judah*. London: T&T Clark, pp. 135–46.

B. Alster (2008), 'Scribes and Wisdom in Ancient Mesopotamia', in L. Perdue (ed.), *Scribes, Sages, and Seers: The Sage in the Eastern Mediterranean World*, FRLANT 219. Göttingen: Vandenhoeck & Ruprecht, pp. 47–63.

P.-A. Beaulieu (2007), 'The Social and Intellectual Setting of Babylonian Wisdom Literature', in R. Clifford (ed.), *Wisdom Literature in Mesopotamia and Israel*, SBLSS 36. Atlanta: Society of Biblical Literature, 2007, pp. 3–20.

P. Bird (1997), 'The Place of Women in Israelite Cultus', *Missing Persons and Mistaken Identities: Women and Gender in Ancient Israel*, OBT. Minneapolis: Fortress Press, pp. 81–102.

J. Blenkinsopp (1995a), *Sage, Priest, Prophet: Religious and Intellectual Leadership in Ancient Israel*, LAI. Louisville: Westminster John Knox Press.

J. Blenkinsopp (1995b), *Wisdom and Law in the Old Testament: The Ordering of Life in Israel and Early Judaism*, rev. edn, OBS. Oxford: Oxford University Press.

J. Blenkinsopp (1996), *A History of Prophecy in Israel: Revised and Enlarged*. Louisville: Westminster John Knox Press.

J. Blenkinsopp (1997), 'The Family in First Temple Israel', in L. Perdue, J. Blenkinsopp, J. Collins and C. Meyers (eds), *Families in Ancient Israel*. Louisville: Westminster John Knox Press, pp. 48–103.

E. Bloch-Smith (1992), *Judahite Burial Practices and Beliefs about the Dead*, JSOTSS 123. Sheffield: JSOT Press.

J. Bodel and S. Olyan (eds) (2008), *Household and Family Religion in Antiquity*. Malden: Blackwell Publishing.

O. Borowski (2003), *Daily Life in Biblical Times*, SBLABS 5. Atlanta: Society of Biblical Literature, 2003.

H. Bosman (1997), 'Sabbath', in W.A. VanGemeren (ed.), *New International Dictionary of Old Testament Theology and Exegesis*, vol. 4. Grand Rapids: Zondervan, 1997, pp. 1157–62.

C. Camp (1990), 'The Female Sage in Ancient Israel and in the Biblical Wisdom Literature', in J. Gammie and L. Perdue (eds), *The Sage in Israel and the Ancient Near East*. Winona Lake: Eisenbrauns, pp. 185–204.

D. Carr (2005), *Writing on the Tablet of the Heart: Origins of Scripture and Literature*. Oxford: Oxford University Press.

M. Civil (1992), 'Education (Mesopotamia)', in D.N. Freedman (ed.), *Anchor Bible Dictionary*, vol. 2. New York: Doubleday, pp. 301–5.

R. Clements (1997), 'Max Weber, Charisma and Biblical Prophecy', in Y. Gitay (ed.), *Prophecy and Prophets: The Diversity of Contemporary Issues in Scholarship*, SBLSS. Atlanta: Scholars Press, pp. 89–108.

J. Conrad (1980), '*zāqēn*', in G. Botterweck and H. Ringgren (eds), *Theological Dictionary of the Old Testament*, vol. 4, trans. D. Green. Grand Rapids: Eerdmans, pp. 122–31.

M. Coogan (1978), *Stories from Ancient Canaan*, Louisville: Westminster Press.

J. Crenshaw (1976), 'Prolegomenon', in J. Crenshaw (ed.), *Studies in Ancient Israelite Wisdom*. New York: KTAV, pp. 1–60.

J. Crenshaw (1990), 'The Sage in Proverbs', in J. Gammie and L. Perdue (eds), *The Sage in Israel and the Ancient Near East*, Winona Lake: Eisenbrauns, pp. 205–16.

J. Crenshaw (1998), *Education in Ancient Israel: Across the Deadening Silence*, ABRL. New York: Doubleday.

J. Crenshaw (2007), 'Education, OT', in K.D. Sakenfeld (ed.), *New Interpreters Dictionary of the Bible*, vol. 2. Nashville: Abingdon, pp. 195–205.

J. Crenshaw (2010), *Old Testament Wisdom: An Introduction*. 3rd edn, Louisville: Westminster John Knox Press, 2010.

G. Davies (1995), 'Were there schools in ancient Israel?', in J. Day, R. Gordon and H. Williamson (eds), *Wisdom in Ancient Israel: Essays in Honour of J.A. Emerton*, Cambridge: Cambridge University Press, pp. 199–211.

P. Davies (1992), *In Search of 'Ancient Israel'*. JSOTSS 148. Sheffield: JSOT Press.

P. Davies (2007), 'Josiah and the Law Book', in L. Grabbe (ed.), *Good Kings and Bad Kings: The Kingdom of Judah in the Seventh Century BCE*. London: T&T Clark, pp. 65–77.

P. Davies (2008), *Memories of Ancient Israel: An Introduction to Biblical History – Ancient and Modern*. Louisville: Westminster John Knox Press.

J. Day (1992), 'Baal (Deity)', in D.N. Freedman (ed.), *Anchor Bible Dictionary*, vol. 1. New York: Doubleday, pp. 545–9.

J. Day (1998), 'The Canaanite Inheritance of the Israelite Monarchy', in J. Day (ed.), *King and Messiah in Israel and the Ancient Near East: Proceedings of the Oxford Old Testament Seminar*, JSOTSS 270. Sheffield: Sheffield Academic Press, pp. 72–90.

J. Day (2000), *Yahweh and the Gods and Goddesses of Canaan*, JSOTSS 265. Sheffield: Sheffield Academic Press.

J. Day, R.P. Gordon and H.G.M. Williamson (eds) (1995), *Wisdom in Ancient Israel: Essays in Honour of J.A. Emerton*, Cambridge: Cambridge University Press.

R. de Vaux (1965), *Ancient Israel: Its Life and Institutions*, 2nd edn, trans. J. McHugh. London: Darton, Longman & Todd.

G. del Olmo Lete and J. Sanmartin (2004), *A Dictionary of the Ugaritic Language in the Alphabetic Tradition*, 2nd rev. edn, trans. W. Watson, HdO 67. Leiden: Brill.

K. Dell (2006), *The Book of Proverbs in Social and Theological Context*. Cambridge: Cambridge University Press.

K. Dell (2008), 'Scribes, Sages, and Seers in the First Temple', in L. Perdue (ed.), *Scribes, Sages, and Seers: The Sage in the Eastern Mediterranean World*, FRLANT 219. Göttingen: Vandenhoeck & Ruprecht, pp. 125–44.

W. Dever (2001), *What Did the Biblical Writers Know and When Did They Know It? What Archaeology Can Tell Us about the Reality of Ancient Israel*. Grand Rapids: Eerdmans.

W. Dever (2003), *Who Were the Early Israelites and Where Did They Come From?* Grand Rapids: Eerdmans.

W. Dever (2005), *Did God Have a Wife? Archaeology and Folk Religion in Ancient Israel*. Grand Rapids: Eerdmans.

R. Duke (2003), 'Priests, Priesthood', in T.D. Alexander and D. Baker (eds), *Dictionary of the Old Testament: Pentateuch*. Downers Grove: IVP, pp. 645–55.

D. Edelman (2010), 'Cultic Sites and Complexes beyond the Jerusalem Temple', in F. Stavrakopolou and J. Barton (eds), *Religious Diversity in Ancient Israel and Judah*. London: T&T Clark, pp. 82–103.

W. Eichrodt (1961), *Theology of the Old Testament*, vol. 1, trans. J. Baker, OTL. London: SCM Press.

H.-J. Fabry (1998), '*marzēaḥ*', in G. Botterweck, H. Ringgren and H.-J. Fabry (eds), *Theological Dictionary of the Old Testament*, vol. 9, trans. D. Green. Grand Rapids: Eerdmans, pp. 10–15.

A. Faust (2003), 'Abandonment, Urbanization, Resettlement and the Formation of the Israelite State', *NEA* 66:4, pp. 147–61.

A. Faust and S. Bunimovitz (2003), 'The Four Room House: Embodying Iron Age Israelite Society', *NEA* 66:1–2, pp. 22–31.

M. Floyd (2009), 'Vow', in K.D. Sakenfeld (ed.), *New Interpreters Dictionary of the Bible*, vol. 5. Nashville: Abingdon, pp. 793–4.

K. Follett (2010), *Fall of Giants*. London: Macmillan.

C. Fontaine (1990), 'The Sage in Family and Tribe', in J. Gammie and L. Perdue (eds), *The Sage in Israel and the Ancient Near East*. Winona Lake: Eisenbrauns, pp. 155–64.

C. Fontaine (2002), *Smooth Words: Women, Proverbs and Performance in Biblical Wisdom*, JSOTSS 356. London: Sheffield Academic Press.

D. Freedman (1997), 'Between God and Man: Prophets in Ancient Israel', in Y. Gitay (ed.), *Prophecy and Prophets: The Diversity of Contemporary Issues in Scholarship*, SBLSS. Atlanta: Scholars Press, pp. 57–88.

J. Gammie and L. Perdue (eds) (1990), *The Sage in Israel and the Ancient Near East*, Winona Lake: Eisenbrauns.

E. Gerstenberger (2002), *Theologies in the Old Testament*, trans. J. Bowden. Edinburgh: T&T Clark.

J. Gibson (1978), *Canaanite Myths and Legends*, 2nd edn. Edinburgh: T&T Clark.

L. Grabbe (1995), *Priests, Prophets, Diviners, Sages: A Socio-Historical Study of Religious Specialists in Ancient Israel*. Valley Forge: Trinity Press.

L. Grabbe (ed.) (2007), *Good Kings and Bad Kings: The Kingdom of Judah in the Seventh Century BCE*. London: T&T Clark.

N. Habel (1965), 'The Form and Significance of the Call Narratives', *ZAW* 77, pp. 297–323.

L. Handy (1992), 'Serpent, Bronze', in D.N. Freedman (ed.), *Anchor Bible Dictionary*, vol. 5. New York: Doubleday, p. 1117.

J. Hardin (2004), 'Understanding Domestic Space: An Example from Iron Age Tel Halif', *NEA* 67:2, pp. 71–83.

R. Harris (1990), 'The Female "Sage" in Mesopotamian Literature (with an Appendix on Egypt)', in J. Gammie and L. Perdue (eds), *The Sage in Israel and the Ancient Near East*. Winona Lake: Eisenbrauns, pp. 3–18.

M. Heiser (2008), 'Monotheism, Polytheism, Monolatry, or Henotheism? Toward an Assessment of Divine Plurality in the Hebrew Bible', *Bulletin for Biblical Research* 18:1, pp. 1–30.

R. Hendel (1999), 'Nehushtan', in K. van der Toorn, B. Becking and P. van der Horst (eds), *Dictionary of Deities and Demons in the Bible*, 2nd rev. edn. Leiden: E.J. Brill, pp. 615–16.

R. Hess (2007), *Israelite Religions: An Archaeological and Biblical Survey*. Grand Rapids: Baker Academic.

C. Houtman (1999), 'Queen of Heaven', in K. van der Toorn, B. Becking and P. van der Horst (eds), *Dictionary of Deities and Demons in the Bible*, 2nd rev. edn. Leiden: E.J. Brill, pp. 678–80.

A. Hunter (2006), *Wisdom Literature*, SCM Core Texts. London: SCM Press.

R. Hutton (1994), *Charisma and Authority in Israelite Society*. Minneapolis: Fortress Press.

P. Johnston (2002), *Shades of Sheol: Death and Afterlife in the Old Testament*. Leicester: Apollos.

O. Kaiser (1998), '*nādar*', in G. Botterweck, H. Ringgren and H.-J. Fabry (eds), *Theological Dictionary of the Old Testament*, vol. 9, trans. D. Green. Grand Rapids: Eerdmans, pp. 242–55.

O. Keel and C. Uehlinger (1998), *Gods, Goddesses, and Images of God in Ancient Israel*, trans. T. Trapp. Edinburgh: T&T Clark.

R. Kessler (2008), *The Social History of Ancient Israel: An Introduction*, trans. L. Maloney. Minneapolis: Fortress Press.

P. King and L. Stager (2001), *Life in Biblical Israel*, LAI. Louisville: Westminster John Knox Press.

R. Kletter (1996), *The Judean Pillar-Figurines and the Archaeology of Asherah*. Oxford: Tempus Reparatum.

I. Kottsieper (2008), 'The Aramaic Tradition: Ahikar', in L. Perdue (ed.), *Scribes, Sages, and Seers: The Sage in the Eastern Mediterranean World*, FRLANT 219. Göttingen: Vandenhoeck & Ruprecht, pp. 109–24.

B. Lang (1983), *Monotheism and the Prophetic Minority: An Essay in Biblical History and Sociology*, SWBAS 1. Sheffield: Almond Press.

A. Lemaire (1990), 'The Sage in School and Temple', in J. Gammie and L. Perdue (eds), *The Sage in Israel and the Ancient Near East*. Winona Lake: Eisenbrauns, pp. 165–84.

A. Lemaire (1992), 'Education (Israel)', in D.N. Freedman (ed.), *Anchor Bible Dictionary*, vol. 2. New York: Doubleday, pp. 305–12.

A. Lemaire (1995), 'Wisdom in Solomonic Historiography', in J. Day, R. Gordon and H. Williamson (eds), *Wisdom in Ancient Israel: Essays in Honour of J.A. Emerton*. Cambridge: Cambridge University Press, pp. 106–18.

J. Lindblom (1962), *Prophecy in Ancient Israel*. Oxford: Basil Blackwell.

G. McConville (2002), *Exploring the Old Testament: The Prophets*. London: SPCK.

W. McKane (1965), *Prophets and Wise Men*. London: SCM Press.

W. McKane (1995), 'Jeremiah and the Wise', in J. Day, R. Gordon and H. Williamson (eds), *Wisdom in Ancient Israel: Essays in Honour of J.A. Emerton*. Cambridge: Cambridge University Press, pp. 142–51.

P. McNutt (1999), *Reconstructing the Society of Ancient Israel*, LAI. Louisville: Westminster John Knox Press.

V. Matthews and D. Benjamin (1993), *Social World of Ancient Israel, 1250–587 BC*. Peabody: Hendrickson.

S. Meier (1999), 'Destroyer', in K. van der Toorn, B. Becking and P. van der Horst (eds), *Dictionary of Deities and Demons in the Bible*, 2nd rev. edn. Leiden: E.J. Brill, pp. 240–4.

S. Meier (2009), *Themes and Transformations in Old Testament Prophecy*. Downers Grove: IVP.

T. Mettinger (1999), 'Seraphim', in K. van der Toorn, B. Becking and P. van der Horst (eds), *Dictionary of Deities and Demons in the Bible*, 2nd rev. edn. Leiden: E.J. Brill, pp. 742–4.

C. Meyers (1987), 'David as Temple Builder', in P. Miller, P. Hanson and S. Dean McBride (eds), *Ancient Israelite Religion: Essays in Honor of Frank Moore Cross*. Philadelphia: Fortress Press, pp. 357–76.

C. Meyers (1996), 'Procreation, Production, and Protection: Male–Female Balance in Early Israel', in C. Carter and C. Meyers (eds), *Community, Identity and Ideology: Social Science Approaches to the Hebrew Bible*, SBTS 6. Winona Lake: Eisebrauns, pp. 489–514.

C. Meyers (1997), 'The Family in Early Israel', in L. Perdue, J. Blenkinsopp, J. Collins and C. Meyers (eds), *Families in Ancient Israel*. Louisville: Westminster John Knox Press, pp. 1–47.

C. Meyers (2005), *Households and Holiness: The Religious Culture of Israelite Women*. Minneapolis: Fortress Press.

C. Meyers (2010), 'Household Religion', in F. Stavrakopolou and J. Barton (eds), *Religious Diversity in Ancient Israel and Judah*. London: T&T Clark, pp. 118–34.

J. Milgrom (1993), 'Notes on Leviticus', in W. Meeks (ed.), *The HarperCollins Study Bible*. New York: HarperCollins, pp. 151–97.

P. Miller (2000), *The Religion of Ancient Israel*, LAI. Louisville: Westminster John Knox Press.

M. Moore and B. Kelle (2011), *Biblical History and Israel's Past: The Changing Study of the Bible and History*. Grand Rapids: Eerdmans.

H. Müller (1998), 'nābî'', in G. Botterweck, H. Ringgren and H.-J. Fabry (eds), *Theological Dictionary of the Old Testament*, vol. 9, trans. D. Green. Grand Rapids: Eerdmans, pp. 129–50.

R. Murphy (1983), *Wisdom Literature and Psalms*, IBT. Nashville: Abingdon.

R. Murphy (2002), *The Tree of Life: An Exploration of Biblical Wisdom Literature*, 3rd edn. Grand Rapids: Eerdmans.

R. Nelson (1993), *Raising up a Faithful Priest: Community and Priesthood in Biblical Theology*. Louisville: Westminster John Knox Press.

J. Niehaus (1992), 'Amos', in T. McComiskey (ed.), *The Minor Prophets: An Exegetical and Expository Commentary*, vol. 1. Grand Rapids: Baker Academic, pp. 315–494.

S. Olyan (2008), 'Family Religion in Israel and the Wider Levant of the First Millennium BCE', in J. Bodel and S. Olyan (eds), *Household and Family Religion in Antiquity*. Malden: Blackwell Publishing, pp. 113–26.

L. Perdue (1997), 'The Israelite and Early Jewish Family: Summary and Conclusions', in L. Perdue, J. Blenkinsopp, J. Collins and C. Meyers (eds), *Families in Ancient Israel*. Louisville: Westminster John Knox Press, pp. 163–222.

L. Perdue (2008a), 'Sages, Scribes, and Seers in Israel and the Ancient Near East: An Introduction', in L. Perdue (ed.), *Scribes, Sages, and Seers: The Sage in the Eastern Mediterranean World*, FRLANT 219. Göttingen: Vandenhoeck & Ruprecht, pp. 1–34.

L. Perdue (2008b), *The Sword and the Stylus: An Introduction to Wisdom in the Age of Empires*. Grand Rapids: Eerdmans.

L. Perdue, J. Blenkinsopp, J. Collins and C. Meyers (eds) (1997), *Families in Ancient Israel*. Louisville: Westminster John Knox Press.

D. Petter (2005), 'High Places', in B. Arnold and H. Williamson (eds), *Dictionary of the Old Testament: Historical Books*. Downers Grove: IVP, pp. 413–18.

I. Provan, V.P. Long and T. Longman III (2003), *A Biblical History of Israel*. Louisville: Westminster John Knox Press.

D. Rooke (1998), 'Kingship as Priesthood: The Relationship between the High Priesthood and the Monarchy', in J. Day (ed.), *King and Messiah in Israel and the Ancient Near East: Proceedings of the Oxford Old Testament Seminar*, JSOTSS 270. Sheffield: Sheffield Academic Press, pp. 187–208.

I. Rowe (2008), 'Scribes, Sages, and Seers in Ugarit', in L. Perdue (ed.), *Scribes, Sages, and Seers: The Sage in the Eastern Mediterranean World*, FRLANT 219. Göttingen: Vandenhoeck & Ruprecht, pp. 95–108.

L. Sabourin (1973), *Priesthood: A Comparative Study*. Leiden: E.J. Brill.

M. Smith (2002), *The Early History of God*, 2nd edn, BRS. Grand Rapids: Eerdmans.

J.A. Soggin (2001), *Israel in the Biblical Period: Institutions, Festivals, Ceremonies, Rituals*, trans. J. Bowden. Edinburgh: T&T Clark.

L. Stager (1985), 'The Archaeology of Family in Ancient Israel', *BASOR* 260, pp. 1–35.

H.-P. Stähli (1997), '*yṣ*', in E. Jenni and C. Westermann (eds), *Theological Lexicon of the Old Testament*, vol. 2, trans. M. Biddle. Peabody: Hendrickson, pp. 556–9.

F. Stavrakopolou and J. Barton (eds) (2010), *Religious Diversity in Ancient Israel and Judah*, London: T&T Clark.

R. Sweet (1990a), 'The Sage in Akkadian Literature: A Philological Study', in J. Gammie and L. Perdue (eds), *The Sage in Israel and the Ancient Near East*. Winona Lake: Eisenbrauns, pp. 45–66.

R. Sweet (1990b), 'The Sage in Mesopotamian Palaces and Royal Courts', in J. Gammie and L. Perdue (eds), *The Sage in Israel and the Ancient Near East*. Winona Lake: Eisenbrauns, pp. 99–108.

W. Toews (1993), *Monarchy and Religious Institution in Israel under Jeroboam I*, SBLMS 47. Atlanta: Scholars Press.

C. Uehlinger (2007), 'Was There a Cult Reform under King Josiah? The Case for a Well-Grounded Minimum', in L. Grabbe (ed.), *Good Kings and Bad Kings: The Kingdom of Judah in the Seventh Century BCE*. London: T&T Clark, pp. 279–316.

K. van der Toorn (2006), 'Baal', in K.D. Sakenfeld (ed.), *New Interpreters Dictionary of the Bible*, vol. 1. Nashville: Abingdon, pp. 367–9.

K. van der Toorn (2008), 'Family Religion in Second Millennium West Asia (Mesopotamia, Emar, Nuzi)', in J. Bodel and S. Olyan (eds), *Household and Family Religion in Antiquity*. Malden: Blackwell Publishing, pp. 20–36.

K. van der Toorn and T. Lewis (2006), '*těrāpîm*', in G. Botterweck, H. Ringgren and H-J. Fabry (eds), *Theological Dictionary of the Old Testament*, vol. 15. Grand Rapids: Eerdmans, pp. 777–89.

R. van Leeuwen (1990), 'The Sage in the Prophetic Literature', in J. Gammie and L. Perdue (eds), *The Sage in Israel and the Ancient Near East*. Winona Lake: Eisenbrauns, pp. 295–306.

P. Verhoef (1997), 'Prophecy', in W.A. VanGemeren (ed.), *New International Dictionary of Old Testament Theology and Exegesis*, vol. 4. Grand Rapids: Zondervan, pp. 1067–78.

G. von Rad (1968), *The Message of the Prophets*. London: SCM Press.

G. von Rad (1984), *The Problem of the Hexateuch and Other Essays*. London: SCM Press.

J. Walton (2006), *Ancient Near Eastern Thought and the Old Testament: Introducing the Conceptual World of the Hebrew Bible*. Grand Rapids: Baker Academic.

M. Weber (1978), *Economy and Society*, vol. 1. Berkeley: University of California Press.

J. Wellhausen (1885), *Prolegomena to the History of Israel*, trans. J.S. Black and A. Menzies. Edinburgh: Adam & Charles Black.

K. Whitelam (1992), 'King and Kingship', in D.N. Freedman (ed.), *Anchor Bible Dictionary*, vol. 4. New York: Doubleday, pp. 40–8.

R. Whybray (1989), 'The Social World of the Wisdom Writers', in R. Clements (ed.), *The World of Ancient Israel: Sociological, Anthropological and Political Perspectives*. Cambridge: Cambridge University Press, pp. 227–50.

R. Whybray (1990), 'The Sage in the Israelite Royal Court', in J. Gammie and L. Perdue (eds), *The Sage in Israel and the Ancient Near East*. Winona Lake: Eisenbrauns, pp. 133–40.

R. Whybray (1995), *The Book of Proverbs: A Survey of Modern Study*, HBIS 1. Leiden: E.J. Brill.

E. Willett (2002), 'Infant Mortality and Family Religion in the Biblical Periods', *DavarLogos* 1:1, pp. 27–42.

R. Williams (1990a), 'The Functions of the Sage in the Egyptian Royal Court', in J. Gammie and L. Perdue (eds), *The Sage in Israel and the Ancient Near East*. Winona Lake: Eisenbrauns, pp. 95–8.

R. Williams (1990b), 'The Sage in Egyptian Literature', in J. Gammie and L. Perdue (eds), *The Sage in Israel and the Ancient Near East*. Winona Lake: Eisenbrauns, pp. 19–30.

T. Willis (2001), *The Elders of the City: A Study of the Elders-Laws in Deuteronomy*, SBLMS 55. Atlanta: Society of Biblical Literature.

T. Willis (2007), 'Elder in the OT', in K.D. Sakenfeld (ed.), *New Interpreters Dictionary of the Bible*, vol. 2. Nashville: Abingdon, pp. 233–4.

R. Wilson (1980), *Prophecy and Society in Ancient Israel*. Philadelphia: Fortress Press.

R. Wilson (1987), 'Early Israelite Prophecy', in J. Mays and P. Achtemeier (eds), *Interpreting the Prophets*. Philadephia: Fortress Press, pp. 1–13.

N. Wyatt (1998), *Religious Texts from Ugarit: The Words of Ilimilku and His Colleagues*, BS 53. Sheffield: Sheffield Academic Press.

N. Wyatt (1999), 'Asherah', in K. van der Toorn, B. Becking and P. van der Horst (eds), *Dictionary of Deities and Demons in the Bible*, 2nd rev. edn. Leiden: E.J. Brill, pp. 99–105.

N. Wyatt (2010), 'Royal Religion in Ancient Judah', in F. Stavrakopolou and J. Barton (eds), *Religious Diversity in Ancient Israel and Judah*. London: T&T Clark, pp. 61–81.

Z. Zevit (2001), *The Religions of Ancient Israel: A Synthesis of Parallactic Approaches*. London: Continuum.

# INDEX OF BIBLICAL REFERENCES

OLD TESTAMENT

**Genesis**
14 96
17:9–14 22, 125
18:11 86
20:7 62
20:17 124
23 126
23:10 76
23:18 76
24:27 103
24:35–48 52
25:21 123
28:18 32
29:33 125
31 113
31:19–54 113
31:53 113
32:3–4 58
34:14–16 125
35:20 127
37:25 14
38:21–22 23
39—50 71
41 68
50:2–3 126

**Exodus**
3 50
3:10 57
3:11 52
3:15–18 65
4:1–9 62
4:24–26 126
6:2–3 106
7:11 68

12 121
12:3–4 121
12:4 121
12:7 121
12:11 120
12:26 88
12:43 100
12:44 22
12:47–48 125
12:48 22
12:48–49 100
13:8 88
15:20 23
20:3 114
20:8–10 122
20:24–25 28
21:6 116
23:17 22
29 24
29:9 20
32 63
34:6 106
35:25–26 23
38:8 23
38:26 134

**Leviticus**
1—7 15, 25, 29, 37
1—14 15
2:1–10 30
6:14–18 30
8—9 24
9:22 30
10:10–11 25, 27
11—14 15
12 22
12:3 126

15 22
16:8–10 37
17:11 29
17:15 100
19:27 129
19:31 130
20:6 130
22:10–16 30
22:12–13 23
26:1 33
27:1–8 86

**Numbers**
1:47–53 20
3:6–9 20
3:12 18
3:39 134
4:3 23
4:23 23
4:35 23
4:39 23
4:43 23
4:48 134
6:3–4 123
6:5 123
6:6–7 123
6:23 25
6:24–26 31
8:16 18
8:24–26 86
9:14 100, 121
11:16–30 60
16 20
16:8–11 20
16:40 20
18:1–7 20
18:8–20 19

18:11 23
18:13 23
21:4–9 93
21:6 51
21:8 51
21:29 34
22—24 41
26:5–51 134
26:62 134
27:21 26

**Deuteronomy**
1:13–18 80
4:10 83
4:19 111
5:12–14 122
6:4–9 83
8:15 51
10:8 25, 30
11:19 83
12:2 34
12:7 135
12:12 135
13:1–5 62
14:1 129
14:21 100
16:16 22
16:18–19 80
16:22 33
17:3–4 111
17:8–13 28, 139
17:9 19
17:10–12 28
17:18 19
18:1 19
18:3 19, 30
18:5–7 19

*18:11* 130
*18:20* 50
*19* 79
*19:11–12* 80
*21:1–9* 79, 80
*21:5* 19, 27
*21:18–21* 76, 79, 80
*22:13–21* 76, 79, 80
*23:3–7* 100
*23:17–18* 23
*23:21–23* 123
*24:8* 19, 27
*25:5–10* 76, 79, 80
*26:14* 129
*27:1* 77
*27:6* 28
*27:9* 19
*31:9* 19, 27
*31:9–13* 77
*32:7* 77, 88
*33:8–10* 19
*33:8–11* 25
*33:9* 19
*34:9–12* 62
*34:10–12* 64

**Joshua**
*4:21–22* 88
*5:14–15* 112
*6:19* 99
*7:14–18* 99
*8* 13
*8:31* 28
*13:14* 19
*18:7* 20
*18:30* 20
*20:1–6* 80
*20:4* 76
*20:23* 76
*24:26–27* 33
*24:30* 136
*24:32* 136
*24:33* 136

**Judges**
*2:13* 134
*3:7* 107
*4:4–5* 56
*6* 119
*6:19* 119
*6:25–26* 107
*8:25* 119
*8:27* 119
*8:33* 134

*11:24* 34
*13:6* 41
*13:8* 41
*17* 18, 19, 117
*17—18* 25, 113
*17:1* 18
*17:3–4* 118
*17:5* 18, 117
*17:5—18:6* 26
*17:7–13* 19
*17:10* 30
*18:14* 113
*18:15* 118

**Ruth**
*1:16* 103
*4* 76
*4:1–12* 79, 80

**1 Samuel**
*1:1* 18
*1:7–9* 121
*1:9–20* 31, 124
*1:12* 124
*1:21* 121
*2* 30
*2:12–17* 17
*2:22* 23
*2:28* 25
*3* 53
*3:1* 21, 53, 139
*3:1—4:1* 64
*3:20* 139
*4:21* 104
*7:8–11* 62
*7:15–16* 139
*8:5* 90
*9* 56
*9:7* 56
*9:8* 56
*9:9* 42
*9:15* 59
*9:18–24* 54
*9:22* 34
*10:5* 43
*10:5–6* 60
*10:5–13* 60
*10:10–13* 60
*12:17–18* 62
*12:19* 63
*12:23* 63
*13* 90, 139
*14:36–46* 26
*14:37* 26

*14:41* 26
*15:23* 113
*16:4* 75
*18:6–7* 23
*19* 113
*19:11–17* 113
*19:20–24* 60
*20* 122
*20:5–6* 121, 136
*20:26* 122
*23:6–12* 26–7
*28* 130
*28:6* 26
*28:13* 130
*28:14* 126
*30:7–8* 27

**2 Samuel**
*6* 139
*6:13* 94
*6:17–18* 94, 96
*6:18* 139
*7:1–3* 65
*8:16–18* 70, 71
*8:17* 91
*8:18* 18
*14* 80
*14:3* 80
*15:12* 79
*16:23* 79
*18:18* 126
*20* 80
*20:14* 81
*20:16–17* 81
*20:18* 81
*20:21–22* 81
*20:23–26* 70, 71
*20:26* 18
*24:11* 44
*24:16* 121
*24:25* 94, 95

**1 Kings**
*2:26–27* 91
*2:35* 91
*3* 80, 86, 139
*3:3–4* 36
*3:4* 94
*3:9* 80
*3:10–14* 80
*3:16–28* 80
*3:28* 80
*4:1–5* 70
*4:1–6* 71

*4:2* 91
*4:5* 36
*4:29–34* 86
*4:33* 85
*5:12* 86
*8:5* 94
*8:14* 96
*8:62–64* 94
*9* 36
*9:25* 96
*10:24* 86
*11:7* 34
*11:7–8* 91
*12* 35, 90
*12:6–11* 78
*12:8–10* 73
*12:29* 35
*12:31* 18, 35
*12:32* 94, 95
*13:1* 94, 95
*13:1–6* 64
*13:6* 131
*13:32* 34
*13:33* 18, 32
*14* 56, 132
*14:1–18* 57
*14:2–3* 131
*14:23* 34
*15:9–24* 93
*16:7* 54
*16:31* 89
*16:32* 91
*17* 56
*17—19* 107
*17:1–17* 107
*17:14–16* 62
*17:17–24* 63
*17:19–21* 131
*17:20* 64
*17:24* 64
*18* 107, 139
*18:18* 70, 71, 134
*18:19* 45, 56, 108, 134
*18:26–29* 60
*18:27* 107
*18:37* 70, 71
*18:38* 6
*18:41–46* 107
*19* 56
*19:10* 133
*19:19* 48
*19:19–20* 56
*20:7–12* 78
*21* 101

21:8 75
21:8–14 80
22 44, 45, 46, 57
22:1–8 112
22:6 40
22:11 61
22:19–22 59
22:19–23 46
22:20–21 46, 47
22:22 46
22:41–51 93

**2 Kings**
1:2–4 57
1:2–12 62
2:1–18 54
2:19–22 62
2:3 43
3:4 49
3:14–19 60
3:15 60
4 56
4:1 54
4:1–7 54
4:8–37 43
4:18–37 63, 131
4:22–23 132
4:23 43, 122
4:33 64
4:33–35 131
4:38 43, 54
4:42–44 56, 62
5 56
5:1–19 63
6:1–2 54
6:1–7 54, 62
6:8–23 45
6:17 112
8:7–10 45, 57
8:7–15 137
8:10 58
10:1 73
10:5–6 73
11 93
12:1–16 92
12:1–17 93
12:2 138
12:2–3 73
13:21 63
16 95
16:4 34
16:13 95
17:9–10 34
17:10 34

17:13 65
17:16 111, 134
17:27–28 37
17:29–32 36
18 58, 71, 93
18:4 93
18:19 58
18:26 84
19:3 58
19:6 58
19:35 121
20:1 57
20:1–3 131
20:7 63
21 94
21:3 111
22 49, 84
22:3–7 92
22:8 24
22:12–20 57
23 93, 94
23:1 75
23:4 108
23:4–5 111
23:5 32
23:6 136
23:7 23
23:8 34, 36
23:12 117
23:24 113
23:25 34

**1 Chronicles**
2:55 84
6:18–23 36
16:39–40 32
21 121
23:13 30
23:23 25

**2 Chronicles**
16:7 54
17:7–9 73
22—26 96
26:16–21 90

**Ezra**
7:6 71
7:11 71

**Job**
1—2 46
1:20 128
2:22 46
4:3 75, 88

4:7–8 85
4:12–21 59
5:27 85
6:24 88
8:8–10 85
9:4 86
12:12 74, 85
12:13 78, 86
13:1 85
15:2–3 76
15:7–10 74
15:17 85
15:17–19 85, 88
15:18–19 85
21:17 85
26:3 79
27:11 75, 88
28:27 85
29 75
29:7–17 79
29:21 76, 79
31 75
31:13–15 79
32:7 74, 85
32:9 74
33:33 88
34:32 88
35:11 86

**Psalms**
2:7 96
20:3 97
20:6 97
20:9 97
22:9–11 132
29:1 46
60 55
65 55
68:24–26 23
78:5 83
82 55
82:6 46
89:7 46
90:10 86
105:22 74
106:28 136
110 55
110:4 89, 139
115:14–15 31
118:26 31
119:100 74
121 135
121:7–8 31
134:3 31

**Proverbs**
1—9 77
1:2–4 77
1:8 81, 82, 83
2:1–5 87
2:1–6 86
2:4–5 87
2:6 87
3:12 84
4 82
4:5 82
4:7 82
5:13 72
6:6 85
6:20 81, 82, 83
8:5 82
8:14 78
10:1 82
11:14 79
13:14 76
15:2 76
15:7 76
15:20 82
15:22 79
15:31 72
17:16 72
18:5 79
18:17 79
20:20 82
22:17 80
22:17—24:22 72
22:24 72
23:2 82
23:10 72
23:13–14 84
24:6 79
24:7 76
24:23 80
25:2 85
25:14 85
27:8 85
29:15 84
30:11 82
30:15–33 85
30:17 82, 83
31 76, 83
31:1–2 83
31:1–9 81
31:26 83
31:28 83

**Ecclesiastes**
3:13 85
4:13 74
5:4–5 123

**Isaiah**
*1:13* 122
*1:26* 79
*2:2* 59
*3:1–4* 79
*5:9* 29
*6* 47, 50, 51
*6:1* 47
*6:1–13* 59
*6:8* 47
*8:19* 130
*8:19–20* 130
*11:2* 78
*14:29* 51
*15:2* 128
*16:12* 32
*19:11* 68–9
*19:11–12* 77
*20* 61
*21* 57
*22:12* 128
*22:14* 59
*22:15–19* 127
*28:7–13* 73
*28:9–10* 84
*28:13* 84
*28:23–29* 67
*29:10* 65
*29:14* 70
*30:1–5* 70
*30:2* 70
*30:6* 51
*31:1–3* 70
*31:2* 70, 86
*36* 71
*36—39* 62
*37:1–7* 57
*37:3–10* 57
*38:21* 63, 131
*45:6b–7* 114
*53:3* 42
*57:6* 131, 137
*66:23* 122

**Jeremiah**
*1* 50
*1:1* 48, 138
*1:6* 52
*1:7* 58
*1:10b* 52
*2:1–3* 58
*2:23* 134
*2:28* 112

*3:3* 67
*4:19* 60
*7* 44
*7:16* 63, 66
*7:16–20* 109
*7:18* 23, 110
*8:1* 112
*8:8–9* 71
*9:13–14* 134
*9:16–20* 126
*9:17–18* 67
*10:6–8* 86
*11:13* 112
*13:1–11* 61
*13:12–14* 61
*14:11* 66
*14:14* 50
*15:1–2* 66
*16:1–13* 61
*16:5–9* 127
*16:6* 128
*18* 74
*18:7–9* 52
*18:18* 27, 67, 70, 74, 77
*19:13* 111, 116, 117
*20:1* 65
*20:6* 65
*21* 45
*22* 45
*23:9* 60
*23:11* 44
*23:16–22* 47
*24:6* 52
*26:17–19* 80
*26:20–23* 40
*27:1–15* 41, 57
*27:18* 63
*28* 44
*28:1–17* 40
*28:8–9* 54
*29:3* 88
*29:21–23* 40
*29:31* 40
*29:56* 60
*32:29* 116
*33:18* 20
*35:4* 44
*36:10* 84
*37:3* 63
*38:4* 40
*41:5* 128
*42:2* 63
*42:4* 63

*44* 110
*44:15* 110
*44:15–30* 109
*44:17* 109
*44:19* 110
*47:5* 128
*48:35* 32
*48:37* 128
*49:1* 34
*49:7* 79

**Lamentations**
*2:20* 44

**Ezekiel**
*1—3* 50
*1:1* 49
*1:1–3* 49
*1:3* 138
*1:16* 47
*2:2* 60
*3:14* 60
*3:22* 60
*4* 61
*7* 74
*7:11* 139
*7:14* 49
*7:18* 128
*7:26* 37, 74, 78
*9:1* 59
*9:5* 59
*12* 61
*13:4–5* 63
*13:6* 50
*16:44* 83
*22:30* 63
*24* 61
*27:8* 67
*27:31* 128
*44* 20
*44:5–9* 100
*44:10* 20
*44:14* 20
*44:15–16* 20
*44:17* 37
*44:24* 37
*45:17* 122
*46:1* 122
*46:3* 122

**Daniel**
*1:5* 87
*1:17* 87

**Hosea**
*2:8* 106, 134
*2:16* 134
*3:4* 113
*4:14* 23
*6:5* 40
*9:7* 60
*11:2* 134
*12:13* 64

**Amos**
*1:1* 49, 59
*2:11–12* 40
*6:4–7* 127
*7* 46, 59
*7:1–6* 63
*7:1–9* 47
*7:10–17* 42, 53
*7:13* 57, 90
*7:15* 50, 56
*8:5* 122
*8:10* 128

**Micah**
*1:1* 59
*1:16* 128
*3:7* 65

**Zephaniah**
*1:4* 134
*1:5* 111, 116

**Haggai**
*2:10–13* 27

**Zechariah**
*10:2* 113

**Malachi**
*2:4–9* 37
*3:11* 56

APOCRYPHAL/
DEUTEROCANONICAL
BOOKS

**Sirach**
*30:18* 131

NEW TESTAMENT

**John**
*9:17* 66

# INDEX OF NAMES AND SUBJECTS

Ackerman, Susan 101, 109, 135
Ahiqar 68, 69, 73, 77, 84
Ahlström, Gösta 91, 92, 94
Ai 116
Albertz, Rainer 10, 103–4, 110, 112–13, 117, 132, 134, 136
Alt, Albrecht 103
altar 28, 29, 30, 32, 35, 95, 116, 118
'ancient Israel': meanings of 3
Ancient Near Eastern texts: as source for historical reconstruction 9–10, 13, 90
Arad 33
archaeology, Syro-Palestinian: as source for historical reconstruction 2, 3, 8, 10–13, 99; see also inscriptions, Hebrew
Asherah 11, 12, 13, 33, 56, 107–9, 111, 121, 124; as El / Yahweh's consort 108, 109; represented by female figurines 125
'ăšērîm, 32–4; see also Asherah
astragali 118

Baal 34, 89, 91, 94, 104, 106–7, 108, 109, 116, 119, 120, 132; as alternative title for Yahweh 134; Cycle 9, 107; prophets of 56, 60, 133; Yahweh's supremacy over 107
Balaam 41
Bes 124, 126
Bethel 32, 35, 36, 43, 46, 53, 57, 90, 91, 94, 114
biblical text: as source for historical reconstruction 2, 6–8, 11–12, 13, 42, 90, 98–9
Bird, Phyllis 22, 23, 49
Blenkinsopp, Joseph 21, 39, 40, 41, 42, 44, 47, 48, 49, 53, 64, 65, 69, 76, 77
blessing 25, 30–2, 94, 96
'bull site' 119–20
burial see tomb; mourning practices

Canaanite 9, 23, 33, 93, 97
Chemosh 34
childbirth 22, 123, 126; see also pregnancy
circumcision 125–6, 136
'clan' (mišpāḥâ) 101, 121; sacrifice (zebaḥ hayyāmîm) 121–2, 136
council, divine 46–7, 53; see also host of heaven
Crenshaw, James 68, 72, 84, 85, 87, 88
cult: corner 118, 135; niche 115, 118; room 116, 117–18, 135; see also shrines

Dan 20, 26, 32, 35, 36, 90, 91, 118
Day, John 89, 106, 107
de Vaux, Roland 17, 27, 36, 37, 96, 120, 122, 123
dead, offerings for 129–31, 136
Deir 'Alla 41
destroyer 121
Dever, William 6–7, 10–12, 13, 99, 101, 108, 113, 116, 118, 124, 125, 127, 135
divination: as priestly role 26–7; use of astragali 118; use of teraphim 113

Ebal, Mount 12
El 33, 104–6, 116, 120; relationship with Yahweh 106
elders 74–6, 85, 87; female 81; Job as example 75–6; as judges 28, 79–80; location 76; roles 74–5, 77–8
ephod 25, 26–7, 113, 118, 119

figurines, female (pillar) 11, 109, 111, 118, 124–5; from Tell Halif 115
figurines, horse and rider 111
Fontaine, Carol 76, 80, 81, 83
food and meals 23, 118
foreigners 100

god of the family ('God of my/your father') 102–7, 113
Grabbe, Lester 7, 13, 14, 44, 57, 59, 71, 82, 86, 95, 138

Hess, Richard 9, 23, 120, 125
Hezekiah 28, 36, 57, 58, 62, 63, 69, 93–4, 94, 97, 131
'high places' (*bāmôt*) 18, 32, 33, 34, 36, 38, 43, 93, 94, 97; *bêth bāmâ* 34–6; bull site as example 119–20; location of 33–4; *see also* shrines
Hinnom Valley 31
host of heaven 46, 111–12, 117; and horse and rider figurines 111
household (*bêt 'āb*) 99–101; god of 102–4, 134; gods (teraphim) 113; inheritance (*naḥălâ*) 101, 126, 136; as location of cultic practice 115–18; size and composition 100–1; tomb 118, 126, 136
Hutton, Rodney 27, 37, 42, 44, 48, 66, 85

incense 20, 28, 29, 30, 33, 35, 90, 94, 95, 116, 118
inscriptions, Hebrew 8, 10, 103, 108, 127, 134; *see also* Lachish ostraca
*Instructions of Amenemope* 72
intercession 62–3, 64, 66, 131; *see also* prayer

Jeroboam I 18, 32, 35, 56, 64, 90, 91, 94, 131
Josiah 36, 92–4, 108, 117

Keret 105, 116
King, Philip and Lawrence Stager 7, 25, 29, 33, 35, 86, 100, 110, 116, 130, 136
kings: and blessing the people 96; as builder of religious sanctuaries 90–1; and maintenance of religious sanctuaries 92; and offering of sacrifices 94–6, 97, 139; as organizers of the cult 91, 96; as priests 89; as reformers of the cult 92–4; elationship to Yahweh 96
*kispu* rite 129
Kuntillet Ajrud: image of female lyre player 12–13; image of worshippers 63; inscription mentioning a/Asherah 108

Lachish ostraca 40
lamp / light 124
Lang, Bernhard 53, 54, 55, 58, 62
Lemaire, André 21–4, 68, 72, 84, 87
Levites 18–20, 23, 98, 101, 134
*liškâ* 34

Manasseh 94
Mari 44, 49, 57, 60, 75, 91
marriage 125, 136
*marzēaḥ* (funerary feast) 127–8, 136
Matthews, Victor and Don Benjamin xiii, 31, 61, 75, 76, 87, 140
maximalists 8
Meier, Sam 46, 47, 56, 65, 121
Mesha Stele 32, 34

Meyers, Carol 91, 100, 101, 102, 115, 120–1, 122, 123, 124, 125, 126, 135, 136
Milcom 34
Miller, Patrick 16, 19, 38, 40, 43, 46, 47, 53, 56, 59, 71, 92, 96, 103, 104, 105, 106, 109, 119, 125, 132, 135
minimalists 6, 8, 13
monotheism 114
Mot 107
'mother's teaching' 82, 83
mourning practices 61, 126–31; *see also* dead, offerings for
Mowinckel, Sigmund 43, 55

names, personal 103–4, 112–13, 125, 134
necromancy 130
Nehushtan 93
Nelson, Richard 17, 22, 23, 24, 27, 30, 36
new moon 43, 122

offering stands 115, 116, 118, 120
old age 86

parallelomania 9–10
parallelophobia 9–10
Passover 114, 121; observed by 'resident aliens' 100; pre-history 120
Perdue, Leo 78, 87
Phoenicia 9, 17, 41, 57, 89
pilgrimage 22, 36, 114, 121, 135
pillars, sacred *see* 'standing stones'
prayer 59, 62–3, 64, 123–4, 125, 131, 132
pregnancy 123–5; *see also* childbirth
priests / priesthood: any Israelite 18; appointed by king 17, 91, 96; blessing 25, 30–2; clothing 24, 37; divination 26–7; eligibility 17–21; female 22–3; as hereditary office 17–18, 21; income 24, 29–30, 37; installation ceremony 24; as judges 27–8; Levitical priests 18–20; location 32–6; negative view of 15–16; and prophets 64, 138–9; roles 24–32; sacrifice 25, 28–30; schools for 21, 24, 73; sons of Aaron 20; as tax-men 31; as teachers 25, 27–8, 37–8; training 20–4
prophetic bands / guilds *see* 'sons of the prophets'
prophets / prophecy: call 50–3, 65; cult 43, 53–4, 55, 57; and divine council 46–7, 53; early versus classical 40, 64; ecstasy 60; eligibility 47–50; as envoys / diplomats / messengers 47, 53, 57–8; and healing 63–4, 131–2; Hebrew titles 41–2, 50, 59, 65; as hereditary office 54; income 56; independent 45–6; intercession 62–3, 64, 66; location 42–6; and miracles 62, 64, 65; misconceptions 1; numbers of 39–40; and priests 65, 138–9; reception of revelation 59; and religious centres 43–4;

roles 46–7, 55–64; and the royal court 44–5, 65; symbolic actions 60–2; training 53–5, 65; and word of the Lord 27, 55–62; *see also* 'sons of the prophets'

prostitute, sacred / cult (*qĕdēšâ*) 23

Queen of Heaven 23, 109–11; cakes 110

'resident aliens' (*gērîm*) 100, 101
rooftops 116–17

Sabbath 43, 122; observed by 'resident aliens' 100
sacrifice 20, 25, 28–30, 32, 35, 36, 90, 94–6, 97, 100, 113, 116, 118, 119, 121, 123, 132; *see also* altar
sage *see* wise / wisdom
schools: priestly 21, 24; prophetic 53–4; royal / scribal 71, 72–3, 84, 87
scribes 68, 71, 81–2, 84, 88; and priests 21, 28, 139
seraphim 51
Sheol 130
shrines: clan 119–20; gate 35; household 18, 117–18, 135; town 118–19; *see also* 'high places'
sickness 45, 56, 57, 63–4, 123, 131–3, 137
social scientific research: as a source for historical reconstruction 14
society, structure of Israelite 99; *see also* 'clan', household
sons of God *see* council, divine
'sons of the prophets' (*bᵉnē hannᵉbî'îm*) 43, 48, 54
'standing stones' (*maṣṣēbôt*) 32–3, 113, 115, 118, 119; as memorial stele 126–7, 130

Tell Halif 115
temple, Jerusalem 20, 24, 32, 34, 36, 43, 44, 53, 55, 90, 94, 95, 98, 108, 114
teraphim 113, 115, 118
thanksgiving ceremony 131–2
tomb 31, 127, 129; family 118, 126, 136; plan of typical 128

Ugarit 49, 74, 116; location and significance 9; schools 73; texts as evidence regarding El, Baal and Asherah 74, 104–7, 109, 120
Urim and Thummim 25–6, 37

van der Toorn, Karel 107, 113, 115, 129
von Rad, Gerhard 51, 53, 59, 65, 69, 71
votives 120, 124, 125; *see also* figurines, female (pillar)
vow 110, 123, 124

Walton, John 57, 104, 129
Weber, Max 46, 48
Wellhausen, Julius 15, 16, 103
Wilson, Robert 45, 60, 63
wise / wisdom: as advisers / counsellors 77–9; as arbiters of disputes 79–80, 81; as composers of documents 80–2; as divine attribute and gift 78, 86; as hereditary office 84, 88; Joseph as example 71, 87; location 68–76; and priests 138–9; prophetic critique of 70–1; roles 76–82; and the royal court 68–71, 77, 78–9, 84; and schools 72–3, 84; and scribes 71, 81–2; as teachers 76–7, 87–8; terminology 67; training 72–3, 82–7
women 10, 103, 110, 124, 125, 136; as composers of texts 81; as makers of vows 123; as priests 22–3; as prophets 49; roles in the Israelite cult 23, 135; as singers of laments 126; wise 80–1; *see also* childbirth; pregnancy
Wyatt, Nicolas 90, 96, 108

Yahweh 34, 51, 58, 59, 61, 85, 112, 114, 116, 120, 122; and Asherah 108, 109; and blessing 31, 108; as god of the family 104, 134; and Nehushtan 93; relationship with El 106, 109; relationship with Israelite king 96; supremacy over Baal 107; and vows 123, 124

Zadok 20, 91
Zevit, Ziony 5, 119–20, 124, 135
*zukru* festival 120